D0084827

WITHDRAWN

Lyric Contingencies

VILLA JULIE COLLEGE LIBRARY
STEVENSON, MD 21153

Lyric Contingencies

EMILY DICKINSON
AND WALLACE STEVENS

MARGARET DICKIE

upp

University of Pennsylvania Press   *Philadelphia*

COPYRIGHT © 1991 BY THE UNIVERSITY OF PENNSYLVANIA PRESS
ALL RIGHTS RESERVED
Printed in the United States of America

Library of Congress Cataloging-in-Publication Data

Dickie, Margaret, 1935–
    Lyric contingencies: Emily Dickinson and Wallace Stevens/
Margaret Dickie.
      p. cm.
    Includes bibliographical references and index.
    ISBN 0–8122–3077–9
    1. American poetry—History and criticism. 2. Dickinson, Emily,
1830–1886—Criticism and interpretation. 3. Stevens, Wallace,
1879–1955—Criticism and interpretation. I. Title.
  PS303.D53 1991
  811'.4—dc20

90–48495
CIP

22.75

67116

For Arnold Stein

Contents

Acknowledgments

This book began during a sabbatical leave from the University of Illinois and an appointment to the Center for Advanced Studies there. It was completed during residence at the Rockefeller Study and Conference Center at Bellagio. I am grateful to both these institutions for their aid and to the University of Georgia, which has generously supported my research. I should also like to thank Mrs. Helen S. Lanier for her interest in literature and for the terms of my appointment at Georgia.

Among friends who have improved the process of writing this book are Ernest Bufkin, Sarah Carter, Dee Anne Gauthier, Penny Martin, William Prokasy, and Frances Teague. I am fortunate too in having had very helpful comments on all or part of the manuscript from Anne Williams, Vivian Pollak, and A. Walton Litz. Dianne Middlebrook and Thomas Parkinson read it for the press and provided valuable suggestions for revision. Two graduate students, Ellen Brown and Catherine Rogers, provided necessary help with details. I am especially thankful to Jerome Singerman of the University of Pennsylvania Press for his skillful and cheerful handling of the editorial process. And, finally, although I have seldom been more than reproved, I have never been less than improved by a conversation with Arnold Stein.

An early version of Chapter II was published in *American Literature*.

Athens, Georgia   Margaret Dickie

Abbreviations

The following texts have been used in this study and will be cited by the abbreviations listed in parentheses here.

Emily Dickinson, *The Complete Poems of Emily Dickinson*, ed. Thomas H. Johnson. Boston: Little, Brown and Co., 1955 (P); *The Letters of Emily Dickinson*, ed. Thomas H. Johnson and Theodora Ward. 3 vols. Cambridge, Mass.: Harvard University Press, 1958 (L).

Wallace Stevens, *The Collected Poems of Wallace Stevens*. New York: Alfred A. Knopf, 1974 (page number); *Letters of Wallace Stevens*, selected and edited by Holly Stevens. New York: Alfred A. Knopf, 1981 (L); *The Necessary Angel: Essays on Reality and the Imagination*. New York: Vintage, 1951 (NA); *Opus Posthumous: Revised, Enlarged, and Corrected Edition*, ed. Milton J. Bates. New York: Alfred A. Knopf, 1989 (OP); *Souvenirs and Prophecies: The Young Wallace Stevens*, ed. Holly Stevens. New York: Alfred A. Knopf, 1977 (S and P); *Sur Plusieurs Beaux Sujects: Wallace Stevens' Commonplace Book: A Facsimile and Transcription*, ed. Milton J. Bates. Stanford, Calif.: Stanford University Library, 1989.

Quotations from *The Complete Poems of Emily Dickinson* are reprinted by permission of Little, Brown, and Co., the Belknap Press of Harvard University, and the Trustees of Amherst College.

Quotations from *The Collected Poems of Wallace Stevens*, *Letters of Wallace Stevens*, *The Necessary Angel*, *Souvenirs and Prophecies*, *Opus Posthumous* are reprinted by permission of Alfred A. Knopf, Inc.

Chapter 1

"They shut me up in Prose": Introduction

"Poetry is not the same thing as the imagination taken alone. Nothing is itself taken alone. Things are because of interrelations or interactions," Wallace Stevens wrote in "Adagia" (OP 189). This is a book about the importance of interrelations in the poetry of Emily Dickinson and Wallace Stevens. It is not primarily about the interactions between these two poets, although that will figure in the discussion; rather, it is about the importance of interrelations in the American lyric genre they created. It will focus on three topics: the speaker of the lyric, its language, and its audience. The book's aim is to extract Dickinson and Stevens from the Emersonian tradition in which they are conventionally discussed, where those elements of the lyric genre are idealized, and to place their work in the world of contingency where "things are because of interrelations" and not because of an ideal or abstract plan. It will emphasize the interactional nature of the speakers in the poems, the metonymic habit of the lyric language, and the discomforting fear and anticipation that the need for an audience caused Dickinson and Stevens. And it will suggest that these qualities define a distinctive lyric tradition in American literature that is quite different from that of either the American long poem or epic or prose.

Against the teleological ambition of those genres, lyric contingency will appear almost trifling, as Stevens describes it in the late poem "July Mountain":

We live in a constellation
Of patches and of pitches,
Not in a single world,
In things said well in music,
On the piano, and in speech,
As in a page of poetry —
Thinkers without final thoughts
In an always incipient cosmos,
The way, when we climb a mountain,
Vermont throws itself together. (OP 140)

If this Connecticut Valley poet may appear to a native to take a rather casual attitude toward the state of Vermont, he points nonetheless to the constituting feature of his work—its improvisation.[1] For Stevens, Vermont is composed in the enigma of *when*, a term that announces both time and place and yet can signify chance as well as cause. In both instances, it indicates the haphazard nature of all interrelation, even that which precedes poetic composition and on which poetry depends.

This undeliberated pose of improvisation is a Modernist strategy not peculiar to Stevens. It may have its beginnings in the Romantic openness to experience evident, for example, in Dickinson's "I started Early—Took my Dog—" (P 520); but improvisation has an almost staged arbitrariness for the Modernist as if the most unlikely combinations of experience were necessary to express the novelty of life in the twentieth century. It appealed to the poets, and especially to Stevens and William Carlos Williams, because it suited the way in which they composed, as Stevens acknowledges in his introduction to the reissue of Williams' *Kora in Hell: Improvisations*:

> Quick, snatched, not disciplined by the continuous rewriting of the sedentary academician, his work had the freshness of the instant. By the time he had leisure to do otherwise, Williams had established his technique. . . . For Williams, the method was both inevitable and essential.[2]

Stevens too composed in snatches of time taken from a full work day, but his enthusiasm for improvisation had a longer life in his work, and it may have had different and deeper roots.[3] While Williams and Ezra Pound moved from the improvisations of their earliest work toward the sustained treatment and public subjects of their later long poems, Stevens remained devoted to the end to the improvisations that the lyric poem permitted and encouraged. He may have found the variety of style that improvisation offered him suitable to the paradoxical arbitrariness and intimacy of his subjects. The choice of genre that distinguished him from his contemporaries may have been dictated by his sense of antiessentialism. Among his contemporaries, Stevens is the preeminent pragmatist, the one who remained most resistant to what he calls "final thoughts" and most open to the contingent.[4]

Unlike Pound, who would lament at the end of his life's work that he had failed "To make Cosmos— / To achieve the possible" (*Canto* CXVI), and Williams, who would not waken even at the end from "this dream of / the whole poem" (*Paterson* IV, 200), Stevens celebrates the achievement of an end in what he calls in "July Mountain" the oxymoronic "incipient cosmos," the poet's real world, a place that is both still beginning and already completely ordered. The constellation of "pitches" in which "Vermont throws itself together" is part of that cosmos, a place of throwing and throwing oneself together. At once, it is just beginning, as throwing or pitching is a start outward rather then an absorption inward, a trial rather than an achievement, and at the same time it relies on a willingness to believe, on an openness to the scene, on a confirmation as well as a questioning. But it is also working toward an end in order as throwing oneself *together* is something more, a response to pitching perhaps, but quick, unplanned, and haphazard. The poet inhabiting such a constellation will always be open to its opportunities, on the move, always alert to possibilities, never fixed or certain.

But, Stevens claims, we live also in a "constellation / Of patches," a system that is from the very start casual, in need of mending, a pattern, if at all, of scraps. Such a constellation is older, more time-ridden, less "incipient" than the constellation of pitches. In this system, the poet appears as a secondary figure, one who comes after, perhaps in his more conventional role of ordering, but without preeminence. In this combination of pitching and patching, the language of this poem undoes itself, revealing the frantic need of Stevens's old age to keep something still to do, to resist "final thoughts." Yet, as we shall see, this need was lifelong. Stevens points here to a preoccupation with patching things together that has informed his poetry from the beginning and guarantees that there will be no end.

It is neither a consolatory project of old age for Stevens nor a youthful effort to restore some original state. Patching is, early and late, a desperate task, a response to local conditions, a temporary measure. In "Parochial Theme," he finds it necessary because

> There's no such thing as life; or if there is,
>
> It is faster than the weather, faster than
> Any character. It is more than any scene:
>
> Of the guillotine or of any glamorous hanging.
> Piece the world together, boys, but not with your hands.[5] (192)

In the advice of the last line, Stevens indicates the connection between the contingent and the trial of patching and piecing, between the foundation-less unreality of life and the longing for something less final than the guillotine. He called this poem "an experiment at stylizing life," commenting, it "may be summed up by saying that there is no such thing as life; what there is is a style of life from time to time" (L 435).

Here, style seems to have something to do with slowing down a life that, as the weather attests, speeds by too quickly to know or understand. Yet, style is not the full stop of a "glamorous hanging" because it is less an end than a means of living, of connecting one contingent, if fleeting, moment with the next. Or, as Stevens commented, "We cannot ignore or obliterate death, yet we do not live in memory. Life is always new; it is always beginning. The fiction is part of this beginning" (L 434). Here, Stevens sets his style apart from that Romantic ideal of Keats's "Cold Pastoral" and matches it to the "incipient cosmos." Style is improvisation, a means of accommodating rather than arresting change, of discovering what the poet can make of its novelty, and of challenging the "glamorous hanging" on its own terms.

It is precisely Stevens's interest in style or in piecing the world together that has elicited the most controversy among his critics. His early readers thought he was *all* style or too heavily stylized, as Gorham Munson commented in the 1925 *Dial*, "Until the advent of Wallace Stevens, American literature has lacked a dandy."[6] Correcting that view, Frank Doggett presents Stevens in another style, identifying him as the poet of ideas in *Stevens' Poetry of Thought* (1966). When Helen Vendler gives attention again to the subject of Stevens's style in *On Extended Wings: Wallace Stevens' Longer Poems* (1969), it is to retrieve the poet from both the charges of hedonism and the claims of philosophy in order to examine the variety of experiments in style he undertook; but Vendler emphasizes the formalist achievement of style, "the complicate, the amassing harmony" of the late long poems, rather than the experimenting impulse that brought Stevens to that final product.

The argument that continues about Stevens along these familiar divisions between the frivolous and the serious poet has, at its base, questions of style. Hugh Kenner finds Stevens's work too stylized, identifying it as "an Edward Lear poetic, pushed toward all limits," while Harold Bloom can place him squarely in the company of Romantic visionaries.[7] More recently, with a new interest in Stevens's biography, Frank Lentricchia has given the dandy Stevens an updated and very serious treatment, attributing the poet's style to the feminized side of his character occluded in the masculinized profession he chose as an insurance company executive.[8]

This turn of the critical debate about style into questions of gender has been achieved through Lentricchia's argument with what he regards as the essentialist feminist criticism of Sandra Gilbert and Susan Gubar, but it has a longer critical history in American literature.[9] Writing in 1925, William Carlos Williams asked:

> "Poets? Where? They are the test. But a true woman in flower, never. Emily Dickinson, starving of passion in her father's garden, is the very nearest we have ever been—starving.
> Never a woman: never a poet. That's an axiom. Never a poet saw sun here.[10]

In terms quite unlike Lentricchia's but with a similar sentiment, Williams attributes the repression of the woman, the poet, and the passions they both represent, to the Puritan fervor for domination and control.[11] In his mind, the anti-lyric impulse in American culture is combined with, if not the result of, a native antifeminism. Nor is Williams's exasperation entirely new; he quotes Edgar Allan Poe's equal impatience expressed in "Mr. Griswold and the Poets":

> That we are not a poetical people has been asserted so often and so roundly, both at home and abroad that the slander, through mere dint of repetition, has come to be received as truth. Yet nothing can be farther removed from it. . . . Our necessities have been taken for our propensities. Having been forced to make railroads, it has been deemed impossible that we should make verse. . . . But this is purest insanity. (218)

Like Williams, Poe railed against the suppression of the poetic by the practical or the didactic, arguing for poetry as *"The Rhythmical Creation of Beauty"* and claiming its sole arbiter as Taste. His designation of the death of a beautiful woman as the most perfect subject for poetry suggests that, in a somewhat different way from either Lentricchia or Williams, he too links gender and genre.[12]

The suspicion of Stevens, then, that runs its circuitous course from Lentricchia through Kenner to Munson may have its roots in a much older anti-lyric impulse, which Williams identifies with the Puritans and Poe with the practical urgencies of a new country; but it persists and relies even today on an unusual severity of judgment.[13] Why such a sentiment would linger into the twentieth century has been variously explained by Lentricchia's Marxist and Gilbert and Gubar's feminist arguments. That it continues, whatever its origins and despite the creativity of twentieth-century lyric poets, is evident in the critical reception of Stevens, who may be the canonical Modernist but whose place in the period is still seriously debated.[14]

The argument is over Stevens's style, and its intensity may be taken as one indication of a native critical uncertainty about style. In becoming questions of gender, as they have in Stevens criticism, questions of style point to an uneasiness about identity, about expression, and about reception, that lyric poetry has generated in American literary history. Although Harold Bloom has tried to subsume that uneasiness into the tradition in his magisterial reading of Stevens as the twentieth-century inheritor of Emerson and the Romantics, the continuing critical debate over Stevens's poetry suggests that he cannot be so easily abstracted. His poetry challenges those traditional interpretations of American literary history in which the self is imagined as representative, the letter as a symbol of spirit, and the audience as subjects to be persuaded.[15]

This book is an inquiry into that challenge and into the genre that has encouraged it. The engendering of lyric poetry that recent Stevens criticism has attempted suggests that an examination of the genre might best start with a consideration of a poet for whom the female gender is a primary issue. Thus, this book opens with a discussion of Emily Dickinson's poetry, and, after an interchapter, it continues with an exploration of Stevens's work. As I have said, the book will concentrate on three topics in each poet: the speaker of the poem, the poem's language of exchange, and the audience that the poet imagines. In these topics, those questions of gender, which appear to be so important to the genre of lyric poetry in America, will be central. In Dickinson, they are given their boldest, most imaginative, and original responses. As a woman withdrawn from the world, undertaking the unusual act of opening an intercourse with the world, she had to imagine an exchange for which she had few models and create an audience she hoped might exist. In taking up the genre after Dickinson, Stevens had her example, and he could also draw on the ferment in poetry in the early Modernist movement. In distinguishing himself from his contemporaries, he had to find his own way toward answering the questions of gender that the American lyric arouses, and often he chooses to handle them by allowing the woman to speak in his poetry. He reserves for himself the voice of final commentary; it is disembodied, removed, and summative. Nonetheless, the frequency with which women speaking initiate a poem for Stevens, often only to be corrected or reproved, suggests that he too tried to create a new kind of speaker, develop a linkage through language, and work out a viable exchange with an audience about which he had some reservations.

Together, the work of these two poets posits the possibility that American lyric poetry is the genre most in conflict with the culture and most expressive of that culture's conflicts. The sense of self in the lyric speaker, the idea of language as interactional, and the idea of a beloved and feared audience—all these factors are uniquely expressed in these two poets. They do not confirm the sense of American literature that has been derived from its Emersonian tradition, partly because the genre itself has never been a vital part of that tradition.

Lyric poetry has been a neglected genre in American literary history. In the nineteenth century, it was regarded as insufficient to express the new country. The earliest call for an American literature in the 1830s and 1840s emphasized, above all else, length and the need for an impressive form to express a large country. One writer, treating "The Inferiority of American Literature" in the *Southern Literary Messenger*, argued that most of our authors had produced "pieces of little length," when what was needed was magnitude and awe.[16] A writer in *The Knickerbocker* asked, "Where is the American epic?" and lamented that "the present age is incapable of the epic."[17] His hope is that "if writers would focus on our national beauty, we could achieve an immortal national literature. It will happen as age gives us a 'national character'" (388).

The length of the poem was a constant issue in reviews and surveys of the American literary scene in the nineteenth century. In the *North American Review* in January 1830, a reviewer admitted that America could not expect a *Paradise Lost* for a long time, but he called for "a poetical essay, tale, romance, tragedy or comedy" that he could peruse in several hours.[18] Such nineteenth-century tastes that judged quality by the length and the authenticity of its American subject could commend Henry Wadsworth Longfellow because "Hiawatha is the first permanent contribution to the world's *belles-lettres* made from Indian authorities."[19]

The idealism that caused nineteenth-century critics, concerned with the foundation of American literature, to judge the greatness of a work by the greatness of its theme and length, however poorly conceived, lingers in twentieth-century tastes as well. Ezra Pound based his positive assessment of Henry James on "the momentum of his art, the sheer bulk of its processes" that "should heave him out of himself, out of his personal limitations, out of the tangles of heredity and environment, out of the bias of early training, of early predilections, . . . and leave him simply the great true recorder."[20] Williams also had a relish for size, admitting that he wanted to "find an image large enough to embody the whole knowable world about me," to "gain 'profundity'" in order "to write in a larger way than of the birds and flowers."[21]

The emphasis on size and the ambition to be the "great true recorder," which inspired Williams and Eliot no less than Pound, made the brief lyric genre a less significant achievement. The American Modernists seemed tuned to the public, not the private, sphere and therefore willing to suppress imaginative possibilities on which the lyric voice depends. In American poetry, this view has a long history. It finds confirmation of its logic in Puritan hermeneutics. There, the sense of the unique self as inescapably limited and its corollary that this limited self can be converted into a representative self by suppressing its individuality minimize all but the didactic value of art. As these ideas came into the American literature of the Romantic period, Ralph Waldo Emerson conflated the private with the public dream, arguing for the *American* scholar, for self-reliance as reliance on God within, for the dependence of language on the American landscape, and for a prophetic fulfillment of the scriptures here and now.[22] Such a sense of self made the private valuable only as it could be publicized.

Dickinson's break with this tradition may have come about because she wrote most of her poetry in a crisis of culture. The thirty odd years that separate the bulk of Dickinson's writing from Emerson's was crucial. Emerson wrote in the pre-Civil War period when culture could still be considered as a single evolutionary process, ending in the bourgeois ideal of autonomous individuality.[23] Dickinson wrote during the war and afterward, when that idea of culture was being severely challenged, and eventually would give way to the idea of cultures in the plural without a necessary evolutionary pattern, suggesting a world of separate, distinctive, and diversely meaningful ways of life. Dickinson's experience was part of that changing sense of culture, and her work became an early expression of its possibilities.

For its guiding sense of self, language, and audience, Dickinson's poetry points in the direction of what was to be called pragmatism more clearly than it looks back to Romanticism. First, in the genre itself, the sense of self is crucial, and by devoting herself exclusively to that genre, Dickinson had to abandon the help she might have received from the formulations of the public and representative self that served Emerson in his essays and Walt Whitman in his epic poetry. Where Whitman could claim, "And what I assume, you shall assume, / For every atom belonging to me as good belongs to you," Dickinson could never make that identification, writing rather, "I never felt at Home—Below— / And in the Handsome Skies / I shall not feel at Home—I know—" (P 413). Her sense is of the always changing self that cannot be described by that Transcendental state beyond activity to which Emerson aspired.[24] Her project is much closer to that of the pragmatists, which is, in Richard Rorty's words, to "de-divinize" the world and the self, "to say that one no longer thinks of either as speaking to us, as having a language of its own, as a rival poet."[25]

Held up against the Transcendental ideal, Dickinson's lyric speakers will appear changeable and duplicitous.[26] Far from reaching that stasis that Emerson idealized in his "transparent eyeball" passage, Dickinson's lyric speakers are always in process, moving, and struck by the discontinuity of their experience. For her, continuity is figured as dejection, as in "From Blank to Blank— / A Threadless Way / I pushed Mechanic feet—" (P 761).

Furthermore, Dickinson's speakers do not expand and grow in a narrative of self-development such as Henry David Thoreau could generate, partly because her lyrics are too brief to trace such a process and partly because she does not model her own development after natural processes. Her sense of self and of the world depends upon contingency, and her dominant trope is metonymy not metaphor.

If individuality is a cultural construct, then Dickinson had the advantage of a gender that would not permit her to use the Emersonian language of the centered self. She had to investigate an unmapped and private territory of the self where the individual might be truly unique and, if not original, then certainly eccentric.[27] In writing as a means of identifying herself to herself alone, Dickinson opposed the cultural restraints imposed on her as a woman with an imaginative ferocity equal to the powerfully repressive cultural force she met.[28]

Like Stevens but more lonely, she confirms nonetheless the idea that poetry is not the imagination taken alone.[29] It comes from those fortuitous interactions that make and unmake experience. To regulate these imaginative possibilities is for Dickinson a loss, as she writes:

Perception of an object costs
Precise the Object's loss—

Perception in itself a Gain
Replying to its Price—

The Object Absolute—is nought—
Perception sets it fair
And then upbraids a Perfectness
That situates so far— (P 1071)

She does not wish to dominate, but to remain open to experience. In this poem, as Robert Weisbuch has noted, "dualism is replaced by an idea of imperfect, partial relatedness."[30] That interaction of subject and object in Dickinson's poems, which has occasioned as varied a critical debate as that between imagination and reality in Stevens's poetry, is both arbitrary and intimate.[31] She eschewed the far-off "Perfectness" of perception in favor of the near and intimate where chance rather than purpose prevails. "Within my reach! / I could have touched! / I might have chanced that way!" is a common exclamation in her poetry (P 90).

She exemplifies that readiness for experience that characterized the other Romantics, but she lacks their aptitude for drawing conclusions of direct public relevance, preferring rather the puzzlement that intimacy always involves. For Dickinson, the choice was not that eighteenth-century and Emersonian one between the private and the public, but the twentieth-century choice between the intimate and the social that Stevens's work also exemplifies.[32] In this, the two poets are linked by their choice of the lyric genre, which does not require the speaker to be organized in a socially viable way or in the cause-and-effect logic of prose. They are also linked by their choice of a female speaker. Dickinson's nineteenth-century female speakers, relieved of the public posture of Emerson's speakers even in his lyrics, can express the discontinuity of moods that composes the self. In Stevens's twentieth-century poems where he often uses a female speaker responding or talking to someone (presumably male) who is absent, this process develops into a sense of the self as interactional, neither coherent nor continuous, but contingent.[33]

A lyric speaker, presented in a poem's brief, repeated, and figurative form, will lack the steadfastness of identity that the novelistic character can have. Without a narrative progression, a lyric speaker will be free to disrupt notions of a coherent and continuous identity. In examining the ways in which Dickinson and Stevens use the lyric genre to develop a variety of fantastic and eccentric speakers, this book will investigate the radical conception of identity that the lyric genre allows. Neither rooted in biography, as Dickinson's speakers have been, nor abstracted by the philosophy of idealism into "central man" as Stevens's speakers often are, the speakers of their lyric poems represent rather a sense of selfhood as contingent, changeable, aleatory, discontinuous. Critics who have identified a narrative of repression in Dickinson's lyric speakers and a narrative of centrality in Stevens's have severely limited the radical nature of the poets' imaginative resources by restraining them to prose models of character.

If the lyric speakers of their poems are not centered characters, neither can their language be centered in a symbolic system. This book will look at the two poets' different interests in letters as a language of correspondence distinct from symbolism. Both Dickinson and Stevens were frequent letter writers as well as lyric poets, and an inquiry into the importance of letters in their poetry—letters of the alphabet, letters of correspondence, and poems as letters—will indicate how, in emphasizing the literality of the letter, the lyric genre insists on itself as an artifact, a place, and not simply a transparency through which meaning might pass. A consideration of why Dickinson reveals nothing of the contents of her famous "letter to the world" and why Stevens offers little information beyond the sound of the letter in his *The Comedian as the Letter C* will lead to an exploration of the ways in which the lyric genre might value the letter over the spirit and challenge the tradition of typological reading that has dominated American literature from the Puritans onward.

These poets cause us to arrest attention at the letter itself, both as a character of the alphabet and as a material token, to consider our relation to it, and to gain our bearings from it. Although their critics have been anxious to determine what the letter stands for, the poets themselves appear to be more interested in the ways in which the letters stand in place. The interest in place, in relationships of contingency, in genealogical and generational links, may be regarded as part of a lyric impulse to draw connections that do not depend on a narrative development.

The two poets differ essentially in their use of letters and in their interest in what letters can accomplish. Because Dickinson relied on letters to represent her in a world from which she largely withdrew, she developed an interest in letters as material tokens. Touching them offered pleasures beyond the satisfactions of reading their message. Her poems about sending and receiving letters have an erotic charge that is largely missing from

Stevens's poetry. For her, letters appear to be love tokens, and words signify links between people before they generate referential meaning.

She could write to Thomas Wentworth Higginson, "A Letter always feels to me like immortality because it is the mind alone without corporeal friend. Indebted in our talk to attitude and accent, there seems a spectral power in thought that walks alone" (L, II, 330). However, what interests her is exactly the feelings that letters arouse; their "spectral power" to thrill and terrify, and not their message, focuses her attention.

Stevens's interest in letters is a much more restrained activity. Where Dickinson feels their erotic charge, he writes letters and uses letters in his poetry to establish a sense of community.[34] Stevens sees letters as establishing familial connections and nesting places. In "Two Letters," for example, he describes in "I / *A Letter From*" "Some true interior to which to return, / A home against one's self, a darkness, // An ease in which to live a moment's life" (OP 133); and in "II / *A Letter To*" he identifies the same need: "She wanted a holiday / With someone to speak her dulcied native tongue," "and the two of them in speech, // In a secrecy of words / Opened out within a secrecy of place" (OP 133). The "secrecy" of words or place is valued for the intimacy that it promises and not for the messages it may hide. In a late poem, "Recitation after Dinner," he asks if one's identity in the generations of a family is determined by the order of place:

> Are we characters in an arithmetic
> Or letters of a curious alphabet;
> And is tradition an unfamiliar sum,
> A legend scrawled in script we cannot read? (OP 115)

In part, Stevens's poetry is itself an effort to find a place. In his commonplace book *Sur Plusieurs Beaux Sujets*, he quotes a notice of *The English Flower Garden*:

> "The art of play, as also, I am inclined to think, the art of life itself, consists mainly in the creation of an environment within which we are of some importance. The consciousness of inferiority which characterizes so many people today, destroying their peace and driving them helter-skelter into the barbed-wire entanglements of false philosophies, is due very largely to the neglect of this first principle."[35]

Milton Bates has argued that Stevens used his commonplace book to establish that kind of environment, "a plot to be cultivated and jealously guarded against intrusion by any idiom or idea he could not appropriate wholly for his own purposes" (2). Moreover, he developed in his poetry such an environment. Again, in his commonplace book, Stevens cites a passage from Henry James indicating a way of thinking that is obviously congenial to his own habits of mind:[36]

> ["]To live *in* the world of creation—to get into it and stay in it—to frequent it and haunt it—to *think* intensely and fruitfully—to woo combinations and inspirations into being by a depth and continuity of attention and meditation— this is the only thing[.]" (81)

Yet this separate world of creation in Stevens is never totally isolated from the audience it seeks.[37] Stevens's letter-writing habits and his use both of alphabetic letters and of letters of correspondence in his poems turn his work toward that audience and the community it can create. The final chapter on each poet in this book will investigate that sense of community. The subject is as problematic in Dickinson, who remained largely unpublished, as it is in the publicly recognized Stevens. The imagined audience cannot be easily separated from either the lyric's speaker or the language of correspondence the poem creates. Such interrelations underwrite the lyric, however much the genre resists it.

The next six chapters take up these subjects of speaker, language, and audience, first in Dickinson and then in Stevens. The two poets lived in different times and places, and I have not tried to connect them except through the lyric genre to which they devote themselves in somewhat similar ways. Creating the lyric speaker, both Dickinson and Stevens free themselves from a conception of identity as uniform, continuous, and coherent. Their radical rethinking of identity allows them to consider their work as letters to the world, links rather than simple messages. And they can both imagine that their imaginary audiences will need them, even desire them, because, deeply ingrained in their creative habits remains Stevens's sense that "things are because of interrelations or interactions." This book is a study of the way such "things are."

Chapter 2

"The dazzled Soul / In her unfurnished Rooms": Dickinson and the Lyric Self

Although Ralph Waldo Emerson could express disappointment with his age, acknowledging that men could claim to confirm their existence only by reading what they thought, he retained nonetheless Descartes's faith in the sovereignty of the *Cogito* as the basis of subjectivity.[1] This faith confirmed his concept of individuality. What he thought could be, indeed, should be thought by everyone; even his moods were universal ones. He saw himself as a representative self and wrote as a man at the center of his age.[2]

In him, the culture found its spokesman. Only his aphoristic style gives any hint of the transitory nature of culture and the precariousness of its center. The form more than the content of his work points to the tensions that were to tear apart his firm, even rigid, sense of individuality.[3] In those sentences that do not cohere and the paragraphs that fail to develop in careful stages, Emerson wrote better than he knew. They prove against his own assertions that each is not needed by each one; some, even many, are perfect alone. Emerson appeared to remain impervious to this paradox of thinking about the relationship of each to all in completed fragments. While he may have despaired, he did not doubt.

Writing thirty years after Emerson had started, Emily Dickinson had the advantage of time. Emerson's confidence in his representative self began to erode even in his own lifetime. But she had, in addition, advantages of her female gender and of the lyric genre in which she wrote that allowed her a greater latitude in thinking about the self. Tied as he was to a public certitude and optimism, Emerson could express his private and idiosyncratic self only in the private revelations of style. Emily Dickinson could make it the content of her art. Because she was a woman and a poet, she was freer than he was from the conviction that she was representative and also from the necessity to be so.[4] In nineteenth-century America, the female gender, the lyric genre, and the culture existed in a tension that allowed Dickinson to feel the repressive fiction of the representative self and the hazards it presented to self-expression.

She wrote in the first stage of advance beyond Emerson's thinking about individuality, and, although her work is conventionally read as influenced by his, I want to suggest that it is actually a powerful indictment of his confidence in the discrete subject of the *Cogito*. Woman and poet that she was, she was uniquely situated to revise Emerson's thinking and to express a more radical understanding of individuality. For her, individuality could not be universalized and made to be representative; it had to find its expression in a form, like itself, that could be both fragmented and excessive.

The lyric poem provided the perfect genre for such experimental expression because it was relieved of the narrative order of prose, the moral purpose of the essay, and the persuasive thrust of argument. As Dickinson developed it, the lyric was a brief, repetitive, figurative form that allowed her to explore those same qualities in the puzzle of individuality and thereby to undermine the certainty of the representative self and of representation itself.

Nonetheless, despite Dickinson's insistence on the self as expressed only in brief, repetitive, and figurative form, she has been assimilated by a literary tradition that has remained dominated by an Emersonian conception of the representative self. Effectively "shut up in Prose" by that tradition, she has been frequently read as if her poems could be easily attached to a plot. Although she consistently states her preference for "Possibility" over "Prose," no poetry has been more thoroughly organized into a continuous explanatory narrative than hers. Still, she could write of one range of experience, "Did Our Best Moment last— / 'Twould supersede the Heaven—" (P 393), and of the other, "Pain—has an Element of Blank—" (P 650). And she was haunted by the uncanny return of certain thoughts even when she had to admit:

> Nor where it went—nor why it came
> The second time to me—
> Nor definitely, what it was—
> Have I the Art to say— (P 701)

Dickinson's understanding of individuality fits neither into nineteenth-century ideas of the lyric genre nor into twentieth-century notions of the female gender. She was certainly more radical than that one contemporary reader who wanted to know who was speaking with such a "spasmodic gait" in the poems, and still more radical than twentieth-century readers who organize their responses by conventional models of reading derived from, and most easily applied to, prose. Psychoanalytic, Marxist, feminist theories of identity, for example, all depend to one extent or another upon a plot, upon character, and upon extended development. Applied to a form that is brief, repetitive, and figurative, these models are no more suitable than the formalistic model Thomas Wentworth Higginson was applying when he urged Dickinson not to try to publish her work. They fit uneasily and can be used only when the form itself is neglected in favor of a narrative that can be derived from joining together a number of poems.[5]

By such strategies of reading, Cynthia Griffin Wolff can make Dickinson, the private poet, into a public speaker, arguing against the evidence of several poems that "she did not want the Voice of the verse to be incongruous or susceptible of dismissal; above all, she wanted to speak as a 'Representative Voice,' not querulously—not with the keening voice of the 'overheard soliloquy.'"[6] While Wolff draws her conclusions from a psychoanalytic reading of Dickinson's biography, Alicia Ostriker, writing from a feminist perspective, can comment:

> Dickinson genuinely despises publicity and power, prefers the private and powerless life—and the reverse is equally true. We may say the same about many of her poems in praise of deprivation: they reject what they commend, commend what they reject. Their delight, their strength derives from their doubleness. (41)

But power and deprivation are themes that interest Ostriker, issues central to feminist criticism, and her own claims should suggest that they are not issues equally central to Dickinson.

The brevity with which the lyric "I" is presented in Dickinson's poems alone indicates a conception of identity different from the psychoanalytic or the American feminist model.[7] The fiction of a coherent single identity can be maintained best in a prose form which tends inevitably toward steadfastness of character. Even an effort such as Edgar Allan Poe's to undermine the stalwartness of fictional characters by the use of unreliable narrators relies on a consistency of representation that is foreign to the lyric "I."

In the lyric poem, the "I" is expressed only in limited detail. For a lyric poet of consistent productivity such as Dickinson, that limitation is a deliberate choice of self-presentation, expressive of a particular sense of self and individuality. The repetition and figuration of the lyric also articulate a sense of identity as particular, discontinuous, limited, private, hidden. Such a concept directly subverts the idea that the self is a publicly knowable, organized, single entity. Thus, it challenges all narrative explanations of identity, including the dominant ideology of self-reliance expressed in the prose of nineteenth-century American culture.[8] Dickinson's chief means of revolt against that ideology was her choice of the publicly degraded lyric form.

Only in nineteenth-century American literature, where there was no great lyric tradition, would this easily conventionalized genre be available for subversive expression. Despite Poe's claim for its importance, the lyric was considered a woman's form, judged insufficient to express the grandness of America and the American individual, the central mission of the nineteenth-century American literary establishment.[9] This insufficiency of form was coextensive with the insufficiency of female identity. The precariousness of identity, the unmappable privacy, and the unacknowledged limitations of individuality could then be suggested, evoked, tentatively recognized in the brevity, repetition, and figuration of the lyric because it was a marginalized form. Dickinson's experimental form responded to a new sense of identity. Further, the lyric was uniquely available for self-expression in a society where other literary forms for such expression (the diary, the letter, for example) had been conventionalized and absorbed by the cultural imperatives of the Puritan tradition.

She wrote in that moment before the Civil War when the idea of individualism was losing its sense of comprehensiveness. Her exclusive choice of the lyric genre allowed her to express individuality in an age committed to individualism. The two are not commensurate, as Emerson's self-reliant yet representative individual attests. The concept of individualism includes a commonality and a sense of partaking in the common that threatens the claim of individuality. Individualism is always spoken with a forked tongue, as Werner Hamacher, discussing Nietzsche, has explained:

> Individuality is so fully determined as incommensurability that no individual could correspond to its concept if it were at one with and equal to itself, if it were a thoroughly determined, whole form. *Human, All Too Human* proposes, in the interests of knowledge, that one not uniformize oneself into rigidity of bearing and that one not treat oneself "like a stiff, steadfast *single* individual" (I, 719). Only the individual's non-identity with itself can constitute its individuality. Measured against itself as concept, bearing, and function, the individual proves to be other, to be more—or less—than itself. Its individuality is always only what

reaches out beyond its empirical appearance, its social and psychological identities, and its logical form. Individuality is unaccountable surplus.[10]

This unaccountable surplus is what cannot be made uniform, narrated, and
organized into a single individual. It is best expressed not in prose but in
lyric poetry where a brief and repeated form depends upon the exposure
of particularity and peculiarity. Such limited details rather than extended
narrative development provide relief from the self-defeating ambitions of
a coherent and definitive presentation of the self. The lyric poem does not
mythologize the individual as a readable organization, making coherence
out of isolated moments and fragmentary experience as the novel does;
rather, the lyric makes isolated moments out of coherence and restores
with words the contingency of the self that has been lost to experience.[11]
Unlike the novel, the lyric's "significant form" does not signify social
viability.[12]

It signifies rather the profligacy of individuality. In P 634, Dickinson
describes the value of such profligacy. A riddle, or more accurately a
quasi-riddle, since it is evident from the start that the subject is a bird, the
poem demonstrates the way in which the lyric strains the techniques of
representation by rendering clear details opaque and then creating out of
that opacity the central clarity. The poem's riddling quality is an important
element of its representation because it allows Dickinson to present one
thing in terms of another as an image, and in the instability of the image
to suggest thereby the paradox of identity. What we see best, we see least
well; what we cannot see or refuse to see becomes clearest evidence. Offering instruction on how to know a bird, Dickinson provides too an
inquiry into self-representation.

She starts with alarming confidence in the brief detail: "You'll know
Her—by Her Foot—". And that particularity presents itself as immediately
obstructive since to know *her* by her foot is to know nothing of the
conventional feminine beauty of her face or figure. Nor is it to know much
by symbolic extension. The foot, unlike the hand or the heart, does not
stand for anything except standing. Curiously, however, the first stanza
insists on its own particular way of knowing by metaphorical extension,
developing in apposition:

You'll know Her—by Her Foot—
The smallest Gamboge Hand

With Fingers—where the Toes should be—
Would more affront the Sand—

No poet could make these connections without thinking of how she herself is known by her poetic foot, and in the apposition of the foot/hand Dickinson makes a whimsical connection between bird and poet, hand writing and poetic foot, which will be developed in the final stanza where she meditates on an idea close to the Nietzschean surplus in individuality.

Before that, however, the poem appears to be a detailed taxonomy of the bird, identified by particular details—her foot, her vest, her cap. But these typical parts lose their immediate force in the poet's efforts to maintain the metaphor of bird and woman. The bird's foot described as "this Quaint Creature's Boot" is rendered unknowable as either foot or boot when the speaker says it is "Without a Button—I could vouch—". That testimony guarantees enigma. Without a button it is not a boot, and so the vouching undoes the knowledge that it would confirm. The excursion seems merely decorative, as does the admission that inside her tightly fitting vest she wore a duller jacket when she was born. This aleatory information appears inappropriately applied to a figure described as small, snug, tightly encased, finely plumed.

Like Nietzsche's individual, this bird is something other than its type. Its foot is a boot but not a boot; its orange-brown vest is the opposite of its original jacket; its cap appears from a distance to be no cap at all, and then closer up proves to be a cap that is not a cap since it has no band or brim. By the sixth stanza, Dickinson has demonstrated convincingly the extent to which details do not represent the whole, and concomitantly the uncertainty of ever knowing the whole either by knowledge of parts as in synecdoche, by knowledge derived from identifying one thing in terms of another or relating the familiar to the unfamiliar as in metaphor, or by personal testimony, or by precise description and careful distinction. Even in combination, such ways do not lead to a satisfactory representation of the whole. But the poem does not end with this conclusion toward which it appears to be drawing. Rather, it presents the bird presenting itself:

You'll know Her—by Her Voice—
At first—a doubtful Tone—
A sweet endeavor—but as March
To April—hurries on—

She squanders on your Ear
Such Arguments of Pearl—
You beg the Robin in Your Brain
To keep the other—still—

The "doubtful Tone" that turns into "Arguments of Pearl" is an excessive presentation. And it is perhaps the excess from which the poet imagines the recipient retreating, preferring the idea to this reality.

Such self-presentation as the bird's is always more than enough. It must be excessive if it is to be the expression of an individual, of the "unaccountable surplus" of individuality. This bird of doubtful tone exemplifies Hamacher's description of the Nietzschean individual:

> The individual does not live. It outlives. Its being is being out and being over, an insubstantial remainder and excess beyond every determinable form of human life. Instead of being a social or psychic form of human existence, the individual—the self-surpassing of type, or genius—is the announcement of what, generally translated as 'superman' or 'overman,' is best translated in this context as 'outman'. (Hamacher, 119)

Leaving aside for the moment the absurdity of considering Dickinson's bird an 'outman,' I draw attention to the way in which the poet presents a bird through brief details and then obliterates these details in the verb "squanders" where the bird surpasses the type. Thus, the bird is profligate in Nietzschean terms. And the poet behind the bird knows too that, in its squandering, it is casting pearls before swine, claiming individuality in a world that prefers types.

Thus, the brevity of the lyric allows a certain kind of knowing. It demands the excessive patience and attention that only a poet would possess, and it requires an indulgence that Dickinson had every reason to believe her readers would lack. To know by the foot is not a simple knowledge, nor is it a different way of knowing something that exists outside the poem; it is rather a form of knowing by excesses only available in brief and metrical form.

Such excesses figure in the brevity of lyric representation by distorting syntax and sense. Knowing by the foot means fitting language to form as in the lines, "Nor is it Clasped unto of Band— / Nor held upon—of Brim—". Extracted from the poem, these lines fail to signify anything; they can signify only in an arrangement of language that prizes apposition, parallel structures, or periphrasis, in short, that prizes excessive statement. Or, another example, the opening quatrain with its comparison of foot to hand that "Would more affront the Sand" is a deictic chaos, made necessary and then managed by the only full rhyme in the poem—"Sand" holds "Hand" in place. Here, Dickinson seems to be underscoring the whimsy of knowing in rhyme and rhythm. Like the bird, the poet too is a squanderer and, like the bird's, her squandering is permitted and limited by brief form and the formal repetition it requires.

The lyric's repetition derives from its brevity, but repetition is curiously essential both *to* and *in* the lyric poem. As a way of representation, repetition brought Dickinson's lyrics into conflict with Romantic conceptions of form and subject in nineteenth-century America. A form that depends on the repetition of its formal elements will not be free nor will it necessarily grow by the principle of organic form. Moreover, the subject presented in repetitive images will not be original and new. It will always be a copy and a copy of a copy.

The vulnerability of the lyric to conventional form and subject is well documented in the history of literature. But for Dickinson, it posed a particular problem. She shared with her fellow Romantics a suspicion of convention. She knew, as they did, the limits of the self that was made and the character that was formed in large and in little by repeating familiar patterns of behavior, by repeated professions of faith, by copying over moral precepts both in school books and in embroidery lessons at home, by duties performed and performed again. She resisted in her own life these means through which one generation inculcated into the next its values, its identity, its way of life, and forced the self through repetition to grow into a presentable self. It was this self that Thoreau hoped to wash off each morning in his dips into Walden Pond. It was this self that Emerson intended to escape by writing "Whim" on his lintel post and departing from family and friends for a day. And it was this self that Dickinson drew and satirized in several poems. But while Thoreau could generate a belief in the natural man beyond the social man and Emerson argued for the genius within, Dickinson as a lyric poet had no access to these plots of redemption.

Rather, she was tied by the repetition in and of the lyric to use repetition as the constituent of character. Again, the limits of the genre enlarged her understanding and when in P 443, for example, she takes repetition as her subject, she uses it to express ranges of experience inaccessible to narrative organization. The poem has been enforced into such organization by Barbara Mossberg, who reads it as evidence of the duplicity imposed upon women by the dominant patriarchal culture (Mossberg, 197). The repetitive language and strategies of the poem reveal, however, a miserable lack of duplicity or division between inner and outer actions.

The repetition in the verb tense—"I tie my Hat", "I crease my Shawl", "I put new Blossoms in the Glass", "I push a petal from my Gown", "I have so much to do"—describes particular habits by which the speaker prepares herself and her house for presentation to the world. Yet they are not aids in self-making so much as subterfuges behind which she hides both from the world and from herself. More crucially, the theatricality of these acts is doubled by the theatricality within; the outer self acting is in danger at every point of being upstaged by the dramatic, even melodramatic, inner self who "got a Bomb— / And held it in our Bosom—". By this convergence of outer show and inner show, Dickinson questions the nature of identity. What is real? What is disguise? Do these questions even apply? Is the self only show?

The repetitive gestures of putting on hats and taking off shawls may be obsessive acts, but no more so than the "stinging work— / To cover what we are", the effort of holding a bomb in the bosom. The speaker justifies her "life's labor" by claiming that it holds "our Senses—on". But on to what? What is the center? What is the periphery here? The speaker's sense that she must "simulate" is, as it must be in the lyric, unexplained. Her boast that she only trembles at the bomb that would make others start suggests a fondness for her own dilemma. She is holding on to "Miles on Miles of Nought" by the same effort of will that nullified the self. Both her inner and her outer life reflect a willingness to act as if "the very least / Were infinite—to me—".

Often accused of speaking from beyond the grave, here Dickinson brings the grave into the center of life. Sharon Cameron is perhaps too vigorous in envisioning this poem as one in which life as disruption of stasis "seems like an outbreak around which control keeps trying, unsuccessfully, to close" or where "meaning disrupts both vacuous action and the sententia in which such action takes refuge."[13] It appears rather to be a poem in which control is the only meaning, and meaning the only control.

In this poem where the inner self is fashioned by the same patterns of repetition that fashion the outer self, the collapse of the division between inner and outer in the speaker makes it possible to collapse the division between self and other. "I" becomes "we" at the very point in mid-poem where the speaker turns from her daily duties to announce the unique errand that should have distinguished her from all others. It is not that the catastrophe deprives her of individuality, but that she divests herself of her individuality by surrendering to this single event. "*We* came to Flesh—" and "*we* got a Bomb—" the speaker boasts, as if she were somehow made more grand, indeed "completed", by this dwindling of life into a single purpose which it is now her duty to memorialize (italics added).

In life lived as a duty, there can be no difference between private and public. The repetitive strategies of the lyric are used here to express the dilemma of the self ensnared in its own trap of meaning. The clotting of the lines with internal rhymes, assonance, consonance, alliteration, anaphora, and phrases in apposition suggests the way in which language can be used to impede change, to repeat sameness, even as it seems to press forward.

"I tie my Hat" is not about loss but about the refusal to give up loss. The speaker in this poem appears to account for the unaccountable surplus of individuality by explaining it in terms of a single completed "errand." But insofar as that "errand" is undetailed and only abstractly named, it would appear to be subject to endless repetition.

The "Bomb" in the bosom that somehow mysteriously never goes off, that is paradoxically "calm" is pure melodrama, an image that loses its power the second it fixes itself in the imagination, or rather *should* lose its power. In fact, in critical commentary, it has not. The restitution of order around the bomb, evident in the persistent present of the verb "we do life's labor," has come to signify the speaker's martyrdom for critics who want to see in the poem a cause and effect explanation of character, a narrative that will contrast the liveliness of the bomb to the deadliness of routine existence (Mossberg, 197). But such a reading provides a plot where plot has been deliberately suppressed by repetitive action; it finds biography where Dickinson has placed only habit.

Dickinson's poems have been particularly vulnerable to narrative explanation, specifically to biographical explication. Vivian R. Pollak justifies this practice by arguing that Dickinson's art of self-display and self-advertisement draws attention to the person behind the poems and so calls for an examination of biographical relationships.[14] What Pollak terms self-display and self-advertisement could as easily be called repression as in "I tie my Hat" where the staged performance of daily duties is an evasion of self-knowledge and even the inner faithfulness to the bomb in the bosom has its element of ritual—a display perhaps, but not of the bared self.

The relationship of poet to speaker is not a simple equation; it may be mediated through and suppressed by the lyric's figurative language. Thus, Dickinson points us in a different direction to ask questions that lead away from biography and toward figuration and supposition or, as in P 505, the person supposing. Dickinson's art of self-presentation depends on supposition in "I would not paint—a picture—".

The relationship of speaker to Dickinson is intricate and inadequately understood in Adrienne Rich's powerful reading of the poem that identifies Dickinson with the speaker and with the fear of her poetic power.[15] All that is known about the actual person who wrote this poem, about her difficulties in reaching the kind of appreciative audience she imagines in this speaker, about the doubts that she might have entertained over the breathlessness of this speaker, about her attitude toward art in general and her own poetry in particular, all this information must be added to the poem when it is read as a political and social tract. But if such reading seems reductive in its extraneousness, equally reductive is the view of the speaker here as purified of contingency by the lyric. It is a poet, after all, who is writing, "Nor would I be a Poet" and imagining what the dower of art would be. Hers is a mixed voice, contaminated by its source and, as we shall see, easily blending into its circumstances.

The speaker of this poem is a person supposing, dwelling in supposition, and, as such, she moves in and out of identities. She figures, refigures, and figures again. Now audience, now artist, she is a creature without a core, free to dwell on and in the creator's feelings and the feelings that creation inspires, open to elevation as to fixity, both impotent and privileged. The speaker is all feeling here, and her feeling is dependent on what will arouse it. But it is a productive and willing dependency that drives her to superfluous denials and extravagant affirmations. "I would not paint", "I would not talk" are excessive protestations. Denying herself what she most wants, the speaker intensifies her pleasures by doubling them in creating the occasion for the poem. Sweet torment and sumptuous despair are moods of desire prolonged and longingly anticipated, not evidence of Dickinson's passivity as Rich has argued. The speaker's relishing of her own relishing cannot fit into Rich's narrative of female repression because it is perversely irrepressible—a desire that is always for something else, always reaching out toward something, never satisfying itself except in its repetition and perpetuation. The poet is not frustrated in her desire to be a painter but rather thrilled by the desire to feel what the painter feels. She is not denied art; she has after all "fingers" of her own which stir, as we read, evoking both in the writer and in the reader their own sweet torment.

Again, in the second stanza, the speaker repeats her rapture. Just as in the first stanza where there was an odd disproportion between the "bright impossibility" of paintings and the "fingers" of the painter, so here the speaker as "endued Balloon" launched by "a lip of Metal" presents herself as soaring high from rather low inspiration. The talk of cornets is banal by comparison to the speaker's elevation through "Villages of Ether". The transport of art and the ability to be transported by art thrill the speaker, who marvels at her own powers to be moved by "but a lip". The cornet player is a performer, not a creator, and the performance is rendered remarkable by the response of the "One / Raised softly to the Ceilings—". She too is a performer—and on a higher wire.

The final stanza narrows the gap between creator/performer and audience/performer by endowing the speaker with the "Ear" *for* poetry. Identities blur. The ear of the poet as of her audience is "Enamored—impotent—content—", a passive receiver and willing receptacle. It is through the ear that both will be inspired and stunned by "Bolts of Melody!" The separate identities of the creator and the reverent appreciator of poetry compose a fantasy that had started disingenuously in the speaker's wondering how the painter's fingers feel and how the musician's lips could inspire her, but it is a fantasy of self-empowerment, not self-diminishment. The speaker also has fingers, also has lips, even as she has "the Ear". "What would the Dower be, / Had I the Art to stun myself," she speculates, but only after she has presented herself as stunned and stunnable. She has the "Art".

The supposed person that Dickinson might have called the representative of this verse is less a person than the power of supposition. Drawing up a dramatis personae for the poem or outlining a narrative continuity of envy and renunciation both diminishes and mislocates the power which names itself only in repetition. "I would not paint", "I would not talk", "Nor would I be a Poet" are repeated affirmations of the always unsatisfied, always to be satisifed, desire to create. They celebrate themselves in prolonging the moment of desire just before it is satisfied. The eroticism of the language suggests various possibilities without generating a narrative of sexual longing and consummation, and there is something indeterminate about its reference.

The description of a painter creating a picture by the "rare—celestial—stir—" of fingers is not mimetic. The words move from perceiver to perceived, from effect to affect, along a wayward path that zigzags between sound and sense. Sound alone seems to require the preposterous metaphor "Pontoon" for the self. And finally the wish to know what the dower would be if one could electrify oneself seems willful semantic wandering.

The excess in this language cannot do more than point to the excessiveness in the speaker's fantasy of self. She would be *sweetly* tormented, *sumptuously* despaired, raised and endued, awed and stunned, moved beyond sense. In her state of elevated and extravagant longing, the speaker is wanton with language, disposing lines with abandon as if they were impediments to, rather than expressions of, anticipated ecstasy. If language cannot speak itself, it must appropriate a channel for its transmission. The channel in lyric poetry need not be a fully developed character defined by birth and death dates, by family and a maturation plot; it can be, as here, a voice that speaks from shifting perspectives, that inhabits various frequencies, that has no center but rather many circumferences.

From the robin to the woman of melodramatic routine to this disembodied power of supposition, the examples I have chosen appear—when placed together—random, discontinuous, and uncentered. They are intentionally so because I want to suggest something of Dickinson's profligacy. It is possible to set the poem about the robin in the context of Dickinson's riddles or of her bird poems and to discuss P 505 with other poems in which Dickinson sets out her poetics. Or, all three poems could be adapted to one or more narratives of social repression, artistic restriction, romantic deprivation. But although such order and explanation might justify critical discourse, even my own, it would have to be superimposed and designed to suppress or ignore the fact that the poems are discrete forms, perhaps part of a larger whole that is the poet's imaginative world but deliberately brief, separate, disconnected units of expression.

The brevity of the lyrics she wrote is a form of artistic restraint that relies paradoxically on excess. In an age of sprawling masterpieces that followed the laws of nature, chapters proliferating as branches grow from trunks, in Melville's terms, the brevity, compactness, and convention of the lyric form appear unnecessarily restrictive. Yet Dickinson could use the brevity of the lyric to suggest even more freely than Melville the unaccountability of individuality. Although the lyric speaker can be conventionalized by the form itself, insofar as she is imaged in details rather than as a whole, particularized rather than totalized, she appears not conventional at all.

Such a speaker presents herself partially, not fully; her whole existence is, for us, partial. Measured against Ahab, for example, the lyric speaker suggests a sense of self that is certainly limited and yet remains paradoxically free from the restraints of social viability that will be exerted on the novelistic character. The partial may be, if not all there is, more than we realize. Brevity, then, may be the soul of character.

The brevity of the lyric form enforces its repetition. It encourages a refiguration of the already figured, and so it permits a concept of the self not only as partial but as excessive. In composing over a hundred poems that start with "I," Dickinson could create and recreate a supposed person supposing one way and then another. No single "errand" for her, the lyric speaker is singular, unique, isolated, changeable, not to be made into one composite person by joining poems together. The lyric "I" is not the real-life poet or even part of her, because she will not share her beginning or end, her history. She is not a copy of that original either because, she is always and conventionally partial.

Formally, repetition encourages a predictability that nonetheless permits disruption and gaps. Dickinson establishes a repetitive rhythm or rhyme scheme or organizing grammar and then breaks it, as she does in "I tie my Hat" when she breaks the rhythm with "Stopped—struck—my ticking—through—" and the rhyme in "Too Telescopic Eyes / To bear on us unshaded— / For their—sake—not for Ours—" and the grammar in "But since we got a Bomb— / And held it in our Bosom—". The disruption, made possible only by the expectations of repetitive form, allows the brief lyric to expand its space, to incorporate blanks, to open indeterminately.

Repetition in the lyric as, for example, in the anaphora of "I would not paint—a picture—" becomes a means of obstructing narrative explanation. It also precludes the organization of events in a causal series. And it leaves open the question of what is original, what copy, as, for example, in "I tie my Hat," in which the repetitive routine gestures of the speaker may imitate a deadened inner life or may be themselves the originator of that life.[16]

Finally, the figurative language of a lyric poem represses one term under another and suggests again the profligacy of such repression. The self is not exposed in figurative language but hidden and shielded and thus freed from social definition. Such freedom allows for the whimsy always available in self-presentation. The lyric character may be called "Pontoon" perhaps only to rhyme with "Balloon" or stuck in the improbable pose of holding a bomb in the bosom or singing not a tune but a "tone". The lyric "I" is free because its relationship to even the "I" of a supposed person is of copy to copy. It can proliferate endlessly. Although Dickinson describes one speaker acting "With scrupulous exactness— / To hold our Senses—on—" she actually calls into question the center around which such exactness would accrue both in that particular poem and in a lifetime's accumulation of such poems.

As I have noted, the brevity, the repetition, and the figuration of the lyric form point to the essential qualities of Dickinson's work: its interest in the unaccountable surplus of individuality, in repetition as constituent of character, and in figurative excess as essential to self-presentation. The problems of interpretation that Dickinson's poetry poses are essentially problems of narrative readability which have usually been resolved by the imposition of a master narrative on the work and the life. Feminist critics of Dickinson who have brought so much new energy to the reading of her poetry express only the latest version of this tendency; they have been preceded by psychoanalytic critics, biographers, and cultural historians. Dickinson's work evades them because it represents a much more radical understanding of the self than American feminists, tied as they are to a social explanation of character, can allow.

Dickinson's lyric speakers have no narrative continuity, no social viability, no steadfast identity. In their squandering, melodrama, and excesses, they express an individuality that resists final representation and the control that signifies. Yet Dickinson's lyric presentation of a self that obstructs narrative reading because it is discontinuous, profligate, and excessive may be the nineteenth century's most revolutionary expression of individuality. Thus, it may offer not only a new model for reading the lyric, but a new and perhaps persuasively feminist model of self-presentation.

Chapter 3

"A nearness to Tremendousness": Dickinson and Metonymy

As a lyric poet, Dickinson has an interest in words that is quite different from the essayist Emerson's. Although his aim in reattaching words to things is to restore their original relationship, his final purpose is to master nature by naming it and so, by persuasion, to restore man himself to his original relationship with nature.[1] Words are emblematic because things are emblematic, and Emerson's idea that there can be a right reading of the text of nature derives from a long history of Christian typological interpretation. By contrast, as a lyric poet, Dickinson needs neither to persuade nor to master. She uses words as parts of an arrangement of words, concentrating on the obduracy of their concreteness more than their emblematic force.

Dickinson's choice of the lyric genre itself signifies an advance in the battle that raged over language in nineteenth-century America because it required a new understanding of communication. In part, the difference between Dickinson's lyric speaker and Emerson's essayist is signified by the movement from an older distinction between public and private that Emerson maintained, to the more modern opposition between the social and the intimate. Whereas for him, reading and writing are public acts, for her, reading and writing are acts of intense intimacy.[2]

In expressing its intimacy, Dickinson develops an unusual trope for reading as touching letters.[3] This touch arouses a latent power in the poet that makes the act of reading an erotic experience. The intimacy of this reading, which Dickinson treats in poems about letters, is opposed to a quite different kind of reading or being read into the social world. In a number of marriage poems, Dickinson explores the ways in which words, such as "Wife," that are enforced by social conventions, can kill. These words effect a blank in the reader's consciousness. They mark the intimate as a place of emptiness. Knowing that, Dickinson's genius inheres in her insistence that the intimate might be disruptive, but it alone confirms life.

In concentrating on the sense of touch, she writes as a woman experiences the world, according to Luce Irigaray. The woman "finds pleasure more in touch than in sight."[4] Irigaray goes on, "the prevalence of the gaze, discrimination of form, and individualization of form is particularly foreign to female eroticism." These terms seem ready made to distinguish Emerson, once drawn in caricature by Christopher Cranch as two eyeballs on legs, from Dickinson who had many ways of claiming she could "not see to see." Yet rarely is Dickinson seen in her own particular way of experiencing the world. Approached most consistently in Emersonian terms through his interest in vision, Dickinson's frequent efforts to say that she could neither see nor say have had to be read as the admission of an inaptitude, whereas her sense of touch and interest in contingency have gone unexplored.[5]

For example, E. Miller Budick can acknowledge that for Dickinson "the universe is not a cohesive whole but a collection of incommensurate components," and yet Budick can still claim that Dickinson was "compelled by the structure of the human imagination, and by the exigencies of life in a multifaceted universe" to employ some kind of symbol, acknowledging that "without our correlative language of symbols, there can be no knowledge at all."[6] The convolutions of Budick's argument are essential if we are to understand the "structure of the human imagination" as designed to fix and stabilize the universe in symbols. But, if Irigaray is correct, Dickinson would have no such project in mind nor would she have derived any pleasure from such a vision. Rather, she would express herself through touch and its trope metonymy.[7] Actually, she uses both senses in her poetry; but because her interest in sight fits into conventional views of the period, it has been more thoroughly emphasized than her use of touch.[8]

Just how thoroughly touch as a way of apprehending the world permeates Dickinson's imagination is evident in those poems that she wrote about letters. The sense startles by its unexpectedness here. Letters are read, we imagine, and their content comes to us through sight. For Dickinson, letters are held; they are felt by the touch. Concentrating on how letters are handled rather than on what they say, Dickinson insinuates into her treatment of correspondence a felt sense of the pleasures and dangers of touching and being touched. For her, correspondence links person to person, self to self, and not, as Emerson urged, word to thing and thing to idea.

The prominence of letters in Dickinson's imagination—actual letters of correspondence, letters of the alphabet, and poems as letters—is not surprising, since letters came to stand for her presence in a world from which she gradually retired.[9] They form an odd token of constancy in her eccentric, discontinuous, and guarded life. They have a material existence, as she claimed, "A Letter is a joy of Earth— / It is denied the Gods—" (P 1639). Yet, for all their materiality, letters are for Dickinson a way of being in the world without being in the world, as she told Higginson, "A Letter always feels to me like immortality because it is the mind alone without corporeal friend. Indebted in our talk to attitude and accent, there seems a spectral power in thought that walks alone" (L, II, 460). Whether she is writing or reading a letter, Dickinson's main interest is in its "spectral power," its ability to terrify and exhilarate, to separate the reader from her own "corporeal friend." The sensations aroused by a letter come to her not from its contents but precisely from the ability of its physical presence to move her, to put herself beside herself.

As a writer of such a letter, Dickinson expresses her reasonable fears of what such a touch would bring. She writes:

> This is my letter to the World
> That never wrote to Me—
> The simple News that Nature told—
> With tender Majesty
>
> Her Message is committed
> To Hands I cannot see—
> For love of Her—Sweet—countrymen—
> Judge tenderly—of Me (P 441)

Dickinson's plea that the hands which would touch her letter should judge it and, presumably, handle it tenderly appears to be motivated by her fear of self-exposure as well as by her sense that the hands will "see" her in a way she cannot see them. Their touch and their judgment will penetrate. The exchange itself, so apparently dangerous to her, has nothing to do with the message, which, as "the simple News that Nature told," is news not conveyed but already known both to sender and receiver. It may be the object of the verb "wrote" and thus the world's, or in apposition to the letter and thus the poet's. That it can be both diverts attention from the news itself to the manner in which it is transmitted: by hand, willingly extended by the speaker or grudgingly withheld by the World.

The speaker's interest is in the touch that will manage the exchange. It is mediated through an earlier and different exchange between the "World" and "Nature" which nature "told— / With tender Majesty". In urging the reader to imitate nature and "Judge tenderly" the speaker appears to anticipate harsh treatment and yet insists that her readers judge "For love of" "Her"—a word with multiple referents to the letter's message, nature's message, the letter itself, the writer herself. Touching the letter tenderly and for love, the reader is being prepared to be aroused, and so the hand of the poet reaches out to demonstrate the responsive pleasure she desires. This plea for love is unexpected in the intimacy which it asks of a world first presented as unresponsive and distant. And yet it suggests, in its simplicity, Dickinson's sense of writing as an intimate act that can generate a reciprocal tenderness.

Letters themselves are agents of intimacy for Dickinson. In her mind, writer and reader become connected not just by the common alphabet but in the intimacy of the letter "I" which represents them both. The poet's letter to the world is, on one level, the alphabetic letter with which she intrudes into and thus ceases to exist in the world—the letter "I." The poet's "I" as her letter to the world joins the other meanings the letter has assumed: the letter as a message on which the world will base its judgment and the poem identified as a letter of Nature's news. The poet's letter as the letter "I" by which she is represented to the world signifies the "simple news that Nature told" in her creation.

Written by or committed to "Hands I cannot see," the letter "I" ceases one existence and takes up another. This thought forces the poet to turn abruptly at the end of the poem toward her readers in order to underscore their complicity in the letter "I." "For love of Her—Sweet—countrymen—" becomes "for love of the letter 'I' as you use it yourself." Writer and reader are all countrymen of that country of "I's." The speaker appeals then to the reader's self-love and turns what appears to be an appeal for tenderness into the poet's own tender reception of the reader's self-exposure.

Like Baudelaire's address "hypocrite lecteur, mon semblable, mon frère," Dickinson's approach is a radical revision of the reader's position and his or her relation to letters. What appears to be a lonely act of self-exposure in a world that remains mysteriously unknown is actually a revelation of the common exposure enforced in any exchange of words. The letter "I" insists upon a community and a correspondence that its use appears to deny. In writing it, the poet both succumbs to that community, losing herself in it, and indicates her difference from it. There are dangers here that she both courts and fears. To write is to be read, to be seen where one cannot see. But, the poem's ending warns, to read is also an act of exposure.

The poem works to keep its focus on the exchange between writer and reader rather than on the contents of the message exchanged. There, on the surface, is all the danger and the excitement. Dickinson would have agreed with that other great letter-monger of the nineteenth century, Edgar Allan Poe, who wrote, "There is such a thing as being too profound. Truth is not always in a well. In fact, as regards the most important knowledge, I do believe that she is invariably superficial."[10] The life of the letters that we send back and forth is not the depth they hide or reveal but the linking power they generate at the surface.

In P 441 which identifies itself as a letter, the poet promises tautologically to tell the world the world. In P 636, a letter tells the reader the reader, and again the knowledge comes through touch. Reading a letter, Dickinson's speaker duplicates its writer:

The Way I read a Letter's—this—
'Tis first—I lock the Door—
And push it with my fingers—next—
For transport it be sure—

And then I go the furthest off
To counteract a knock—
Then draw my little Letter forth
And slowly pick the lock—

Then—glancing narrow, at the Wall—
And narrow at the floor
For firm Conviction of a Mouse
Not exorcised before—

Peruse how infinite I am
To no one that You—know—
And sigh for lack of Heaven—but not
The Heaven God bestow—

Here, as in "This is my letter to the World," the letter's reception and not its contents is the subject. And the reception is mediated through the touch: locking doors, pushing with fingers, picking the lock. All these maneuvers which might indicate a desire to hide the letter's message actually serve to intensify the speaker's transport. Also, the letter may be from abroad or the letter "I" she has written to represent herself, and it does not matter which it is because Dickinson is chiefly interested in the materiality of the exchange through which she is transported into a new existence. She reads with her hands, or at least her reading duplicates the acts by which she secludes herself from the world. She locks the door and then picks the lock of the letter, pushes the door shut and pushes her fingers over the letter for "transport", goes "the furthest off" in the room and goes the furthest off into the letter's infinity. The letter's potential for transporting her beyond herself is riveted to the material world and known only by its palpable effects—the "glancing narrow", the sigh.

"The Way I read a Letter's—this" might also be "The Way I write a Letter's—this". Writing even more than reading requires, if not a locked door, at least that solitude or transport from the world that a locked door ensures. It too is an act of stealthy entry into another world, a narrowing of the glance that concentrates the attention. And finally writing more than reading reveals the "infinite I am" to the writer herself, a persona who is "no one that You—know—", indeed no one that the writer herself knows, but someone made known to herself only in the writing-reading. In part, it is this lack for which she sighs as she reads, since the act of reading and writing is short-lived and predicated on the brevity of its duration.

Dickinson appears to draw on the conventions of a sentimental narrative in which a lovesick girl or boy receives a longed-for letter from her or his beloved, retreats into privacy to relish its secrets, enjoys its expected message of idealization, and finishes with regret that she or he cannot live forever in that transported state. But the poem's ending, in which the self-absorbed speaker turns outward to fend off a reader whom she or he has been at such pains to exclude, suggests that the individual is involved in a completely different kind of reading. "Peruse how infinite I am / To no one that You—know—" is a line that flaunts and secures the privacy the speaker has carefully established. All the subterfuge of this reading has had as its aim the secret mission of self-empowerment. In reading herself, she also reads someone unknown or, rather, "no one" known to anyone else, and so reading is not a matter of *seeing* or being *seen* so much as it is a matter of feeling oneself and feeling infinite. "Peruse how infinite I am" seals the poem by reiterating its opening line "The Way I read a Letter's—this—". The process of becoming the "infinite I am" by the arousal of latent power through the agency of touch calls up the parallel between reading and the erotic. To read is to feel. This equation of reading and arousal forces the reader to the literal and corporeal.

Like the poem's reader "glancing narrow, at the Wall" and "narrow at the floor", the reader of the poem is encouraged first to narrow her or his sights, to take the letter of the letter over its spirit, because curiously it is this narrow reading that will allow for the "firm Conviction of a Mouse", the death sentence in the sentence of the small, the minimal, the intrusive. The "Way" to the "infinite I" is straight and narrow, moving from lock, to door, to wall, to floor, along lines that are both contingent and touchable. The way requires exclusion, stealth, exorcism, rather than expansion, freedom, and acceptance. Feeling and touching all the "Way " Dickinson comes to a sense of her own infinite powers not by an idealizing gaze but by a clandestine narrowing into her own body. In this poem Dickinson rewrites the New Testament warning that the letter killeth, the spirit giveth life; she suggests that the letter withdrawn from its strict and orthodox representation of the law can generate a power of its own that is not spiritual but erotic. Reading the letter/the self secretly, one picks the locks of secrets unknown to a public and conventional reading, secrets that contain an erotic charge.

Touching the letter, the poet feels her own power, and that power resides in her own hands quite literally.[11] In P 454, she claims:

It was given to me by the Gods—
When I was a little Girl—
They give us Presents most—you know—
When we are new—and small.
I kept it in my Hand—
I never put it down—
I did not dare to eat—or sleep—
For fear it would be gone—

Like the letter reader retreating behind locked doors, the poet cherishes her God-given talent as if it were a precious secret and simultaneously so valuable that it had to be jealously guarded against theft. Feminist readings of this poem have concentrated on the split between the courage of the woman as poet and the timidity of the woman as woman, whereas the prized privacy of the creative power here appears to derive from the sense of her separation from the social world.[12] The poem goes on:

I heard such words as "Rich"—
When hurrying to school—
From lips at Corners of the Streets—
And wrestled with a smile.
Rich! 'Twas Myself—was rich—
To take the name of Gold—
And Gold to own—in solid Bars—
The Difference—made me bold—

In the first half of the poem, she appears to be afraid that she will lose her touch, lose touch with the "Present" given her. In the second half, she salves that fear by realizing that what she keeps in her hand is not a possession but an identity. It is not something she owns as others own "Gold" "in solid Bars" but something she is that sets her apart and marks her difference. She holds in her hand the power to write words and thus to designate difference, and this power makes her different.

In this context, Irigaray's comments are again pertinent. She writes:

Property and propriety are undoubtedly rather foreign to all that is female. At least sexually. *Nearness*, however, is not foreign to woman, a nearness so close that any identification of one or the other, and therefore any form of property, is impossible. Woman enjoys a closeness with the other that is *so near she cannot possess it, any more than she can possess herself*. She constantly trades herself for the other without any possible identification of either one of them. (Irigaray,104–105)

Although Irigaray is writing about sexuality and Dickinson about words, the twentieth-century critic and the nineteenth-century poet play off against each other as each attempts to define a woman's way of knowing. Irigaray's comments are instructive in indicating how the erotic power of words enlivens and arouses Dickinson's imagination. The problematic of possession and self-possession is as real for Dickinson as for Irigaray, distinguishing them from the presumably male "banker" and from the language of fixity that a sense of property and propriety encourages.

Words such as "Rich " engender one meaning when spoken by "lips at Corners of the Streets" and still another when spoken by and of the poet herself.[13] The difference between naming and owning, between poet and banker, masks another difference between naming names with street-corner lips or taking names into gifted hands, between male ownership and female possession, between symbolic meaning and concreteness. She is rich as soon as she says she is rich because using the word itself makes her so. Bankers, then, are different from poets because they claim to "own" gold; they trust to the solidity of their bars of gold, whereas poets know that all bars will dissolve or be transgressed.

For Dickinson, "rich" to poet is not "rich" to banker, because each handles the word differently and according to her or his particular needs just as in P 300 "'Morning'—means 'Milking'—to the Farmer— / Dawn—to the Teneriffe— / Dice—to the Maid—". Meanings are not given but attached to words by people who touch them under different circumstances. Just as surely as the "Epicures" "date a Breakfast" by "Morning", "Faith" dates it "The Experiment of Our Lord". From the most material to the most spiritual, the definition of the word is established by context rather than by a settled correspondence with the thing it is to represent. Words, then, touch our lives at various angles, and we use them as we feel them.

If meanings are a matter of attachments, they derive from place and they have a place. So Dickinson can boast, "The Robin's my Criterion for Tune— / Because I grow—where Robins do—" (P 285). She has picked up her standards and the language that encodes them from her neighborhood. Thus, when she explains herself in the poem's famous line "Because I see— New Englandly—" she is not so much identifying her purpose with the New England way as she is equating sight with site. She is "Orchard sprung—" she claims. Although that beginning may indicate a peculiarly New England view of life as Eden after the Fall, as Wolff suggests, in this poem Dickinson appears to be more interested in punning on a different kind of falling, in simple things that fall, like nuts and snow, in poets, as in seasons, that fall in place.[14] Such falling is a way of knowing, of sensing what is fit and fitting to her landscape, and it is also a way of marking differences, as language falls one way to the American poet and another to the British. Dickinson has a special eye for those things that flit and designate flitting, because her attention itself follows the same pattern, moving from detail to detail on a whim, as she says, "The Buttercup's, my Whim for Bloom— / Because, we're Orchard sprung—". Because her vision is tied to mutable language rather than to eternal forms, it is whimsical, not fatal as it is for Emerson.

Her language comes from place, she claims, and it seems to justify her divorce from the British literary tradition, although the parallel structures "But, were I Cuckoo born" and "But, were I Britain born" do more than distinguish her by locale. "Cuckoo born" may contain a witty judgment of the British literary tradition, but Dickinson turns her wit on all provincial discernment. Seeing "New Englandly" is just as eccentric in its teaching that "None but the Nut—October fit—". Local wisdom, no matter how solemnly taught, is always a provincial fiction with its basis in the spectacle of sight. For, depending on the "Snow's Tableau" without which "Winter, were lie—to me—" the speaker puts her faith in pageantry and enjoys its fictive splendor. For her, language is made or made up, not found in natural forms.

For Dickinson as for her British counterpart the "Queen" language is not a truth-bearer but a place-marker. In this, Dickinson simply articulates a Romantic faith in the creative imagination that is more English and European than American. A change of locale is a change of language, as Richard Rorty explains:

> What the Romantics expressed as the claim that imagination, rather than reason, is the central human faculty was the realization that a talent for speaking differently, rather than for arguing well, is the chief instrument of cultural change. What political utopians since the French Revolution have sensed is not that an enduring, substratal, human nature has been suppressed or repressed by "unnatural" or "irrational" social institutions but rather that changing languages and other social practices may produce human beings of a sort that had never before existed.[15]

Rorty's assertion that "the human self is created by the use of a vocabulary rather than being adequately or inadequately expressed in a vocabulary" is part of Dickinson's meaning.

Dickinson's hope that a changing language will create a new self finds a problematic expression in those poems she wrote about marriage where the name of "Wife" often does not produce the change desired. In her poetry, rather, the erotic charge encouraged by a letter is more intense than the ceremonial imposition of a new name. Dickinson's marriage poems play with notions of language as a place-marker where the place marked by marriage is a blank. In these troubled and troubling poems, Dickinson's speakers take on not only a language new to them but the identity promised by that language, assuming, as Rorty claims, that languages are made rather than found and "truth is a property of linguistic entities, of sentences." So Dickinson opens a number of poems with the faith that a change of name will mean a change of identity: "I'm 'wife'—I've finished that—" (P 199), "A Wife—at Daybreak I shall be—" (P 461), "Title divine—is mine!" (P 1072). In all these poems, the speaker finds herself negated by the change because the self created by conventional language can only be conventional, and so the woman who thinks she has "finished that— / That other state—" finds her new estate as "'Woman'" "this soft Eclipse". She would like to think it "comfort" and the other "pain" but all she can really say is, "I'm 'Wife'! Stop there!" (P 199).

The identity-creating language of marriage has names but no plots despite woman's frantic effort to create one. "I'm 'Wife'! Stop there!" stops exactly where fairy tales stop. In this poem, Dickinson's speaker is misled by a social language that can make no intimate difference. After an attempt and failure to create that difference between this new and that old identity, she says, "But why compare?" Why indeed, when the new life is imagined in such minimal terms? At most, it is "safer so", a "comfort". Hardly worthy of a new name or the extravagance of the designation "I'm Czar" the new status bears the small comfort of a name full of conventional meaning that has no intimate significance. The woman in this poem colludes in her own objectivization, internalizing that rejection of the female imaginary Irigaray describes as central to a patriarchal sexual economy:

> The rejection, the exclusion of a female imaginary undoubtedly places woman in a position where she can experience herself only fragmentarily as waste or as excess in the little structured margins of a dominant ideology, this mirror entrusted by the [masculine] "subject" with the task of reflecting and redoubling himself. The role of "femininity" is prescribed moreover by this masculine specula[riza]tion and corresponds only slightly to woman's desire, which is recuperated only secretly, in hiding, and in a disturbing and unpardonable manner (Irigaray, 104).

Reading in secret, Dickinson can recuperate her desire. But, in the objectification of the marriage poems, she expresses only the dislocations of herself from her self:

> Title divine—is mine!
> The Wife—without the Sign!
> Acute Degree—conferred on me—
> Empress of Calvary!
> Royal—all but the Crown!
> Betrothed—without the swoon
> God sends us Women—
> When you—hold—Garnet to Garnet—

Gold—to Gold—
Born—Bridalled—Shrouded—
In a Day—
Tri Victory
"My Husband"—women say—
Stroking the Melody—
Is *this*—the way? (P 1072)

Between the exclamatory opening and the coolly satiric ending, the poem is divided by the line "Betrothed—without the swoon" which serves both as summary of the first half and introduction to the second. Dickinson's most energetic language is frequently reversible, designating one thing and its opposite, as the betrothal here may be the unconventional betrothal of the "Empress of Calvary" to her "Acute Degree" or the conventional betrothal without the "swoon" of erotic pleasure for those women whose marriage gives them only the name "Husband" to stroke. Behind this linking phrase, the poem splits in two, and its divisiveness is most clearly articulated in the awkward change of pronoun and tone from exclamation to explanation in the enigmatic line: "God sends us Women—". Here, even as gifts from God, women seem to bear only an exchange value, delivered into this world for the express purpose of the bridal-bridle day.

The distinction in the poem is not so much between a heavenly and an earthly marriage, as Sharon Cameron claims, as between a conventional marriage and an unconventional existence which cannot be exactly articulated in the names available for it.[16] The opening is misleading precisely because, in her desperation, the speaker grasps at words, claiming them in the first half of the line only to disclaim them in the second half. For her condition, there is no proper name, and she casts about for a name that by contrast might explain the dilemma of her own identity. She finds that not everyone experiences herself as a divided character. There are those, "untwisted by the love of things irreconcilable" as Hart Crane said, who hold to one identity and are held by it, "Garnet to Garnet—", "Gold—to Gold—". On their marriage day, they are duplicated, verified, and turned into precious jewels. Giving themselves over completely to the title "wife" these women must spend out their days "stroking the Melody" of the name to which they have given their life. "My Husband" they say, imitating their husbands' own possessiveness and seeking his approval of their adulation. Thus, in Irigaray's terms, the husbands are reflected and redoubled, and the wives are negated.

From the end, the poem's beginning claims seem less confusing. A contrast to the stroking wives whose only identity comes from being able to say the word "Husband" the opening speaker has titles of her own. Divine, they may be, and so not apparent, designations of suffering too, nonetheless these titles by which the speaker gropes to define her unique identity admit of no conventional meaning. Not "Bridalled" by any lexical particularities, the speaker makes them mean just what she wants them to mean. No outward sign, no crown, these words are conferred from within and carry with them an explosive energy. Unlike the wives at the end, the opening speaker does not have to ask "Is *this*—the way?" because *her* way is *the* way for her.

The difficulties in describing her way are ironed out when she comes at them obliquely through an ironic handling of the conventional way. Gilbert and Gubar note the "insistent ambiguity" with which Dickinson reconciles the opposites of female submission and poetic assertion. But like the speaker of P 479 who "dealt her pretty words like Blades—" Dickinson can be cutting when she writes about the self-sacrifice and silence of marriage in a poem such as "She rose to His Requirement—dropt" (P 732). There the "honorable Work / Of Woman, and of Wife—" would cost "Amplitude" and "Awe" and even "Gold" and, one must assume, no poet would be willing to exchange such possibilities for the honor.

More problematic among Dickinson's poems of self-naming, however, is a poem that Adrienne Rich reads as a poem of great pride and of "*self*-confirmation" in which the poet transcends the patriarchal condition (Rich, 172). The self-confirmation is, however, scant here. This poem may be unlike the other marriage poems since it does not specifically designate the new status the speaker assumes; but, like the marriage poems, it tells us nothing of the new rank confirmed:

I'm ceded—I've stopped being Theirs—
The name They dropped upon my face
With water, in the country church
Is finished using, now,
And They can put it with my Dolls,
My childhood, and the string of spools,
I've finished threading—too—

Baptized, before, without the choice,
But this time, consciously, of Grace—

Unto supremest name—
Called to my Full—The Crescent dropped—
Existence's whole Arc, filled up,
With one small Diadem.

My second Rank—too small the first—
Crowned—Crowing—on my Father's breast—
A half unconscious Queen—
But this time—Adequate—Erect,
With Will to choose, or to reject,
And I choose, just a Crown—(P 508)

Yielding or yielded, the speaker of "I'm ceded" rises to her choice expectantly, but the poem, like the marriage poems, tells us more about the childhood she renounces than the new title she chooses. Can this poet not imagine the world of the imagination? Rich claims that because the poem was written in the year that Dickinson wrote to Higginson about her poems, it may articulate the poet's sense of her own measure, independent of the judgment of others. First, however, we do not know definitely the chronology of Dickinson's writing. And, we must ask, why does she insist on using the same *measure* to mark out crucial stages of her own independent, rebellious, and self-empowering life which she finds ready made for her by the patriarchal religious culture which she seeks to escape?

The identity that yields itself to "supremest name" has not gained a new language by which to denominate her change; she has simply marked her change of status by the familiar religious language of baptism, grace, will, crown. Indeed, so conventional is her language that she might be using it to describe a religious conversion, were it not for the fact that she designates a change of family name, an exchange from "Father's breast" where she was a "half unconscious Queen" to, presumably, her vocation as conscious Queen. Despite her insistence that she is "this time—Adequate—Erect, / With Will to choose, or to reject," she appears to accede to a choice as conventional as her family's choice to baptize her. While the "just" of her choice "just a Crown" is loaded with irony, the poem ends with the choice as if she cannot project a life beyond it. Like the marriage poems to which it is allied, this poem of naming stops short of elaborating on the identity that might come from such a change of language. "Called to my Full" the speaker here enjoys no plenitude, reads no messages of the "infinite I am"; rather, she sacrifices "Existence's whole Arc" for "one small Diadem".

Yet this reading is not entirely satisfactory. The energy in the will to choose sets this poem apart from those poems of marriage, and the tremendous force of the opening line that separates her decisively from "Theirs" lends credence to Rich's reading. Moreover, this new identity may be told in conventional terms, but it is freshly told, as we may see in the repetition of "dropped" in the second stanza. "Called to my Full—the Crescent dropped—" indicates a deliberate shedding of the old half-life in favor of the full, and forms a powerful contrast to the almost hapless first christening: "The name They dropped upon my face / With water".

Something of the same energy is evident in another poem of self-naming:

Mine—by the Right of the White Election!
Mine—by the Royal Seal!
Mine—by the Sign in the Scarlet prison—
Bars—cannot conceal!

Mine—here—in Vision—and in Veto!
Mine—by the Grave's Repeal—
Titled—Confirmed—
Delirious Charter!
Mine—long as Ages steal! (P 528)

Wolff points out that in the first line the speaker appears to be thrown into a territorial dispute (197), and it may be that the energy of the poem comes from the opposition of this undesignated antagonist. But it comes too from the speaker's insistence on self-possession. In the marriage poems and even "I'm ceded," where she might be confirming an unconventional existence, the speaker sacrifices herself for a word; by contrast, here she insists on herself, sacrificing words, as it were, to her own overpowering sense of herself. Not "Wife—without the Sign" this woman says "Mine—by the Royal Seal!" "Mine—by the Sign in the Scarlet prison—". Although it may have something of the "Me-Me-Me" of childhood in it, this confirmation of her circumstances indicates, more than hoarding, a powerful sense of self-assertion that is lacking in the marriage poems. Although here too she dwells more on how she came to her present condition than on its actual details or future plot, she insists that she is "Titled—Confirmed—". Yet, because this "Delirious Charter" has been conferred by a series of rights, seals, and signs, rather than deliberately chosen, it shares with these place-markers its own end. "Titled—Confirmed" then may suggest fixed and settled in time ("long as Ages steal!") and thus dead.

These poems of entitlement in which the speaker takes on the name of wife or some unspecified crown and title express a fear that a change in vocabulary is not always a change in identity. Like the gaze, words may transfix and objectify, and, even if a number of Dickinson's speakers seem to collude in this process by longing for and affirming the names they have been forced to accept, the abrupt endings of the poems suggest the way in which words have the power to stop the process of being and becoming.

By contrast to empty names, touch encourages new life, as Dickinson suggests in the following poem:

> He touched me, so I live to know
> That such a day, permitted so,
> I groped upon his breast—
> It was a boundless place to me
> And silenced, as the awful sea
> Puts minor streams to rest.
>
> And now, I'm different from before,
> As if I breathed superior air—
> Or brushed a Royal Gown—
> My feet, too that had wandered so—
> My Gypsy face—transfigured now—
> To tenderer Renown—
>
> Into this Port, if I might come,
> Rebecca, to Jerusalem,
> Would not so ravished turn—
> Nor Persian, baffled at her shrine
> Lift such a Crucifixal sign
> To her imperial Sun. (P 506)

This touch is life-giving because it is transgressive. Unlike the title that settles and confirms, the touch disrupts and changes. Touch "gropes," it enters into the dark to feel its way, permitting that darkness to deliver its secrets. Through touch, the speaker here can designate a difference of status, a new identity. Even when the desire to settle overtakes the speaker who wants only to come "Into this Port," she wants an exotic port like Jerusalem or Persia. The unfamiliar, the dark, the baffling, are suggested here. The very opposite of "Port," the exotic is close to the erotic.

The desire to be near to the faraway, to join company with the royal and exclusive, is the desire of touch. It finds expression in longing where the speaker says, "I envy Seas, whereon He rides— / I envy Spokes of Wheels / Of Chariots that Him convey—" (P 498). Dickinson's speaker longs to touch her absent lover, as the sparrows dot his eaves, the fly touches his pane; she wants what they so happily enjoy and "What is forbidden utterly" to her. But why is she forbidden? That ideal nearness that she could imagine in "Forever at His side to walk—" (P 246) where she would spend "All life—to know each other— / Whom we can never learn—" promises both the knowledge and the pleasure Irigaray described as woman's way of experiencing. "Two lives—One Being—now—" indicates neither a gain of status nor a loss of identity but rather a process of becoming that is the sum of the woman's erotic existence.

The diffusion of erotic pleasure so much remarked in "Come slowly— Eden!" (P 211) is also at the center of "We learned the Whole of Love" (P 568), where the lovers move from alphabet to words to chapter and "then the mighty Book— / Then—Revelation closed—" and they are allowed to begin all over again in ignorance "Diviner than the Childhood's". "Alas, that Wisdom is so large—", the poem ends in tantalizing regret. The erotic element in Dickinson inheres in this endlessly repetitive gesture of reading lovers. This desire to know the whole of love by learning another human being is a desire to erase the discontinuity between human beings and to establish a sense of continuity which, Bataille says, is at the heart of eroticism.[17] And it is this desire that links eroticism and death, as Bataille explains, "Erotic activity, by dissolving the separate beings that participate in it, reveals their fundamental continuity, like the waves of a stormy sea" (Bataille, 22) and "death, in that it destroys the discontinuous being, leaves intact the general continuity of existence outside ourselves" (21).

For Dickinson, there was a stage this side of death that, like eroticism, could disrupt her settled world and, like death, could place its continuity over her own. She describes this stage by place in the following poem:

A nearness to Tremendousness—
An Agony procures—
Affliction ranges Boundlessness—
Vicinity to Laws

> Contentment's quiet Suburb—
> Affliction cannot stay
> In Acres—Its Location
> Is Illocality—(P 963)

Bataille notes the way eroticism interjects into an ordered, shuttered, and parsimonious existence a plethoric disorder, and this poem relies on that violence to boundaries and place. Its opening line "A nearness to Tremendousness—" introduces that disordering of measurement that points to the moment of erotic pleasure when the discontinuous self will surrender utterly; the line relishes desire and hope in juxtaposing briefly these two disparate measures. Delaying the announcement that it is not eroticism but "Agony" that not only has caused this state but "procures" it illicitly does not exactly erase the expectation of erotic pleasure in the opening line; rather it suggests the connection between pain and eroticism. Examining this phenomenon, Bataille says:

> In human life on the other hand sexual violence causes a wound that rarely heals of its own accord; it has to be closed, and will not even remain closed without constant attention based on anguish. Primary anguish bound up with sexual disturbance signifies death. The violence of this disturbance reopens in the mind of the man experiencing it, who also knows what death is, the abyss that death once revealed. (Bataille, 104)

The disruption of the normal order in Dickinson's poem is caused by an unspecified agony and affliction that are close, in their effects at least, to Bataille's sexual violence. Dickinson had the iron nerve that Bataille claimed was necessary to perceive the connection between the promise of life implicit in eroticism and the sensuous aspect of death, between life as a swelling tumult continuously on the verge of explosion and death as the necessary "orgy of annihilation," both equal manifestations of the boundless wastage of nature's resources (61). In their excesses, both eroticism and death exist outside "Contentment's quiet Suburb". Affliction's "Boundlessness" and "Illocality" are evidence of its terror and simultaneously of a state beyond terror which makes terror no longer seem unlimited and wholly dominant.

Dickinson plays on the double meanings in affliction: the boundlessness of pain intensifies its state, but the boundlessness of being overthrown or cast down may nullify its injury or intensify its pleasure. The pain of one and the imagining of the other may be related, as Elaine Scarry suggests, as "extreme conditions of, on the one hand, intentionality as a state and, on the other, intentionality as self-objectification."[18] Scarry explains, "The more a habitual form of perception is experienced as itself rather than its external object, the closer it lies to pain; conversely, the more completely a state is experienced as its object, the closer it lies to imaginative self-transformation" (Scarry, 165). She cites as an example the difference between touching a thorn where one feels one's body hurting more than one feels the thorn, and touching or feeling the touch of the body of one's beloved where one senses a feeling of self-displacing and self-transforming objectification. In Dickinson's poem, there is an odd conflation of the two states of pain and imagining in which the speaker appears to be feeling the "Agony" as a process of self-transformation.

When Dickinson redefines "Agony" as death in the following poem, she makes explicit the connection between pain and imagining:

> I tried to think a lonelier Thing
> Than any I had seen—
> Some Polar Expiation—An Omen in the Bone
> Of Death's tremendous nearness—
>
> I probed Retrieveless things
> My Duplicate—to borrow—
> A Haggard Comfort springs
>
> From the belief that Somewhere—
> Within the Clutch of Thought—
> There dwells one other Creature
> Of Heavenly Love—forgot—(P 532)

Although the poem trails off into considerations of pity's consolations, its opening brings into play the connection between pain and imagining, between "nearness" and "tremendousness" as those two terms are associated with death and with living creatures. What will console the speaker here in her pain and isolation is imagining that she is not alone but shares her condition with one other creature. The concluding stanza opens, "I almost strove to clasp his Hand," indicating her awareness of the healing power of touch or, as Scarry claims, the self-transformation possible in feeling the presence of another's body. Pain is bypassed by this strategy of imagining first its intensification, second its duplicate, and third someone who shares it. In all these ways, it is objectified, placed into an imagined rather than felt order, and thus cast out.

And, if the imagination is active, it works this triumph over pain and loss often unconsciously. There are, as Wallace Stevens said, "moments of awakening." Dickinson had such moments, as she relates:

Of nearness to her sundered Things
The Soul has special times—
When Dimness—looks the Oddity—
Distinctness—easy—seems—

The Shapes we buried, dwell about,
Familiar, in the Rooms—
Untarnished by the Sepulchre,
The Mouldering Playmate comes—(P 607)

Like the nearness to tremendousness, this sudden nearness of sundered things is evidence of the imagination's desperate effort to offer its consolation in the face of loss and pain. Here as "The Grave yields back her Robberies" the imagination imitating the robber implicates itself in this violent exchange. It too will eventually have to yield back its findings.

Yet the tenacity of the imagination is all that shields us from pain and loss, and it could be adamant in its resistance to mourning. In the following poem, Dickinson places together many of the elements I have been discussing separately. Here the touch, the letter, the place, and the consolation that their contiguity promises combine in a desperate effort to forestall a loss that is guaranteed in the beginning. Dickinson writes:

A single Screw of Flesh
Is all that pins the Soul
That stands for Deity, to Mine,
Upon my side the Veil—

Once witnessed of the Gauze—
Its name is put away
As far from mine, as if no plight
Had printed yesterday,

In tender—solemn Alphabet,
My eyes just turned to see,
When it was smuggled by my sight
Into Eternity—

More Hands—to hold—These are but Two—
One more new-mailed Nerve
Just granted, for the Peril's sake—
Some striding—Giant—Love—

So greater than the Gods can show,
They slink before the Clay,
That not for all their Heaven can boast
Will let its Keepsake—go (P 263)

This poem about loss is obsessed with place and with those sleight of hand tricks that can make things disappear from their appointed places. The speaker located on one side of the veil finds the name of her beloved put "far from mine " "smuggled by my sight". By way of compensation, she is to receive "More Hands—to hold" and "One more new-mailed Nerve". Thus, in the orthodox order of things, the Lord giveth and the Lord taketh away, and the speaker witnessing this magic show is expected to accede to its inevitability. That she will not, despite the evidence of her eyes, let her keepsake go is surprising enough, but that she insists on her invulnerability to loss through the power resident in "Some striding—Giant—Love— / So greater than the Gods can show " might appear foolhardy were it not for the fact that in matters of touch she has all the power. "A single Screw of Flesh" is all that "pins the Soul" but the same single screw unites forever flesh to flesh. The "gift of Screws" Dickinson could call it in "Essential Oils—are wrung" (P 675), the "Screw of Flesh" welds body to body more irrevocably than it holds body to soul. In naming the split between body and soul, Dickinson calls into being the community of body to body. In the same way, the name "witnessed of the Gauze" and thus erased remains "printed" "In tender—solemn Alphabet". The "plight" of the speaker and her beloved is the "gift of Screws", again the human effort to craft and fix in letters and thus to memorialize the union of lovers. All these human efforts to contain and possess the beloved seem helpless before the Deity's superior powers of subterfuge and force until the Giant

Love came striding, and then, in a reversal of "Annabel Lee," this human giant scares off the predatory Gods. In slinking before the Clay, these Gods must acquiesce to the superiority of the flesh in matters of erotic love.

The clay and screw of flesh guarantee a life along the nerve ends of those who, knowing pain, can also imagine pleasure. The touch remembers and locates its pleasure and can refuse to surrender it as long as flesh survives. Just so, the alphabet gets printed and translates invisible plights into tangible form. Hands hold onto such keepsakes.

What prevails in Dickinson's poetry is the word that can be touched, exchanged, lost, and recovered. The full extent of Dickinson's radical approach to language is difficult to discern because she expresses herself in religious terms that are themselves often puzzling but appear to point in the direction of faith, as in the poem that opens: "A Word made Flesh is seldom / And tremblingly partook " (P 1651). The incarnation is conflated with transubstantiation, as the spirit is converted to flesh and then the flesh is reconverted into spiritual food as it appears to be partaken by the faithful. Almost immediately, however, these tropes are dismissed in favor of the poet's real interest, which is not the body of Christ eaten in remembrance of His death and passion, but the body "tasted / With ecstasies of stealth" as "food debated / To our specific strength—". Here a deliberate despiritualizing of the Word is only the beginning stage of an invigoration of the fleshly passions. The poem's second stanza dismisses the incarnation and the metaphysics of presence that it requires:

> A Word that breathes distinctly
> Has not the power to die
> Cohesive as the Spirit
> It may expire if He—
> "Made Flesh and dwelt among us"
> Could condescension be
> Like this consent of Language
> This loved Philology. (P 1651)

For those who do not believe that the Word was "'Made Flesh and dwelt among us'" the Word is not the Word of God but of man. It is, as a creation of man, both as fictive and as "Cohesive" as that other creation of man, the "Spirit." It may "expire" only if at some future time there might be an incarnation. Even then, the "condescension" of God to man would have to be "Like this consent of Language" if it were to prevail.

Dickinson's interest in the word is an interest not in what the word can be made to symbolize or even what it has symbolized, but rather an interest in the power of language to bind together, to strengthen links between the self and the other. "This loved Philology" is a love not only of words but of words as love tokens, partaken tremblingly and ecstatically.[19] No thought of absence or presence can occlude her conviction that the word is as real as the rare touch of flesh to flesh.

Chapter 4

"Who goes to dine must take his Feast": Dickinson and Her Audience

The intimacy essential to Dickinson's idea of reading and writing informs her sense of that relationship she might have with her readers. For a poet who had essentially no public audience, this private speculation indicates how much writing implies reading and how terrifying the self-exposure of writing can be. Dickinson's fears on this point are overlooked when she is assimilated to a more public model of reading. For example, in "Words and Wounds," Geoffrey Hartman writes, "Emily Dickinson could call her poems 'my letter to the world'; so the literary text or artifact is a gift for which the interpreter must find words, both to recognize the gift, and then to allow it to create a reciprocating dialogue, one that might overcome the embarrassment inspired by art's riddling strength."[1] The idea has an honorable history. Montaigne argued that "speech belongs half to the speaker, half to the listener. The latter must prepare to receive it according to the motion given it. As among tennis-players, the receiver moves and makes ready according to the motion of the striker and the nature of the stroke."[2] In Dickinson's own time, Emerson claimed that there was a creative reading as well as a creative writing.[3] The poignancy of Hartman's statement is not in his idea, but in his choice of Dickinson as an example. He uses her to make a point about the need for a language exchange that her own work cannot support. Her poems called up no reciprocating dialogue. Her "letter to the world" went unanswered except as her own poetry came to imagine, create, and incorporate the silence and evasion around it.

The history of creative reading in which Hartman places himself is dominated by a code of contest. He talks of art's riddling *strength* and the embarrassment that must be *overcome* in confronting it. Montaigne too relies, in his analogy, on the power of opposition between striker and receiver. Even Emerson develops his idea by insisting that "When the mind is *braced* by labor and invention, the page of whatever book we read becomes luminous with manifold allusion" (44) (italics added). The terms here do not specifically exclude women, but they encourage association with male contests. There is, also, an element of male camaraderie inherent in the reading and speaking described here. Hartman cites the mock defense scene in Act IV of *King Lear* in which the maddened Lear demands of Edgar, "Give me the word," and, recognizing the game, Edgar gives a nonsense word that nonetheless allows them to continue the game and so keep up appearances (134). Even in getting past the guard, it is more important that the speaker be privy to the rules of the game than that he have the correct word. In his discussion of the language exchange, Montaigne also relies on codes, claiming, "There is a voice for instructing, a voice for flattering, or for scolding. I want my voice not only to reach him, but perhaps to strike him and pierce him" (324).

To these contests and codes, Dickinson, as a woman poet, had no access. Even her art's riddling strength could not gain her entry to the contest. There was no corresponding recipient for her strikes; men cannot play tennis with women even when the woman is a formidable striker. No match at all for Dickinson, Higginson, the editor to whom she sent her poems, revealed his manners by trying to stop the game. He failed in this, as in his reading, but he effectively excluded Dickinson from ever attempting another match. Years after she sent him her poems, he wrote, "The impression of a wholly new and original poetic genius was as distinct on my mind at the first reading of these four poems as it is now, after thirty years of further knowledge; and with it came the problem never yet solved, what place ought to be assigned in literature to what is so remarkable, yet so elusive of criticism."[4] He solved the problem by valorizing the circumstances of creativity he had enforced, writing:

> Emerson said, many years since in the DIAL, that the most interesting department of poetry would hereafter be found in what might be called "The Poetry of the Portfolio"; the work, that is, of persons who wrote for the relief of their own minds, and without thought of publication. Such poetry, when accumulated for years, will have at least the merit of perfect freedom; accompanied, of course, by whatever drawback from the habitual absence of criticism. Thought will have its full strength and uplifting, but without the proper control and chastening of literary expression; there will be wonderful strokes and felicities, and yet an incomplete and unsatisfactory whole.[5]

Thus, Dickinson was politely excluded from the public debate. But, if she could not enter the contest, even more was she denied the exclusive camaraderie of the male language game. Beyond that, she lacked the willingness to indulge in the give-and-take of such games. Part of Higginson's objection to her poetry was that it did not flow in the normal rhythms.

"You think my gait 'spasmodic'— I am in danger—Sir—You think me 'uncontrolled'—I have no Tribunal," Dickinson wrote in reply to his criticism, accepting his point at the same time that she confirmed her own choices (L, II, 409).[6] In a later letter, she was even more insistent on her own exclusiveness, writing, "I marked a line in One Verse—because I met it after I made it—and never consciously touch a paint, mixed by another person" (L, II, 415).

If engendering a reciprocating dialogue meant mixing with other people or their paint, Dickinson would not participate. In that sense, she chose her fate and acceded to the inevitability of not publishing. But despite her disclaimer to Higginson ("I smile when you suggest that I delay 'to publish'—that being foreign to my thought, as Firmament to Fin" [II, 408]), she did appear to write in this early and burgeoning stage of her career in the perhaps naive hope of opening a correspondence with the world. She wrote early poems to specific people, and throughout her life, in the letters that she wrote, she enclosed poems that might take as their subject the difficulty of communication.[7] More than that, she was concerned with poetry as a gift, both a gift to her and from her, and she had particular notions of the protocol of exchange.

However, in contrast to the code of contest used by Hartman, Emerson, and Montaigne, among others, she tended to express her understanding of the language exchange in the metaphor of appetite and desire. Eating, drinking, desiring, willing seduction, are the analogues she uses for her own reading and writing. No tennis player, Dickinson's reader or writer is not so much a single striker as a mass of needs and passions, something like Thoreau's "parcel of vain strivings tied / By a chance bond together." Her desire is fluid, polymorphic, unfocused. The "spasmodic" quality that Higginson saw in her poetry was part of her sense of the writer and reader. Even in her own character, she gave and took according to the particular rhythm of her own desire rather than in response to a strike from an opponent. Recounting his first visit to her, Higginson might easily be describing one of her poem's speakers. He writes:

> She came to me with two day lilies which she put in a sort of childlike way into my hand & said "These are my introduction" in a soft frightened breathless childlike voice—& added under her breath Forgive me if I am frightened; I never see strangers & hardly know what I say—but she talked soon & thenceforward continuously—& deferentially—sometimes stopping to ask me to talk instead of her. (L, II, 473)

Higginson presents himself in this encounter as a passive observer, even a victim of her energy. He wrote at the time, "I never was with one who drained my nerve power so much. Without touching her, she drew from me. I am glad not to live near here. She often thought me tired & seemed very thoughtful of others" (L, II, 476). Some twenty years later he would write, "She was much too enigmatical a being for me to solve in an hour's interview, and an instinct told me that the slightest attempt at direct cross-examination would make her withdraw into her shell; I could only sit and watch" (L, II, 476).

By contrast, Dickinson describes the meeting in the gustatory terms she would use in her poems to express her appetite for words.[8] She wrote to him immediately, "Enough is so vast a sweetness I suppose it never occurs—only pathetic counterfeits—Fabulous to me as the men of the Revelations who 'shall not hunger any more.' Even the Possible has it's [*sic*] insoluble particle" (L, II, 479). Later, in a draft of a letter addressed but perhaps not sent to Higginson, she said, "Thank you for Greatness—I will have deserved it in a longer time!"

Evident in these different accounts are the inequities Dickinson would experience in any exchange based on Montaigne's tennis match analogy. She did not engage in a game of hitting and returning strikes but rather in an experience of emotional elevation. She enjoyed and apparently communicated to Higginson the undifferentiated desire of a woman who was hungry to feed and be fed. Confronted by such needs, Higginson moved to save himself by instinctively putting up his guard. With reason, he came away exhausted from the effort.

Dickinson saw none of Higginson's own wish to defend himself from her company. Deferential she may have been out of some enforced model of courtesy, but she was certainly unschooled in the contest of conversation, the sport of sending and receiving messages. She took from him the surge of energy that his presence supplied her. She expected to talk of literary matters with this literary man, and if she rose high above his requirements, she did so in response to her own sense of the exhilarating interchange about poetry that she might expect from him. It must be admitted too that Higginson probably also had his expectations of their meeting, and that she validated his reasonable fears.

This meeting in which the man held back and the woman exposed herself may serve as a paradigm for Dickinson's dialogue with the world. Neither contests nor language games, her public appearances were more in the nature of strip shows, bountiful banquets, love feasts. Personal contacts were rare, but she had the same kind of intimate contact and derived a similar exhilaration from contacts with other minds through reading, as she described it to Higginson again in physical terms: "If I read a book [and] it makes my whole body so cold no fire ever can warm me I know *that* is poetry. If I feel physically as if the top of my head were taken off, I know *that* is poetry. These are the only way I know it. Is there any other way" (II, 473–474). She simply had no more moderate means of responding to what she perceived to be art's strength. She opened herself to art, was overcome by it, and through it exposed herself to the world. Enchanted and bewitched, she considered herself at the mercy of the text she read, nourished sumptuously by it as she had imagined herself in Higginson's presence. There were, nonetheless, pleasures in such ingestion, which she records in a poem about reading Elizabeth Barrett Browning:

I think I was enchanted
When first a sombre Girl—
I read that Foreign Lady—
The Dark—felt beautiful—

And whether it was noon at night—
Or only Heaven—at Noon—
For very Lunacy of Light
I had not power to tell—

The Bees—became as Butterflies—
The Butterflies—as Swans—
Approached—and spurned the narrow Grass—
And just the meanest Tunes

That Nature murmured to herself
To keep herself in Cheer—
I took for Giants—practising
Titanic Opera—

The Days—To Mighty Metres stept—
The Homeliest—adorned
As if unto a Jubilee
'Twere suddenly confirmed—

I could not have defined the change—
Conversion of the Mind
Like Sanctifying in the Soul—
Is witnessed—not explained—

'Twas a Divine Insanity—
The Danger to be Sane
Should I again experience—
'Tis Antidote to turn—

To Tomes of solid Witchcraft—
Magicians be asleep—
But Magic—hath an Element
Like Deity—to keep— (P 593)

Reading that is enchantment and books that are witchcraft assert the primacy of the word over the receiver of the word and endorse an ideal of reading that appears disastrously passive for a writer. But Dickinson's passivity had its imaginative uses; she actively colluded with her seducer, converting the model of reading she might have taken from the Judaeo-Christian tradition of reading sacred texts into a means of perverse delights. Satisfying an appetite for "Greatness," she could also deny this dangerous desire by attributing her conversion to the devil's party to the seductive power of the word. Through reading, she was led into an unnatural world where "The Dark—felt beautiful", a world also made artful where the "meanest Tunes" became "Titanic Opera", "Mighty Metres", a "Jubilee". Reading for Dickinson became then a means of inspiration, of seeing more fully, more grandly, more deeply.[9]

A world enlarged and transformed by conversion through the word had a Puritan history that Dickinson knew. From Edward Dickinson, she would have learned that reading is valuable as instruction.[10] Dickinson appeared to be a ready student of at least part of the lesson. Schooled in passivity, she demonstrates how dangerously liberating such habits might be. The obedient girl becomes the obedient reader, a "sombre Girl" submitting to "the Foreign Lady" and forever lost to her "Witchcraft".

The seduction of reading was an old-fashioned fear in nineteenth-century Amherst, which Dickinson flaunts in this parable. This particular girl was not necessarily an innocent or unwilling victim. "Sombre" she may have been, but she already had the makings of the dark lady in her character, and she rose naturally, in the manner of Hester Prynne, by falling. Dickinson's openness to reading had its intention. She had a roving eye for just that "Divine Insanity" she desired because she wanted to live "adorned / As if unto a Jubilee ". The common did not nourish her, and she had to read to survive.

She could use the drinking metaphor that served to describe the excitement of her meeting with Higginson to express a basic need for sustenance. She writes:

> Strong Draughts of Their Refreshing Minds
> To drink—enables Mine
> Through Desert or the Wilderness
> As bore it Sealed Wine—
>
> To go elastic—Or as One
> The Camel's trait—attained—
> How powerful the Stimulus
> Of an Hermetic Mind— (P 711)

Far from "Jubilee" this reader requires the means to survive in the desert of daily life that stretched out endlessly before her. Rather than instant enchantment, she needs a powerful stimulus that can provide sustenance for a long time. And she turns for nourishment to congenial company, as the "sombre Girl" turned to the dark lady. The "Hermetic Mind" of the final line belongs to the speaker as well as to those she reads. The speaker bears what she reads as "Sealed Wine" hermetically preserved against the evaporation of its contents by exposure to the common air or company. By these means she can "go elastic" and, like the camel, survive without nourishment from an environment that provided none. The "Hermetic Mind" as the magic stimulus of her reading belongs to those "Refreshing Minds" she matches with her own. The creative act of the reader, nourishing what she is nourished on, finds a more direct expression in this poem:

> Who goes to dine must take his Feast
> Or find the Banquet mean—
> The Table is not laid without
> Till it is laid within.

For Pattern is the Mind bestowed
That imitating her
Our most ignoble Services
Exhibit worthier. (P 1223)

Again, in P 1587 she writes, "He ate and drank the precious Words— / His Spirit grew robust—". Like Dickinson reading Barrett Browning, this man found himself released from tedium so that "He danced along the dingy Days."

Behind her eating metaphor may be the Christian tradition of communion, but it is deliberately subverted. These poems' intensity as well as their imagery recalls Edward Taylor's meditations on the "living bread," but their end is not the preparation of the soul. The feast here feeds the imagination's appetite. Laying the table within before it is laid without may be an act of discipline or it may be a channeling of desire. The appetite that will create its own banquet is lust. And appetency drives both the mind that bestows its pattern, moving in its desire toward the world, and the spirit that grows robust on words, taking what it desires from the world.

This metaphor, which appears removed from the decorum of the sombre girl enchanted by her reading, shares nonetheless with that reading a preference for sumptuousness, for swans over bees, for opera over homely tunes.[11] The poet discovered early enough that enchantments would be few unless she created them.[12] She lived almost alone in her desire, rarely finding it reciprocated or even shared by another desirer. No Emerson convinced that the mind could make the world conform to the ideal within, Dickinson always wanted more than the world ever had to offer. She wanted to be overpowered by "Titanic Opera" in a world that everywhere threatened to be mean, ignoble, unworthy.

Her disappointment had its ghoulish moments, as in P 773:

Deprived of other Banquet,
I entertained Myself—
At first—a scant nutrition—
An insufficient Loaf—

But grown by slender addings
To so esteemed a size
'Tis sumptuous enough for me—
And almost to suffice

A Robin's famine able
Red Pilgrim, He and I—
A Berry from our table
Reserve—for charity—

Dining on herself, the speaker enjoys a particular kind of addition through subtraction.[13] Her lines here echo across the century in another woman poet. Adrienne Rich writes:

I refuse to become a seeker for cures.
Everything that has ever
helped me has come through what already
lay stored in me. Old things, diffuse, unnamed, lie strong across my heart.
        This is from where
my strength comes, even when I miss my strength
even when it turns on me
like a violent master (*Sources*, II, 10)

Characteristically, Dickinson presents her speaker as the waif and Rich presents hers as self-willed and defiant, yet the speakers are alike in their isolation and their self-containment. They both must depend on their own resources to thrive. This is the familiar habit of self-reliance, but not in the Emersonian tradition. No divinity within sustains them; they feed on their own will to survive and on their own generosity. Dickinson's loaf is "insufficient" but it grows by dividing and its "slender addings" increase to "sumptuous enough" not only for herself but for the needs of others.

Dickinson turns within, as Rich does, out of need, but also out of preference. The banquet within may be scant, but once she has grown used to it, it is more satisfying than the lavish banquet of which she imagines herself deprived. Deprivation is a stimulus to appetite for the wrong food both for Dickinson and for Rich. In Dickinson, it inspires an appetite for food that can neither satisfy her nor be digested, as she tells in P 579 where "hungry, all the Years—" her "Noon had Come—to dine—". She found:

The Plenty hurt me—'twas so new—
Myself felt ill—and odd—

As Berry—of a Mountain Bush—
Transplanted—to the Road—

Nor was I hungry—so I found
That Hunger—was a way
Of Persons outside Windows—
The Entering—takes away—(P 579)

It is easy to see this poem as an expression of Dickinson's Puritan habit of living in the world with weaned affections. Her parsimonious "Plenty hurt me" sounds also like Benjamin Franklin. But behind this relish for little is the more original realization that the "ample Bread" is "so unlike the Crumb".[14] The banquet of which Dickinson feels deprived would not be at all nourishing, she realizes. She has been "hungry" all the years for the wrong food. She anticipates Rich's resolve in the final section of *Sources*: "When I speak of an end to suffering, I don't mean anesthesia. I mean knowing the world, and my place in it, not in order to stare with bitterness or detachment, but as a powerful and womanly series of choices" (Rich, 35). Like Rich's, Dickinson's speaker "outside Windows" has been staring with longing at a world that can never satisfy her need. Her great need to find her place in the world depends upon passing up the plentiful feast set for the crowd in preference for that table reserved for those refined and disciplined appetites like her own. Her hunger is an indication of her difference, her status as an outsider. Not a sensation that can be satisfied, it is her mark of distinction, and she has to learn to wear it, like Rich, without "bitterness or detachment."

The whole question of what she can take from the world and what she must find stored within herself assumes a slightly different cast when Dickinson considers that passive ingestion she experiences through the ear. Not going out to dine now, she is still served up a special fare. Fortunately, she has the habit of a large and gracious hospitality whether she shares a berry or takes the feast in going to dine, and she finds that she has to exercise it often in the cacophonous world.[15]

The poet's ear has special powers of adornment or, as she writes in one poem, the "License" to adorn. But, like the generous appetite, the attiring ear belongs to the guest as well as the host, the reader as well as the poet. She writes:

The Fashion of the Ear
Attireth that it hear
In Dun, or fair—

So whether it be Rune,
Or whether it be none
Is of within. (P 526)

Wittily forcing us to hear the variations of the rhyme scheme (ear/hear/
fair and rune/none/within), Dickinson insists that we attire what we hear
in dun or fair. Although this sounds like Emerson's "What we are, that
only can we see," Dickinson, using the more passive organ, seems less
interested in converting the world to the pure idea in the mind than in
indicating the intimacy between the the word and the ear, the poet and
her audience.

Dickinson's ear, unlike Emerson's eye, is both passive and doubled.
Conception through the ear cannot really be resisted, but that conception
depends on an earlier one in the poet's own ear. Emerson's eye looks out
apparently on an inert world which it animates; Dickinson's ear attires
what is already attired by another's art. Emerson feels that the conversion
of things to the mind will bring about a correspondent revolution and "so
fast will disagreeable appearances, swine, spiders, snakes, pests, mad-
houses, prisons, enemies vanish; they are temporary and shall be no more
seen."[16] But in Dickinson, dun and fair are not moral choices because they
are not opposites. Her language indicates connective links of rhyme between "Dun" and "none," but links of parallel structures between "Dun"
and "Rune," "none" and "fair." The words whispered in the ear may be
then blankly dark or fairly magical, but they may also be murky secrets or
sweet nothings. The listener may take in secrets or block them; she may
want the world dark or light.

Although in this poem it is an oriole singing that elicits the commentary,
the oriole which "sings the same, unheard, / As unto Crowd—" duplicates
this particular poet's circumstance exactly. Like the poet's letter to the
world, this bird's tune is committed to ears it cannot see, and the poem
turns on its vulnerability as well as that of the listener whose ear, whatever
its fashion, is always open. Dickinson acknowledges this double vulnerability in P 505 where she writes:

Nor would I be a Poet—
It's finer—own the Ear—
Enamored—impotent—content
The License to revere,

Because she writes these lines as a poet, she already owns the ear to revere the license she enjoys. Her disclaimer of that role is an extravagance that reverses itself in exaggeration. Without the "Fashion" of the poet's own ear, few would be able to fashion their own ear.

In the oriole poem, the point is made more forcefully. "The Fashion of the Ear / Attireth that it hear" may suggest that the ear attires not only what it hears but so that it might hear. Nothing will come of nothing; the hearing of the poet as of her listener is improved by their adorning of language.

Yet how could the ear in its openness and accessibility manage to cover up what it hears? In activating the most passive of senses, Dickinson points to the intimacy and potential identification between singer and listener, between poet and audience, as well as to the extreme defensiveness between them. In a letter to Higginson, she wrote about the vulnerability of the ear: "Death obtains the Rose, but the News of Dying goes no further than the Breeze. The Ear is the last Face. We hear after we see" (L, II, 518).

Thus, in attiring so that it can hear, the ear exerts itself against what it cannot resist. The poet too attires so that she can be heard, because such attire titillates the lust of the listener for the exposure of the word and the lust of the singer for the one perfect respondent to her self-exposure. The give-and-take here between listener and speaker shares something of Hartman's reciprocating dialogue, but with a basis in desire and not, as he would have it, in the opposition of strength. The embarrassment he notes is there in the effort of the ear to cover up what it hears and would have heard, but Dickinson's sympathies are with the self-revealing speaker rather than with Hartman's self-protecting listener. She would never be convinced either of the perfect sympathy between poet and listener that the English Romantic poets celebrated or of the conviction of her compatriots Emerson and Thoreau that the poet was the namer and sayer for all men.

And she turned this lack of assurance to her benefit. As an unread poet, Dickinson had yet another use for the attiring ear. She could rely on the fashion of the ear among poetry readers of her generation to protect her from her song's helpless stripping away of her own defenses, from art's blatant and unstoppable self-exposure. The fashion of her own ear was to attire too little and against the prevailing styles so that she had to depend on her listeners' fashionable obtuseness to cover what she may have left too exposed. Especially as the game between poet and reader became a hunt to the kill, she had to hope that she could hide behind her own unfashionable attire. She could claim, "Good to hide, and hear 'em hunt!" Such defensiveness was the reverse side of a great need. Her art's secrecy grew out of its openness just as her exclusion of the general reader came from her intense longing for the intimacy that perfect expression might offer, as she admits finally:

> Good to know, and not tell,
> Best, to know and tell,
> Can one find the rare Ear
> Not too dull— (P 842)

Every poet longs for the rare ear attuned to her own, but Dickinson wanted even more. She wanted not just a passive audience but one that actively sought her. Her exclusivity had its plaintive side: "I've none to tell me to but Thee / So when Thou failest, nobody." But it had also a corresponding demand. She goes on:

> If things were opposite—and Me
> And Me it were—that ebbed from Thee
> On some unanswering Shore—
> Would'st Thou seek so—just say
> That I the Answer may pursue
> Unto the lips it eddied through—
> So—overtaking Thee— (P 881)

Here in the oceanic imagery of ebbing and eddying that recalls her own experience of enchanted reading, she names her desire and sets up the formidable forces that work against her "little tie" of poetry and love that "just held Two, nor those it held / Since Somewhere thy sweet Face has spilled / Beyond my Boundary—". Casting no spells, tying no one to her, the poet in her telling as in her reading is more desiring than desired.

"I've none to tell me to but Thee" is a love poem in which the lover sees herself as bound and in flux, caught but in an experience that ebbs and spills. In this, the lover resembles the poet, bound to words that can in no way bind either her feelings or their object, but a poet made plaintive by the need to do exactly what she knows words will fail to do.

The pathos of the poet's longing here is her knowledge that "if things were opposite" neither her reader nor her lover would seek for her. Few were the readers in nineteenth-century America sufficiently skilled and desiring, and Dickinson, who had, with rare exceptions, neither the intimate reader she exclusively chose nor the general readers she excluded, was not alone in her loneliness. Even Emerson, with his much more modest hope of "hooking" "like-minded men" by publishing his thoughts and so giving men whom he valued "one hour of stimulated thought," even he despaired of a responsive reader, claiming, "Yet, how few! Who in Concord cares for the first philosophy in a book? The woman whose child is to be suckled? The man at Nine-acre-Corner who is to cart sixty loads of gravel on his meadow?"[17] Thoreau too could complain that "men have learned to read to serve a paltry convenience" "but of reading as a noble intellectual exercise they know little or nothing."[18]

For all their complaints, however, Emerson and Thoreau lacked Dickinson's temerity toward the reader. They were intent on argument, on stimulating thought and encouraging a noble intellectual exercise, and, for such ends, they had to rely on the persuasiveness of their rhetoric. Dickinson did not want to persuade, but to enthrall as she herself was enthralled by her reading. Her appeal was direct, personal, and total. Thoreau wanted readers who stood on tiptoe, alert and wakeful, poised to exercise and willing to strain every muscle to action, like Montaigne's tennis player but of Olympic quality. Dickinson's model is the reader in love, moved not only by poetry but by the poet herself, and, of course, in that sense, the reader totally in the power of the poet. Poetry and love are, as she writes, "coeval":

> To pile like Thunder to its close
> Then crumble grand away
> While Everything created hid
> This—would be Poetry—
>
> Or Love—the two coeval come—
> We both and neither prove—

Experience either and consume—
For None see God and live— (P 1247)

Even Whitman in his expansive moods was more tentative, asserting "I give you my love more precious than money," but waiting to ask, "Will you give me yourself? will you come travel with me?" ("Song of the Open Road"). Dickinson's embrace is insistent: "Poetry— / Or Love—the two coeval come—". Poetry, like love, can be neither resisted nor argued. "Conversion of the Mind" "Is witnessed—not explained—" Dickinson said of her own reading in P 593. And here to her readers as to herself, she says of poetry as of love, "We both and neither prove—".

By these tactics, Dickinson removes poetry from persuasion and the poet from attempts to win an audience. That would be the province of prose, a narrow task in which the poet would feel herself captive, "shut up" as she had been as a little girl because some wanted her "'still'" (P 613). She preferred the openness of poetry, "The spreading wide my narrow Hands / To gather Paradise—" (P 657), to the "Captivity" of prose.

Nonetheless, her open hands were not like Whitman's spread wide to embrace multitudes; they intended rather to gather into themselves extremities of experience and experience of the extreme. Poetry and love are for Dickinson neither a union of two spirits nor a communion of lover and beloved. They are rather an excitation, a visitation of power so enthralling that it forces everything else to hide, a surge of energy that gathers and then even as it crumbles, moves "grand away." As Margaret Homans has argued, this poem describes poetry as "post-linguistic" and love as "post-experiential." She says, "The moment at which language becomes poetry is precisely the moment when we cease to be able to understand it."[19]

But like the thunder, poetry and love are just effects, neither lightning nor storm. They announce rather than consummate the possibilites. Thus, if the verb in the penultimate line is in the imperative "Experience either and consume—" Dickinson seems to be offering a conventional argument for poetry and love as an anticipation of heaven, a gathering of paradise, and at the same time warning her readers against such experience.

If the verb "experience" is not in the imperative, it can be read on from "We prove" as "We experience either and consume." Then we consume and are consumed become a continuum. In the grammatical blur of these middle lines of the second stanza, Dickinson also suggests that "we"—both poet and reader—are helpless before the experience of love and poetry.

Reading and writing as consuming and all consuming cannot be resisted; the poet need not encourage the "experience" of poetry. It will happen and, in its happening, it will overwhelm. But, like the thunder, it comes and goes, gathers and crumbles, announces and departs, and in this it resembles nothing so much as the "spasmodic gait" of the poet.

The spasm that gathers and eases is the rhythm of poetry, of both the poet's and the reader's experience with the poem, and of the poet's relationship with her audience. Intense, brief, but repeatable, the spasmodic lyric poem is enjoyed in its coming and in its coming again. In this art of titillation, the end is not consummation but increased excitement.

Far from the straight line of logic in the narrow development of an argument, poetry follows those strategies by which love grows and thrives on loss, absence, and inaccessibility. The poet-lover knows "To disappear enhances—". So "impotent to cherish / We hasten to adorn—" until:

Of Death the sternest function
That just as we discern
The Excellence defies us—
Securest gathered then

The Fruit perverse to plucking,
But leaning to the Sight
With the ecstatic limit
Of unobtained Delight— (P 1209)

"Death", "Excellence", and "Fruit" combine in an odd list of appositives to suggest that the inaccessible is the desired. In the equation of death's "sternest function" with the "ecstatic limit" of fruit "perverse to plucking " Dickinson underscores the connection between forbidding and ecstasy. In this scheme, deprivation becomes a means of enhanced delight. "Hungry, all the Years" this speaker has been nourished rather than depleted by her appetite for "unobtained Delight". In the moment "just as we discern" and, like the fruit, "leaning to the Sight," we are both denied and reassured that we have "Securest gathered then / The Fruit perverse to plucking". Perversity to plucking is an attribute of the fruit, excellence, and death, which the speaker shares. She is obstinate in her desire not to pick the fruit that will not be picked, because she would rather extend the "ecstatic limit" of her longing than attain it. "We tamper with 'Again'" she writes, "But 'Never' far as Honor / Withdraws the Worthless thing".

Her appetite for unpluckable fruit drives her poetry as it does the poetry of Wallace Stevens. "Death is the mother of beauty," he writes, echoing Dickinson. She knows, as he does, that "We do not prove the existence of the poem," "It is, and it / Is not and, therefore, is" ("A Primitive Like an Orb"). Although such an appetite gives them both a taste for exotic fruit and extreme ranges of feeling, it grew out of an aversion to the attainable, the public, and the common.[20] Like Stevens, Dickinson aimed to "make the visible a little hard / To see" ("The Creations of Sound").

Not that the visible did not interest Dickinson, rather she was tantalized by what it hid, claiming both that the poet "Distills amazing sense / From ordinary Meanings—" (P 448) and equally that "To see the Summer Sky / Is Poetry, though never in a Book it lie— / True Poems flee—" (P 1472). The poet's relationship to "ordinary Meanings" as to "the Summer Sky" is one of amazement, which she expresses both by claiming to distill it and by admitting that it has escaped her. "Poetry" no less than "ordinary Meanings" relies on preserving its "amazing" sense by hiding it. For Dickinson, "The Riddle we can guess / We speedily despise—" (P 1222).

Because Dickinson ardently longed for the "rare Ear" of the true and beloved reader and yet knew that in writing she opened herself fearlessly not only to that special audience but to the world, she had to find a way of being herself visible and yet hard to see, of raising the requirements for full reading. For this reason, the half light was more congenial to her, and she claimed:

By a departing light
We see acuter, quite,
Than by a wick that stays.
There's something in the flight
That clarifies the sight
And decks the rays. (P 1714)

Clarity becomes then a product of half-glimpses, of fleeting glances, and of darkness. In a "departing light" she can both stay and flee, reveal herself to "acuter" sight and escape the full light. Yet everything in the riveting rhyme scheme of the poem negates what is being said. No half rhymes or off rhymes imitate the flight of light, as the poem's music thumps out its beat. Direct statement cannot suggest the clarity of indirection; it must work against itself and depend on a contrived syntax ("acuter, quite") or a vague "There's something" to carry its sense. More suggestively, in the well-known poem "Tell all the Truth" clarity comes only in a gradual light. To brighten is to blind, and she insists that "The Truth's superb surprise" "must dazzle gradually / Or every man be blind—" (P 1129).

The half-light is only part of clarity's requirement, however; its movement in flight, never coming but always just departing, is the other part. Like Stevens in "Le Monocle de Mon Oncle," Dickinson knew that "fluttering things have so distinct a shade." And she could even entertain the possibility that words which might arrest the flight of sensations would also "decrease" and "demean" them, as she writes:

> To tell the Beauty would decrease
> To state the Spell demean—
> There is a syllable-less Sea
> Of which it is the sign—
> My will endeavors for its word
> And fails, but entertains
> A Rapture as of Legacies—
> Of introspective Mines— (P 1700)

The success that "in Circuit lies" in "Tell all the Truth" resides here in that failure of the will as it gestures toward words. Yet the failure must be half willed and the endeavor fainthearted at best since its failure is so supremely rewarded. The "Beauty", the "Spell", a "Rapture" are "introspective" movements and treasures neither to be arrested nor externalized in words. The "sign" is not the word, but the sensation.

Again, Dickinson's determination to "tell" that she cannot tell sets this poem at odds with itself. Its iambic regularity, uncharacteristic of her verse, also works to suggest the static quality of the will's successful endeavor for words.[21] And thus the poem turns on itself; the statement that demeans is demeaning in its prosaic argument and its conventional meter. Poetry belongs elsewhere, not with telling and stating but with that movement of the spirit that Dickinson entitles rapture. By indicating just how stultifying conventional form can be, she subverts the Romantic habit of making dejection a subject that denies its exhaustion of power.

Coming into form may be a diminishment and a limitation, but it could also be an enlarged hazard. Dickinson insisted that the poet writing could not control the movement of her words even when she knew where they are going, and this uncertainty enforced some caution. So overwhelmed with the power of words was she herself that Dickinson had reason not only to prefer the shadow to the full light, fluttering things to constancy, she could value silence over telling. "A Secret told— / Ceases to be a Secret—" she admits and claims "Better of it—continual be afraid— / Than it— / And Whom you told it to—beside—" (P 381). The fear of revealing harmful truths is counterbalanced by the other fear of doing harm with words. "A Word dropped careless on a Page / May stimulate an eye " she warns, adding:

> Infection in the sentence breeds
> We may inhale Despair
> At distances of Centuries
> From the Malaria— (P 1261)

Against the infection of writing, the reader is inoculated only by his or her obtuseness. If the writer may be careless, the reader may be inept, as Dickinson writes:

> Could mortal lip divine
> The undeveloped Freight
> Of a delivered syllable
> 'Twould crumble with the weight. (P 1409)

The "mortal lip" here, like the ear which "attireth that it hear", may belong to writer or reader. Both the one who delivers the syllable and the one who receives it must depend equally on the inability of the other to "divine" the "undeveloped". Mortal lips are not divine nor can they foretell all that they tell, and mercifully so. They would cease talking if they understood perfectly what they were saying, and they would be unable to listen if they heard well.

In this extreme of mutual carelessness and ineptitude, Dickinson suggests that the vulnerability of audience to poet can neither be calculated nor arrested. Breeding and developing, the word's fecundity is deadly. There is a compensatory vulnerability of poet to audience. What is written will be read; what is said will be heard. And in this inexorable process, time proves the enemy of artistic control. Future readers cannot be guessed nor the life they will bring to the poem measured. Dickinson acknowledges this donated immortality:

A word is dead
When it is said,
Some say.

I say it just
Begins to live
That day. (P 1212)

Because the listener gives the word the only life that it will have, the sayer, even of such homely adages as Poem 1212, is almost incidental. The poet is completely at the mercy of her listeners or readers.

It is not wise, then, to say too much. Nor, Dickinson suggests in the following poem, can too much be said.

"Secrets" is a daily word
Yet does not exist—
Muffled—it remits surmise—
Murmured—it has ceased—
Dungeoned in the Human Breast
Doubtless secrets lie—
But that Grate inviolate—
Goes nor comes away
Nothing with a Tongue or Ear—
Secrets stapled there
Will emerge but once—and dumb—
To the Sepulchre— (P 1385)

The "daily" word that does not exist is a paradigm of the language exchange, as Dickinson understood it. As she said in a letter to her sister-in-law Sue Gilbert Dickinson, "Subjects hinder talk" (L, II, 512). Talk for Dickinson was that subjectless communication between kindred spirits and not a matter of giving or sending even secret messages.

The fear that Dickinson entertained toward her audience—both the fear of it and the fear for it—may have inspired this faith in the paradox of secrets. If telling can decrease Beauty, it will kill a secret—if indeed it were possible to tell a secret, which it is not. The power to tell is self-canceling. Art, for all its riddling strength, can wrest no secrets from the dungeon of the human breast.

Interchapter

This book divides in two here, and, although the next three chapters on Stevens's poetry will take up the issues just discussed in Dickinson's work— the self, the letter, and the audience—the terms and treatment will shift somewhat in response to a different poetry and time. The basic difference is that Stevens is not what Emerson called a portfolio poet, writing in private and without thought of publication, and even if Dickinson does not fit that category so fully as her contemporary Higginson imagined she did, she is closer to it than he is. Stevens has then, of necessity, a much less private and radical sense of self than she has and, correspondingly, a greater social sense. Because he is, for all the aloofness and divisions in his character, a more public figure than Dickinson, he will be less frantically reliant on the letter for contact with the world and probably less intensely and erotically charged by it. And, although he can be anxious about his audience, he will lack the passionate need for contact through the written word that Dickinson's life of seclusion encouraged.

The privacy in Dickinson's work, evidenced, as we have seen, in the sense of the discontinuous self, is a way of avoiding conventional plots of character development, of guarding the unmappable areas of privacy, of selecting rather than being coerced into bonds of love and communion. Moreover, for her, the sense of the discontinuous is an experience of the ordinary and the contingent, the very elements of continuity, and not of the universal or nontemporal. How much this sense of discontinuity is part of her experience as a woman living in the nineteenth century, how much it is a part of lyric expression in any age, and how much it is particularly American, remain undecidable. Feminists have argued for her unique status as a woman writer, formalists for her poetry as representative of the genre, and cultural historians for her embodiment of nineteenth-century America.[1] Placing her work next to Stevens's poetry provides an opportunity to see her anew in all these roles and to see his work in the American lyric tradition she can be credited with initiating.

What unites these two poets is, I shall argue, not the Romanticism with which they are usually linked through Emerson, but pragmatism, that philosophical counterpart of literary modernism which denies a preexistent or essential truth that can be represented, takes language as part of the behavior of human beings and not as referring adequately to some world, and accepts "the contingent character of starting-points."[2] Dickinson's place in this movement is less certain than that of Stevens, who had direct contact with its founders as a Harvard undergraduate; yet it seems to me that her work points in that direction more clearly than it looks back to Romanticism for its guiding sense of self, language, and world. It does so largely because she was a private poet, constrained by both her own inclination and the advice of Higginson from publishing. She was thus freed from the restraints that the Romantic movement placed on women writers.[3]

First, Dickinson and Stevens are linked by a sense of the self that is closer to the pragmatists than to the Romantics. Because Stevens does not compose in the brief form that attracted Dickinson, the various strategies by which she expresses the discontinuities and superfluities of individuality are not available to him. Yet, as we shall see, the repetitive action, the brief and multiple anecdotes, inverted dramatic monologues, and varied speakers in his long poems are ways he uses to disrupt the integrity of the lyric speaker. I do not mean to suggest that Dickinson's work is the source of these developments in Stevens. Rather, her efforts to break the lyric "I" into a discontinuous series of gestures or imaginings appear to be the first stage in the reconception of the self as an interactional process, rather than a discrete entity, that twentieth-century American poets and philosophers have continued to develop.

But why would Dickinson rather than Whitman, say, have made this breakthrough? And why would Stevens rather than Williams have continued it? The answers to these two questions are both the same and different. The single answer is that, unlike Whitman and Williams, Dickinson and Stevens devoted themselves exclusively to the lyric genre where the conception of the self is crucial, revisionary, and essential. By contrast, in their long experimental American epics, Whitman and Williams could rely on a more generalized sense of self, the democratic ideal in which self and other are merged, as in Whitman's identification with his democratic audience or Williams's "Whenever I say 'I' I mean also 'you.' And so, together, as one, we shall begin."

The reasons that Dickinson began to reconceive the self, however, are different from the reasons that Stevens continued the process, and these differences are more complicated to explain. Dickinson began to develop what was to be a pragmatic sense of the "contingency of selfhood" out of necessity. There were no available descriptions of the world that fit her experience or, rather, her sense of her self and the world forced her to attempt a redescription. She wrote poem after poem about the failure of what she took to be "The One Right Description" to satisfy her needs. This dissatisfaction moved her to start from her own experience rather than from ideas to describe what she herself knew and felt, what was around her at the moment, what came to her by chance. As a result, she created a way of describing ranges of emotion, such as pain, that probe experience in, for example, "After great pain, a formal feeling comes—" (P 341) or "'Twas like a Maelstrom, with a notch " (P 414). She made poems of the near-at-hand, such homely subjects as the blackberry (P 554), the snake (P 986), the mushroom (P 1298). Or she could admit that she could find no right description, looking out, for example, at "Four Trees—upon a solitary Acre— / Without Design" and concluding, "What Plan / They severally— retard—or further—/ Unknown" (P 742). For her, knowledge was never certain, always a process of questioning: "Why—do they shut Me out of Heaven?" (P 248) or "Afraid! Of whom am I afraid?" (P 608). Or it was a matter for conjecture: "Not seeing, still we know—" (P 1518) or "My Worthiness is all my Doubt—" (P 751).

In her poetry, groping for her own way, she began to work toward a view of the self and world that would be more fully developed by the philosophy of pragmatism. In some sense, Dickinson, the questioning, doubting, troubling poet, is far removed from the optimism of a pragmatist philosopher like William James. She lacked his will to believe, and yet, as I have suggested earlier in discussing the difference between her speakers and the Transcendentalist hero, she would subscribe to the activism that such a belief encouraged. James's famous image of man on a mountain pass in the midst of a whirling snowstorm and blinding mist in "The Will to Believe," who could get only glimpses of paths that might be deceptive can stand for Dickinson's sense of the self.[4] She would agree both with James's warning that such a man if he stood still would freeze to death, and if he moved might be dashed to pieces, and also with James's advice that, despite all, such a man had to act for the best, hope for the best, and take what might come. Her experience taught her the antiessentialism of notions like "truth" and the uselessness of hoping that objects will constrain us to believe the truth about them.

Like James, and for somewhat the same reasons, she built her world on the certain truth that the phenomenon of consciousness exists. Convinced, as James was, of the uncertain validity of all human knowledge, Dickinson did not take the risk of assenting to a religious hypothesis, but she did risk assenting to the words she could put together. She was not moved, as we have seen, by the conventional notions of faith, the "condescension" of the Word "'Made Flesh and dwelt among us'"; rather she placed her faith in the human community of language, "this consent of Language / This loved Philology" (P 1651).

The risk of assenting to language led her to put words together, to attend to the way such linkages worked or failed, and to an interest in metonymy. This interest has been tied to Roman Jakobson's identification of a preference for metonymy with a contiguity disorder.[5] It might also and more productively be seen as part of her desire to start from the particular, from the four trees upon a solitary acre or "Of Bronze— and Blaze— / The North—Tonight—" (P 290) and, from there, to indicate gaps that she would not connect with consoling, because consolidating, ideas. Far from a contiguity disorder, she appears to have had an unusually strong interest in things that stand next to other things or people.

Like Dickinson, Stevens also had an interest in metonymy, as he writes in "Theory," "I am what is around me" (86). In contrast to Whitman and Williams, Dickinson and Stevens insist not on the communal but on the particularity of the "I," and Stevens continues, "One is not duchess / A hundred yards from a carriage." The aristocratic pose belongs to a fantastic, exaggerated, melodramatic range of experience that deliberately sets his speakers off from the common and communal just as the strutting, emoting, and dramatic poses of Dickinson's speakers serve to suggest their uniqueness. The reader is not enjoined to assume what they assume, to identify with them, but rather to witness, if not their originality, at least the particularity of their surroundings and their elegance. It is the individuality, the oddity, or the eccentricity of these speakers that becomes the distinctive quality of these lyric poems and sets the genre apart from the epic or poetic narrative. The anti-democratic quality of this kind of individuality is a powerful reminder of the separateness of the lyric speaker, but it also points to the uniqueness of the individual that often offsets the leveling aspects of the democratic ideal.

Stevens drew into the lyric genre ideas about the self and the world that came to him from, among a variety of sources, the philosophers George Santayana, Henri Bergson, and William James, and thus, he can be more directly linked to pragmatism than Dickinson. With Santayana, he had immediate contact, as George Lessing points out, and their discussions may have helped him work through his preoccupation with the relationship between fact and ideal in his college years.[6] Stevens agreed with Santayana that the mind begins with facts, but he held more firmly than Santayana to facts, not only as a starting point but also as a pervasive and continuing presence in the exercise of the imagination. From Bergson, Stevens took his stress on change and on the poet's ability to express the novelty of the moment.[7] Although, as Margaret Peterson points out in her discussion of Stevens and the idealist tradition, the theory that novelty manifests the self-creative principle of the mind was a commonplace in the idealist tradition long before Bergson, his distinctive contribution is his identification of change with reality itself, and it is this point that matters to Stevens. James fortified Stevens's own belief in the importance of the will and his conviction expressed in "Adagia" that "The final belief is to believe in a fiction, which you know to be a fiction, there being nothing else. The exquisite truth is to know that it is a fiction and that you believe in it willingly" (OP 189).

Stevens's insistence on facts and on the will to believe in them without the fundamental postulate of the Absolute Idealists in the One, the Whole, or Spiritual Unity as the ultimate reality, allowed him to write without frequent recourse to the lyric "I." Thus he can deflect onto the surroundings some of the intensity and eroticism that Dickinson's speakers experience. For example, the passion of the maiden Bawda in *Notes Toward a Supreme Fiction* is played out in the marriage place rather than in her direct declarations. And "The Woman in Sunshine" is "disembodied" (445). The following chapter on Stevens's sense of self will concentrate not on the discontinuities of a single self but on the way in which he repeatedly projects his sense of self on other figures, often women, as if, as he says in "Theory," "I am what is around me. / / Women understand this" (86).

Stevens differs also from Dickinson in his interest in the letter. In using the poem as a letter of correspondence, Dickinson moves from examining the erotic charge of the letter's touch to poems about marriage names and to a consideration of words as love tokens. Stevens sees the letter as a bond between writer and reader in the more distanced but no less personal and particular scheme of genealogy, of familial ties, of the parent-child relationship established between writer and reader. Here again, the two poets are linked through pragmatism in an interest in the letter not as standing for some ultimate reality but as a token exchanged between reader and writer, one person's description of his or her particular surroundings without reference to a transcendent truth.

Although Stevens lived a much more active life than Dickinson and traveled more widely than she did, he became in his later years almost as dependent as Dickinson on letters of correspondence for exploration of the larger world he never visited.[8] And, to a larger extent than Dickinson, Stevens used the material of his correspondents freely in his poems. For example, he included in *An Ordinary Evening in New Haven* a number of casual messages he received from friends during the summer he was writing the long poem. The lines "Bergamo on a postcard, Rome after dark, / Sweden described, Salzburg with shaded eyes / Or Paris in conversation at a cafe" (486) are drawn from a variety of random letters or cards written by traveling friends, as Lessing suggests. He could use what came to him by chance because, as he explains to one of his most frequent correspondents, Barbara Church:

> It interests me immensely to have you speak of so many places that have been merely names for me. Yet really they have always been a good deal more than names. I practically lived in France when old Mr. Vidal was alive because if I had asked him to procure from an obscure fromagerie in the country some of the cheese with raisins in it of which I read one time, he would have done it and that is almost what living in France or anywhere else amounts to. (L 610)

That Stevens had a more sophisticated and wide ranging circle of friends and that he did not know well, except through letters, many of the people with whom he corresponded make his reliance on letters somewhat less intense than Dickinson's, although, as we see, no less thorough.

Finally, as this study moves along to examine Stevens's relationship with his audience, it will depart still further from the passion and intensity that marked Dickinson's fantasies of that one perfect and loving reader who would take up the lovetokens she sent in her letter-poems. It will move again with the poetry in the direction of family toward the parental and, finally, the brotherly connection. David Bromwich argues for the influence of William James in this connection, claiming that Stevens's engagement with the pragmatic idea of world making in *Parts of a World* was to show how a personal reading of life might include a concern for his fellow readers.[9]

In placing these two poets together, my interest is not that of the lecturer in Stevens's "The Ultimate Poem Is Abstract," who "composes himself / And hems the planet rose and haws it ripe" (429). I want to look rather into the way that Stevens, like Dickinson, uses the lyric genre to particularize his experience, to resist the generalizing tendencies of the culture in which he lived and the critical impulse toward continuity, and yet to insist on his own eccentric description of that cultural moment.

Stevens, next to Dickinson, appears less like the Romantic poet and more like the pragmatic poet content to use his power to redescribe the ordinary, the contingent, to vest "in the serious folds of majesty" "whirroos / And scintillant sizzlings such as children like" (442). Such a Stevens can conceive of "his fated eccentricity, / As part, but part, but tenacious particle, / Of the skeleton of the ether, the total / Of letters, prophecies, perceptions" (443). He might nourish a nostalgia for "the essential poem at the centre of things" (440), but he knows that he is actually engaged in writing "lesser poems" (440).

Part of the value of examining this pragmatic Stevens is to see the importance of neglected poems in his collected works—those poems which take as their subjects the Depression and World War II, experiences that he found resistant to the poetic imagination and yet irresistible in the challenges they presented. In these poems that engaged his creative energies throughout the middle period of his career, his work resembles Dickinson's lyric efforts to make poems out of the near at hand, out of the world as it chances to appear to him. The Stevens who emerges in these poems is a lyric poet of community, a particular man concerned that his imagination become active in the imaginations of his readers.

An entry in Stevens's commonplace book *Sur Plusieurs Beaux Sujects*, a quotation from Edward Sackville-West, might sum up the work of Dickinson and Stevens as it is read in an American lyric tradition: "the later proliferations of romantic and symbolist theory have tended to obscure one of the most valuable functions of poetry: the illumination of the usual."[10] A great benefit of reading these two unique and unusual poets together is to see how fully their poetry fulfills this valuable function.

Chapter 5

"He that of repetition is most master": Stevens and the Lyric Self

The self in Stevens's poetry is almost always a social creation, never private nor intimate but rather porous and open-ended, a part of all that is around it. It may seem that Stevens was developing along more radical lines the discontinuity of self that Dickinson contemplated, but his strategies served a much more conservative end. She experimented with ways to express a self in opposition to her culture's representative, narrated self. By contrast, he had neither a program of opposition nor an eagerness to express the privacy of his own individuality which he found problematic, puzzling, and unacknowledgeable. Yet, the lyric genre forced him to find a voice, and the strategies by which he evaded that pressure led him eventually to find a voice for himself in conversation with others.

Like Dickinson, he uses repetition, unaccountable superfluities of expression, and suppositions to subvert the unified subject. However, while she flaunted the unmappable privacy of the self ("Good to hide, and hear 'em hunt!" [P 842]), he not only devises various means of avoiding direct expression of the self, rarely using the lyric "I" for example, but he also employs such tactics to develop a sense of the self that is interactional.

Paradoxically, his escape into the private world of poetry from his social identity as an insurance company executive brought no escape from the sociability of identity. The conception of the self that he worked out over a lifetime in his poetry might have served him, on another level, in the pragmatic world of business: it was a sense of the interactional nature of every use of "I" and the extent to which neither the person who uses the "I" nor the one who hears it is a unified subject.

In his lengthy development of the idea of the self as a process of changing and becoming, Stevens is not driven by Dickinson's need to find a voice for experiences that are neither culturally representative nor conventionally narrated. He can remain silent and often does in his poetry, allowing only women with views he opposes to speak. This strategy, at first a defense against self-revelation, becomes finally the way in which he can negotiate in the privacy of his poetry with that still more private and problematic area of the self which he cannot stand or understand alone. His reserve goes all the way down, and nothing is trickier than the way, very late in his life, that it eroded and he began to see in the mirror of his grandson the repetitive gestures that constituted not only his character but the most creative part of his imagination. He differs from Dickinson because, frightfully free from the need to find an oppositional voice, he must attempt to speak imaginatively from within the culture. Her sense of the discontinuous self led her to celebration; his, to retreat, evasion, and finally reconciliation.

The most frequent users of the lyric "I" in the poetry of Wallace Stevens are women. Some, in the Dickinson mode of the "Soft—Cherubic Creatures—" (P 401), are described and even overheard but only to be severely judged, such as Mrs. Alfred Uruguay, who is allowed to say, "'I fear that elegance / Must struggle like the rest,'" or the complacent woman in "Sunday Morning" who says, "'But in contentment I still feel / The need of some imperishable bliss'" (248–249, 68). Typically, such a woman is not an individual with a sense of individuality so much as a memorable actress in a brief anecdote who may serve the disembodied speaker as someone to instruct, to oppose, and often to ridicule.

Like Dickinson, Stevens had his didactic side; but, to a much greater extent than Dickinson, he used it as a shield against self-expression, as if he were moved to speak only to correct the expression of someone else. As a female, the lyric "I" can be most easily contained.[1] He allows her to speak in order to silence her, to speak so that she need not be heard again.

Stevens's use of the "I" almost exclusively in an overheard conversation might be identified as a dramatic monologue in reverse, giving voice to the person to whom the poet is actually speaking rather than to the poet himself. In this transaction, Stevens emphasizes the extent to which neither the person who uses the "I" nor the one who hears it is a unified subject. They are rather both part of a process, in which a self is repeatedly changing and becoming.[2] The part who uses the "I" to speak is often, paradoxically, that one most resistant to change. Thus, the stolidity of the "I" in Stevens's female speakers suggests their essential falseness. No "I" is ever so certain as their "I." Stevens's difficult women are not his most interesting characters, but his difficulty with them is centrally interesting to his sense of character and of his own self. The self that never speaks first, yet must speak, points to a lifetime's uneasiness about the self that might be most fully examined at that point when it comes to a crisis in one of the rare moments in his poetry where Stevens speaks in his own voice in the lyric "I"—the final three cantos of his long collection of lyrics, *Notes Toward a Supreme Fiction*. There, with the full weight of the poem behind him, the "I" emerges to settle that central question, "What am I to believe?" (404). Almost immediately, the question is made to turn on *who* it is that will believe because, as the speaker claims:

> I have not but I am and as I am, I am.
>
> These external regions, what do we fill them with
> Except reflections . . . ? (405)

Repetitions of "I am" aggrandize the "I," and so, looking to the self, the lyric speaker suggests:

> Perhaps,
> The man-hero is not the exceptional monster,
> But he that of repetition is most master. (406)

Just what kind of repetition he is to master becomes clear when, immediately testing it, he turns to his mistress, "Fat girl, terrestrial," as he must have done many times before, and discovers, as he must have again and again, that she does not reflect his mastery so much as she inspires its need. He is forced to ask:

> How is it I find you in difference, see you there
> In a moving contour, a change not quite completed? (406)

Concluding in the grammatical enigma of a reference to some future time when "You will have stopped revolving except in crystal," he reinstates repetition as desire (407).

The repetitive nature of the desire of the lyric "I" in this passage has had little attention from Stevens's critics because it does not fit into the idealist framework that informs discussions of his work.[3] For example, when Stevens writes in these final cantos:

> A thing final in itself and, therefore, good:
> One of the vast repetitions final in
> Themselves, and therefore, good, the going round

> And round and round, the merely going round,
> Until merely going round is a final good, (405)

Helen Vendler assumes that here "routine is the final good," and "this deadened statement is one version of a belief in the commonplace which recurs rather often in the last volumes."[4] Harold Bloom agrees and concludes, "'Pleasure' now means to be a master of repetition, and to master repetition you must accept it."[5] But how can one master repetition?

In psychoanalytic terms, to accept repetition is not to master it but to be mastered by it, and to reject repetition leads to the same end. Vendler and Bloom follow Stevens's lyric speaker in his desperate search for the definition of the "man-hero." But such a man does not exist. No one is "of repetition most master" because no matter how repetition is construed, it is never mastered.[6] Neither in the Platonic world of copies, nor in the Nietzschean eternal return, nor in the Freudian pattern of trying either to control a frightening experience or to submit to the return of repressed material, in none of these meanings can repetition be mastered. It is, in fact, the experience of what cannot be mastered. Repetition is desire and desire repetition.

How close the poet veers toward that experience is evident in his reliance on formal repetition as an effort at mastery. He repeats sounds, words, rhymes, as a means of binding his form together and asserting control over it. But, seeing a reflection of his own efforts in the Whitmanian "forced bugler, / That bugles for the mate, nearby the nest " and the "Red robin" "practicing / Mere repetitions " he can advise, "whistle and bugle and stop just short", "stop in your preludes " because he can conclude that the "occupation" is a "thing final in itself and, therefore, good " (405). "An occupation, an exercise, a work", this instinct to repeat is and never can be final (405).

Stevens points to the erotic impulse behind his poetry when he writes in "Adagia," "A poet looks at the world somewhat as a man looks at a woman" (OP 192), or again, "The body is the great poem" (OP 194). In his famous defense of the long poem, he concludes, "I find that this prolonged attention to a single subject has the same result that prolonged attention to a senora has, according to the authorities. All manner of favors drop from it" (L 230). In part, these statements are simply slack talk in the sexist clichés of the era. In part, however, such conflation of the creative with the erotic directs attention to questions of desire: how did this particular man look at a woman? what favors did he expect?

In his defense of poetry, he claimed that he wanted contact: "It is the imagination pressing back against the pressure of reality" (NA 36), or poems are "rubbings of reality," he writes (OP 244). More than that, he considered the desire to write not as an arid evasion of life but as identical to desire in life. In "The Irrational Element in Poetry," Stevens acknowledges the "unwritten rhetoric" of desire. He writes:

> There is, in short, an unwritten rhetoric that is always changing and to which the poet must always be turning. That is the book in which he learns that the desire for literature is the desire for life. The incessant desire for freedom in literature or in any of the arts is a desire for freedom in life. The desire is irrational. The result is the irrational searching the irrational, a conspicuously happy state of affairs, if you are so inclined. (OP 231)

But any desire that is *incessant* is seldom the conspicuously happy state of affairs that Stevens's bravado would claim it to be. As it drives the lyric poet to his brief but insistent efforts at form, his inevitable dissatisfactions with those efforts, and his repeated new efforts, it is the source of his continued dissatisfaction as well as of his creativity.

Desire is always *for* something. It intends an ending in satisfaction. When it is transferred to literature and to acts of narration, desire becomes the need to tell, the need to name that can never quite come to the point. Lyric poems add to this narrative drive toward the end, the hope of substituting word for act, metaphor for consummation. Any poet's repetition of words and sounds will be a trial of such substitution.

Between the poet's formal reliance on repetition and his psychic compulsion to repeat, there is a connection that seems to be more than a coincidence. And when repetition is both the subject of the poem and a stylistic device in its language as in *Notes*, the connection becomes too blatant to dismiss, so blatant in fact that the poet must exert every effort to repress it. The constraint of the psychic by the formal plays against the disruption of the formal by the psychic. In the dynamics of that play, poetry regains its lost original power as the first language, the language of the psyche before the repression of the rational. The lyric speaker's desire to name himself, to construct a self out of the unwritten rhetoric of his desire, retains the trace of poetry's original impulse and points to the correspondence submerged in the pressure of psychic against formal impulses. A difficult connection to acknowledge in poetry as formally self-conscious as Stevens's *Notes*, this correspondence may be most clearly understood in the strategies of repetition employed by the lyric speaker, the "I" who appears so rarely in Stevens's poetry.

Repeating certain words in a desperate burst of self-assertion, the speaker follows the repetitive logic of metaphor, creating himself out of words. "I can / Do all that angels can," he boasts, and then continues:

> I enjoy like them,
> Like men besides, like men in light secluded,
> Enjoying angels (405)

By the repetition of the phrase "Like men" Stevens turns the idea that men enjoy like angels into its opposite: that men enjoy angels. Such reconstitution by repetition allows the speaker to name a self and in the naming discover a different, smaller self. Reversal by repetition can move in the opposite direction too, permitting one word to erase another until the speaker can recapture from ennui its origin in desire: "A thing final in itself and, therefore, good" slides into paradox by a repetitive gesture that appears to be simply a stylistic lapse: "the going round / / And round and round, the merely going round, / Until merely going round is a final good" (405). The commentaries of both Vendler and Bloom miss the movement in the language here, which is not so much patterned as driven by repetition. This passage veers between strain and laxity, wit and witlessness, as it spirals toward its enlarged end, its final good.

Repetition as diminishment and repetition as enlargement chart the ebb and flow of desire that moves in a rhythm coextensive with the rhythm of poetic form. Repetition is a reminder of a level below the formal and, calling attention to itself, it signals the movement of forces barely repressible by formal structures: "he that of repetition is most master" is also most servant, and Stevens's use of the term "master," itself a playful repetition in variation of "monster," points to the dynamics in any repetition.

Master and slave, he who repeats is sometimes one and sometimes the other, but always bound up in that hierarchical relationship. Repetition, as Freud suggests in *Beyond the Pleasure Principle*, can be motivated by both compulsion and choice. It may be the return of an experience or feeling that has not been or cannot be satisfactorily acknowledged. Yet it can also be an effort to master an experience that may have been unpleasant, to replay a frightening experience under terms more favorable to control.

This process of deferral is more easily evident in acts of narration where a recollection or reworking produces a story that does not quite make sense and so encourages a future repetition which will itself leave something out and move the storyteller on and on.

But in lyric poetry the process has been less clear. The verbal control, the nonnarrative presentation, the brevity of the lyric, all work against a psychological interpretation of repetition. Because repetition binds the lyric form, it is read most conventionally as a literary strategy largely cut off from its source in the dynamics of the psyche. Even when it is the subject of the lyric, as in Stevens's *Notes*, for example, repetition is often interpreted in Vendler's manner as tied to the routine or the commonal, all that opposes poetry, rather than to the poetic habits of mind that in fact produce the lyric poem. The two may be joined by using, as a model for repetition in poetry, the one that Freud traced in his discussion of psychic deferral. The brevity and control of the lyric are themselves indications of obsessive psychic pressures to repeat with a difference, as the lyric's figuration is a means of deferring meaning by a repression of one term under the other. The choice of the lyric poem may be a deliberate effort at control and, so, mastery of an experience that is terrifying. The conventional subjects of lyric poetry—love and loss—would appear to verify that possibility.

The final cantos of Stevens's *Notes* can illustrate how desire's intention toward an end and repetitive gestures to avoid that end collide. The disquisition on "going round" in canto ix is followed by a brief narrative in canto x which lays bare the far from routine dynamics of the master repeater. "He that of repetition is most master" turns round only to discover that his mistress is not easily mastered. He asks why he finds her "familiar yet an aberration" and answers himself by asserting his obligation to mastery: "I should name you flatly, waste no words, / / Check your evasions, hold you to yourself" (406).

Bloom may be right that Stevens is most himself when he is most evasive, but here his evasions are of a peculiar sort (216–217). First, they are not his but the fat girl's; his effort, by contrast, seems to be direct, efficient, controlling, and masterful. And yet his address to the fat girl is that of a very evasive lover; he repeats to her not the typical lover's words "I *want* to hold you to myself" but rather "I *should* . . . hold you to yourself" (italics added). The replacement of desire with duty, of intimacy with distance, is, more than evasive, repressive.

Bloom calls this a "knowing evasion, the evasion of Stevens's true muse, the Whitmanian fierce mother of fictive music, by this homely, earthly nurse of a summer night in which a poem is born" (217). Here, for reasons of his own, Bloom evades his own best insight in this peculiar syntax. He is not alone among critics in creating rather than reading this poem's ending. Perhaps the most famous and ingenious reading is that of Frank Doggett, who argues that Stevens is

> expressing in his conclusion, then, the genesis of a poem from the imagination of it pictured in procreant terms ("Fat girl, terrestrial, my summer, my night") through the evasions and transformations of its conception, with the arduous work of composition ("Bent over work, anxious, content, alone") to the realization of his conception in language (calling it by name), when it is fixed in the crystal of a poem.[7]

Bloom's earthly nurse and Doggett's procreant terms are gestures toward an identification that, like Stevens himself, they will not name.[8] This fat girl is not a stranger. She is the same and yet different, changed and yet curiously not changed enough. Stevens's desire to hold her off comes from the sudden recognition that she may be familiar but she is not permitted familiarity; she is the image of the woman as mother which the speaker can neither acknowledge nor transform into the strange but accessible image of the woman as beloved. In his failure to do so, the speaker is led finally to his illogical assertion that "this unprovoked sensation requires / / That I should name you" (406).[9]

The wish to detach the sensation from its provocative source in desire replaces the forbidden impulse with the permitted pleasure of naming or invoking the muse. This fat girl terrestrial is no nurse, but the nursing source of the speaker, the focus of his anguish and creativity. His approach to her follows the narrative pattern, detailed by Peter Brooks in *Reading for the Plot*, of recognition, repression, and repetition. He recognizes her, he attempts to master her by naming her, and she returns to be recognized again.

If to name her is to master her, he will give her a name that he can master and so declares "Even so when I think of you as strong or tired " (406). Denying that she has provoked a sensation in him, he describes that feeling in terms that transform her seductiveness into the more acceptable attribute of industry. She is most easily mastered as the slave: "Bent over work, anxious, content, alone " (406). In that guise, she can be given the double life of past and future which she has in his psyche: "the more than natural figure", "the soft-footed phantom", "the more than rational distortion" (406). She is more than the natural mother and so more than the natural beloved. A ghost in his memory, she cannot become a desired figure in his imagination. She can be recognized only by being given a name that will distort her, a name that will not name her.

"The fiction that results from feeling "—the result of more than natural feelings—will be itself haunted and distorted, their mimetic expression. Thus, the speaker may master the feeling by obsessive attachment of the fat girl to himself (*"my* summer, *my* night", *"my* green, *my* fluent mundo") (italics added), but he expresses himself in metaphors of possessive displacement. He can neither wholly claim her nor wholly disclaim her. Mine and not mine, the "fat girl" is dissolved into strangeness. The speaker's failure to possess her is evident in the puzzling syntax of the final tercet where the fat girl moves on her own axis, apart from him, and will ever enjoy such revolutions until some future time when all movement will have stopped. Feelings that cannot be acknowledged can only result in fiction. Death is the mother when death of the mother cannot be contemplated.

The desire to bring this long poem to an ending equal to its subject is frustrated by the speaker, who defers to others the final word; he is convinced that *they* will "get it straight" at the Sorbonne someday, and the "fluent mundo" will have stopped and will have to stop revolving. *They* will also get him straight in death. Thus he passes on to the authorities in a final and repeated gesture the last word, deferring to the rationalists what he has not been able to rationalize.

Inconclusive endings, or what Barbara Hernnstein Smith calls "anti-closure," are characteristic of much modern poetry, but in Stevens anti-closure is limited to the level of plot. The formal structure of a Stevens's poem, unlike that of most modernist poems, adheres typically to a pattern of strong closure. In *Notes*, for example, the form of seven tercets in each canto, ten cantos in each section, is finished in this address to the fat girl, and, in part, it is this formal finish and repetitive structure that encourages the expectation of a thematic conclusion. The speaker himself seems to want such a conclusion, claiming, "That's it", "Yes, that." But "that" is merely an other round, a repeated evasion of the fat girl and her evasive suitor.

That cannot summarize the plot of "the fiction that results from feeling," which is a movement in this canto from question to question, attribution to attribution, in a string of deferrals that comes to rest eventually only in a formally required tercet. Form runs out here, and its running out in a dynamics of continued deferral is best explained in terms of Lacan's understanding of metonymy as the language of narration. Lacan locates repression in all uses of symbolic language. In his interpretation of the Saussurian analysis of the sign, the bar separating the signifer from the signified becomes the bar of repression, indicating the inaccessibility of the true signified. Thus, the use of signs can only be a construction of a signifying chain in which there is a pressure toward a meaning that can never be reached. The motivating force behind this chain is the desire to name, as in Stevens's poem, and the sense that to name would be to end the movement, and thus a renewed desire to name. Poems are for Lacan extravagant evasions of saying what they mean. He writes:

> And the enigmas that desire seems to pose for a "natural philosophy" —its frenzy mocking the abyss of the infinite, the secret collusion with which it envelops the pleasure of knowing and of dominating with *jouissance*, these amount to no other derangement of instinct than that of being caught in the rails—eternally stretching forth towards the *desire for something else*—of metonymy.[10]

The repeated questionings in Stevens's evocation of the fat girl allow him to create a metonymic chain in which his excesses, distortions, and anecdotal extravagances are nonetheless bound together by a fading memory of this figure and a beckoning desire that is inherently unsatisfiable because it is linked to that memory. The dynamic model in Lacan's description of metonymy promises a purpose or intention toward an end even as the end is deferred, just as Stevens's poem moves forward with requirements, deviations, then insistence, and finally the longed for, if unsatisfying, assurance that there will be an end, a metaphoric naming that will in some far off time suffice.

Notes is a series of anecdotes that comes to depend on the dynamics of desire, at least in its final canto. Traditionally, the poet's desire is the desire for the muse, the desire to be satisfied by her and to be satisfying to her. Stevens fails on both counts, and what fails is the erotics of his art. It is not that his speaker is too "civil," although he is certainly that; it is rather that he is not civilized enough to convert a desire for the forbidden object into a desire for the permitted object.

Such a failure has deeper implications in the long poem and in the creative career that it caps. The poet, finding his muse an aberration, indicates a fundamental uneasiness as the source of his naming, a sense of miserable inadequacy both in himself and in the object of his desire. Writing to defer that self-recognition, he speaks nonetheless repeatedly of its naked anguish. He can never write himself out of his dilemma because writing is the dilemma. He is thus bound in structures of repetition where he is, as Lacan describes it, "eternally stretching forth towards the *desire for something else*."

He reproduces this desire in successive images of desiring and restrained women which develop by repetition and accretion into the frenzied questioning of the final canto. This questioning receives its full force from the series of women in *Notes* whose variety seems aleatory and extravagant and only later necessary and intentional. It is worth examining these anecdotes as Stevens's anatomy of desire. On these women, he projects his own desires, narrates his failures, recuperates his loss in scenes of spiraling intimacy.

But the first question must be: why women? In part, women have always served Stevens as figures on whom he may project his most outrageous and extravagant longings. In part, here desire is ridiculous, and Stevens could depict it in female caricature more safely than in male. But as we follow these anecdotes of desire, we begin to see that in the woman desire finds its most perfect embodiment because she can be most repressed and thus most certain to return.

The series opens with Nanzia Nunzio, the stripper, who appears to be the most brazenly desirous and the most severely frustrated of all women. Her failure to seduce Ozymandias by unveiling, however, is less moving than it might be largely because she is not brazen enough; she takes off the necklace and stone-studded belt only as an exchange for the "spirit's diamond coronal" (396). "Clothe me entire in the final filament," she demands (396). Her desire is desire for the wrong thing; she wants not passion but "precious ornament," to be "precious for your perfecting." Standing before "an inflexible / Order," Nanzia Nunzio, like her name, is its mirror image. "As I am, I am / The spouse," she says in words that echo the statue's tautological self and will be repeated in a later canto by the speaker when he is driven to the same self-sealing self-assertion (395).

Nanzia Nunzio's failure of desire is followed by what Vendler calls the "long restriction of desire" in the canto of "the blue woman" (*On Extended Wings*, 183). The blue woman "did not desire" that one array be exchanged for another, "Nor that the sexual blossoms should repose / Without their fierce addictions" (399). The opposite of Nanzia Nunzio's "burning body," this woman is "linked and lacquered", closed into her "cold and clear" memory; but she shares Nanzia's rigidity. Her demands are themselves "fierce addictions." Next in order of restraint is the maiden Bawda who "loved but would no marriage make" until she could make "a mystic marriage in Catawba," the marriage as "sign" (401). Resembling neither Nanzia's precious ornament nor the blue woman's severe clarity, her desire is nonetheless a deferral of gratification from person to place. Finally, in these portraits of increasingly restrained desire there is the "sensible ecstasy" of the Canon Aspirin's sister. Her "widow's gayety" is so completely contained that, even for her children, "what she felt fought off the barest phrase " (402).

From Nanzia Nunzio's straightforward striptease and jeweled adornment to the sister's reticence and "poverty", the anecdotes allow for distortions, digressions, and elaborations in the poem's development. Unsatisfied and unsatisfiable desire drives this poem and produces its variety. From Nanzia's wish for "perfecting" to the sister's desire for "the unmuddled self of sleep " the women live in their dissatisfactions. Conversely, the men move from the inflexible and undesiring Ozymandias to the oddly restless Canon, who admires his sister at the dinner table but at night cannot enjoy her unmuddled sleep perhaps because he cannot enjoy her. He flits nervously about, ascending to "outer stars" and "Descending to the children's bed". The Canon "had to choose". But he could not choose his sister. Like the speaker of the final canto, the canon must choose "The complicate, the amassing harmony"— the sister *and* her daughters, the "whole" family rather than a single woman (403).

Desirous women, undesiring men, these characters are all ways of constructing a self from restraint and desire, or rather a series of selves, all in particular ways incomplete and yet a part of the "amassing harmony" of selves. From spouse to sister, the women are gradually domesticated in the men's imaginations and simultaneously exiled from them. They cannot be "too near, too clear" if they are to serve as the muse Stevens had identified in "To the One of Fictive Music." The dynamics of craving and spurning in these anecdotes spells out the poet's discomfort with the psychic pressures that they reveal.

These anecdotes of unsatisfied desire are, not surprisingly, all in some way unsatisfying, baffling, and oddly memorable, one following the other in an order of increasing perplexity. The restrained women are various guises of the muse for this poet and at the same time mirror images of himself. Their appearance and reappearance indicate an obsessive pattern of recognition, repression, and repetition, as the speaker approaches the end of his notes toward a supreme fiction with the clear recognition that the forward movement has not been progressive. The muse of adornment, of memory, of mystic signs, or of sensible naming—each muse produces a narrative of unfulfillment that leaves unavailable at the level of the plot the symmetry so evident in the poetic form. The end of each anecdote disrupts its actions. For example, Nanzia's story is abruptly cut off by Ozymandias's reply; the blue woman's cold and clear vision is obscured by the reminder that it is "except for the eye, without intrusion"; Bawda is rendered complete only by deflecting her love to the "marriage-place"; and the Canon's so sensible sister wants unmuddled sleep *only* for her children, not, we see, for herself.

This reversal of the terms at the end of each canto, or deconstruction of the tropes, has a correspondent reversal in the psychic dynamics of these anecdotes where the female figure appears, is recognized, and then must be denied. The first and last appearances—the would-be spouse and the mother-sister—are the most intolerably protracted, because the most frightening, and they are also the most severely repressed. Ozymandias enjoys the stripping until it is complete; the Canon hums a fugue of praise until he realizes the sister has a widow's gayety of which he cannot be seigneur.

Stevens's repeated narratives of desire and his repeated frustration in *Notes* form a metonymic chain that defers the meaning toward which this poem had been pressing in its final section. "It Must Give Pleasure" cannot. The Canon's sister is the extreme of the woman who cannot give pleasure; she is the last extravagance of desire. If "That's it," then that is that. The "fiction that results from feeling" is the end of feeling, not only the end toward which such feeling has been pressing but rather the fictionalizing or evasion of pleasure. The muse as sister and mother cannot provoke expressible feelings, and as he grew older Stevens grew more restive in her power, identifying her as an enchantress and progressively deepening his antagonism to her in such names as "Unreal" ("To the One of Fictive Music"), "wild bitch" ("Puella Parvula"), or "bearded queen, wicked in her dead light" ("Madame La Fleurie").

Stevens's simultaneous attraction to and revulsion from this woman, his muse, has a central place in his imagination. The muse, "my summer, my night," inspires an activity of the night, as Stevens explains in "Two or Three Ideas":

If in the minds of men creativeness was the same thing as creation in the natural world, . . . all the propositions one formulates would be within the scope of that particular domination. The trouble is, however, that men in general do not create in light and warmth alone. They create in darkness and coldness. They create when they are hopeless, in the midst of antagonisms, when they are wrong, when their powers are no longer subject to their control. They create as the ministers of evil. (OP 262)

Creativity, like the repetitive desires of *Notes*, is not a generation of the life force but a compulsion motivated by the fear of death.

If he writes under such circumstances, what then does the poet see when he looks at the world as a man looks at a woman? Cold, wrong, hopeless, can he have any desires at all for that woman, that world? If the body is the great poem, is it the source of generation or simply the residence of uncontrollable powers? These are questions that Stevens evaded in his poetry. The "theory" of "endless elaborating" did not interest Stevens at all, as he explains in *An Ordinary Evening in New Haven*:

> This endlessly elaborating poem
> Displays the theory of poetry,
> As the life of poetry. A more severe,
>
> More harassing master would extemporize
> Subtler, more urgent proof that the theory
> Of poetry is the theory of life, (486)

The *master* who might *extemporize* proof would not be a poet in Stevens's view; he would be someone, unlike the poet, who could be extemporaneous and who could live without the compulsion to substitute words for life. He would live in immediacy a plain life.

Such a *master*, Stevens neither could nor desired to be. Even in "Adagia," he is anxious to separate himself from the extemporary, to cut off his life from life. He writes, "Life is an affair of people and not of places. But for me life is an affair of places and that is the trouble" (OP 185). More precisely, it is no trouble because without such deferral of desire from people to places there would have been no poetry.

An anecdote from his letters may illustrate how much of his life depended on this characteristic act of deferred pleasure. It was his way of having a more than natural pleasure from those things that gave him pleasure. He writes to Barbara Church in June 1949,

When I was in New York on Saturday I bought a lot of fruit in the place on 58th street. One likes to look at fruit as well as to eat it and that is precisely the right spot to find fruit to look at. Then, too, I bought a chocolate cake because it was Saturday and Saturday and cakes are part of the same thing. In any case, last evening Holly and Peter dropped in and as the top of the cake had some sugar on it: a couple of roses, sprays of leaves, we put Peter in a chair and placed the cake in front of him and let him go to it to see what he would do. He had it all over the place. But he liked it and it was a good way to get rid of it because I am afraid that cakes, too, ought merely to be looked at. (L 639)

The interconnection here between people and places is of primary interest as Stevens toys with the intrinsic nature of the self and the world. The edible fruit and cake become something to look at as well as eat. Looking instead of eating seems a willful repression of desire or substitution of one desire for another; but the metonymic organization of his imaginative venture suggests Stevens's delight in deferral, his willingness to stand "apart" and to take satisfaction in a secondary pleasure. He can shift the world for his own pleasure just as, in his insistence that fruit and cake should be looked at as well as eaten, he appears to be shifting the instinctive desires of the self. To say this is to assume that fruit and cakes are primarily enjoyed when eaten, and a human being would rather eat than look—assumptions that Stevens explicitly denies.

Much of the criticism of Stevens falls into the mistake I have just committed, insisting against the evidence of the poet that there is an intrinsic nature on which we can agree and that Stevens's poetry is a delicate working out of the relationship between an incoherent or eccentric self and an elegant world. But, as Richard Rorty argues, "the very idea that the world or the self has an intrinsic nature—one which the physicist or the poet may have glimpsed—is a remnant of the idea that the world is a divine creation, the work of someone who had something in mind, who Himself spoke some language in which He described His own project."[11] Therefore, if neither the self nor the world has an intrinsic nature, the poet's effort will be, like the philosopher's described by Richard Rorty, to try to get to the point "where we treat everything—our language, our conscience, our community—as products of time and chance. To reach that point would be, in Freud's words, to 'treat chance as worthy of determining our fate.'"

Yet there is more than mere chance in Stevens's precious reordering of his Saturday self and world. It is all deliberately if not consciously chosen,

and in this preciosity an erotic element intrudes. The cake not eaten but
looked at is given to his grandson to destroy. The metonymic chain of
narration finds here, as it infrequently does in Stevens's poetry, its metaphoric completion in the transfer from grandfather to grandson of desire
and its deferred gratification. This genealogy of desire traces its always
unsatisfiable nature: the cake exchanged as the daughter has been exchanged for the mother.

The identification of himself in his grandson's desire is not unknown in
Stevens's poetry. This same cake-eating Peter is the source of "Questions
are Remarks": "Peter, the voyant, who says 'Mother, what is that'—" is
overheard by his grandfather, the voyeur, who comments,

> Hear him.
> He does not say, "Mother, my mother who are you,"
> The way the drowsy, infant, old men do. (463)

This doubling of grandfather and grandson, of "adult enfantillages" and
"infant, old men," in allowing a transfer of desire, allows also the grandfather to see his own generative imaginative power in this genealogy. The
child's question "what is that" will be followed by incessant questions of
"what is that" and "what is that." The grandfather says, "It is his own array,
/ His own pageant and procession and display," and it can move forward
only "As far as nothingness permits" (462–463). Like Canon Aspirin's
flight, this procession must come to a "point / / Beyond which fact could
not progress as fact"; "thought could not progress as thought" (402, 403).
That point is where all the words have been said, all facts revealed, all
thoughts thought; it is the end where the final question must be asked: "my
mother, who are you".

It is at that point that the grandfather stands, surveying the chain set off
by the grandson's questioning, and is permitted to see his own procession
and pageantry in that beginning. The doubling of the name "Mother, my
mother" reveals the daughter as the mother, the son as the father, and
reinstates the desire of the son for his mother, the father for his daughter,
the son for his mother. In this repetition, the old man can make a choice
not *between* but *of* and chooses, like the Canon, to include people "That in
each other are included".

"Questions are Remarks" records a transfer of power from grandfather
to grandson back to grandfather, a tranference that allows for new life in

new poems, a relishing once again of desire. Stevens's late poems are full of the spirit of the grandson, "A comic infanta among the tragic drapings," as he is called in "Long and Sluggish Lines" (522). He offsets the sluggish mind which imagines that "It makes so little difference, at so much more / Than seventy, where one looks, one has been there before " (522). The world has been so frequently described that even the trees bear a repetition, "saying over and over one same, same thing". Then, surprisingly, the process reaches its opposite, "a contradiction, / Has enraged them and made them want to talk it down." It is this reversal that the grandfather sees in his grandson who wants to "talk it down" in order to master it.

To the grandfather alone, there has remained a different kind of satis- faction, but one that has come to him nonetheless as a result of his trans- actions with his grandson. Unlike the "comic infanta's" power to generate from "pre-history," the old man's desire comes in "The Plain Sense of Things" from the other end, post-history, the power to imagine or project "an end of the imagination." That is the final novelty out of nothingness, and at that vantage the imagination's old power has come to seem "a repetition / In a repetitiousness of men and flies " (502). Here, at last, is something new and of the minimizing of newness. The compulsion to "choose the adjective" remains, but the choice is restricted in this late phase as it was in its earliest phase, and the poet finds it gladly so. Witnessing his physical decay, the old man dwindles back into youth with the same restrictions: he says, "The great structure has become a minor house." It is a world made minor by its minimal instincts: "expressing silence / / Of a sort, silence of a rat come out to see" (502). This diminishment of self and world is the final test of his imagination, undertaken as always not as a choice but "as a necessity requires." The bitterness in the old man's testing himself against the "rat come out to see" should not obscure the contest, the poet's rising to desire again.

If the grandson has a freedom to choose only "As far as nothingness permits," it is because he can create his own imaginings in a world that "rises with so much rhetoric, / But not for him". Eventually he, like his grandfather, however, will have imagined everything possible to imagine and will then *return* to "a plain sense of things". The plain sense repressed in imagination will of necessity repeat itself, be recognized, and then again be repressed. So old age rounds back to infancy as it moves toward death. The poem is the memory of one, the evocation of the other. "We obey the coaxings of our end" Stevens writes in "The Sail of Ulysses" (OP 130).

By necessity or seduction, we come to the end, driven to the end by the intention of desire, but not unpleasantly so. The final satisfaction such as Stevens imagined in the "intensest rendezvous" of "Final Soliloquy of the Interior Paramour" would be the seduction of warmth at the cold end. And more seductive still, he imagined, would be the endless anticipation of such satisfaction. In "The World as Meditation," Penelope does not "obey" the coaxings of the end, but rather tries to coax into being the end she desires and yet can still enjoy in its deferral, "Repeating his name with its patient syllables, / Never forgetting him that kept coming constantly so near " (521). This "interminable adventurer" Ulysses cannot be coaxed home, and in another poem Stevens turns to him as a figure of resistance to the end. His journeying embodies the longed for "divination, a letting down / From loftiness":

> Yet always there is another life,
> A life beyond this present knowing,
> A life lighter than this present splendor
> Brighter, perfected and distant away,
> Not to be reached but to be known (OP 128)

The "distant away" has always had its attraction for Stevens, allowing him to stretch forth toward something else. It reaches its apotheosis in "The Sail of Ulysses." There a second final soliloquy with the interior paramour identifies the "distant away" where it has always been in Stevens's poetry—in the near. The interior paramour is not the "intensest" figure she had been in the earlier poem. She is away, described by what she is not: "Not, / For a change, the englistered woman, seated / In colorings harmonious"; "gorgeous symbol"; "A summing up of the loftiest lives" (130). None of these things, she is rather "the sibyl of the self". He names her flatly:

> Whose chiefest embracing of all wealth
> Is poverty, whose jewel found
> At the exactest central of the earth
> Is need. For this, the sibyl's shape
> Is a blind thing fumbling for its form,
> A form that is lame, a hand, a back,
> A dream too poor, too destitute

To be remembered, the old shape
Worn and leaning to nothingness,
A woman looking down the road,
A child asleep in its own life. (OP 130)

The "self as sibyl" is the self as other, and in that metaphor the poet is
transformed. The sibyl is unknowable, the woman as enigma and as the
creator of enigmas. She is a seer, an even more interminable adventurer
than Ulysses in worlds beyond, in divinations. As the poet's self, she has
come home, returning to her source from wanderings enforced upon her
by the poet's refusal to identify himself with her. Impoverished and blind,
she comes arrayed in the poet's own blind imagery. As self, she has been
anticipated in "Final Soliloquy" when the poet wraps tightly into one
himself and his interior paramour. But the attributes of blindness, lame-
ness, destitution, dependence, come from earlier figures of women whom
the poet had deliberately distanced from himself. Here, they are reclaimed:
Nanzia Nunzio's dependence, the blue woman's destitution, the fat girl's
bent-over shape, Bawda's convinced blinding of her desire.

Now, identifying with these lacks, the poet identifies too the doubling
in his poetry, the projection onto female figures of his own desires and
needs. The "coaxings" of the end have finally elicited this truth from the old
man who names or rather renames himself finally as the woman and the
child. At the end, the poet acknowledging the "self as sibyl" is comforted.
The poet can then re-envision and redescribe a new identity for himself, the
woman, the muse:

The englistered woman is now seen
In an isolation, separate
From the human in humanity,
A part of the inhuman more,
The still inhuman more, and yet
An inhuman of our features, known
And unknown, inhuman for a little while,
Inhuman for a little, lesser time. (OP 131)

Stevens's pleasure in repetition of words does not diminish as he fumbles
for a form here, nor does his doubling of images slacken. The woman
"englistered" by the poet, the painted muse of poetry, is pitted against her

opposite, the common woman looking down the road. The one is human and inhuman, known and unknown, the same and separate; the other, no less so. The identity blinds in its insight: "misgivings dazzlingly / Resolved in dazzling discovery."

If Stevens relies here on familiar formal patterns of repetition to express the identity he no longer need defer by repetitive efforts at self-creation, it is because those patterns have worked their cure: "just to name, is to create / A help, a right to help, a right / To know what helps and to attain, / By right of knowing, another plane." He moves here, as in *Notes*, through repetitions of words that allow him to dissolve one meaning into its opposite. The right to name becomes the right to know, and thus the common need creates the uncommon pleasure. The poet as the woman looking down the road sees another woman in another life lighter than this present splendor, the woman he will become when he attains that other plane.

Stevens in old age had finally invented a self that he could be. He had drawn and been drawn toward this self from the beginning of his career, and yet he had always denied himself to her. In her he recognized himself. "We give ourselves our likest issuance," he says in "To the One of Fictive Music" and adds:

Yet not too like, yet not so like to be
Too near, too clear, saving a little to endow
Our feigning with the strange unlike, (88)

Likest yet not too like, Stevens in this early poem toys with this self as stranger. The self as "Sister and mother and diviner love, / And of the sisterhood of the living dead" had to wait for recognition through a long lifetime of recognition and repression before she came into being as the sibyl. The frenzy of Stevens's creativity mocks the abyss of the infinite out of which he snatches "the old shape".

"The Sail of Ulysses" is a late poem, and one that little satisfied Stevens. Its sibyl would not have charmed him forever, and, even as she appears, *"The great sail of Ulysses seemed, / In the breathings of this soliloquy, / Alive with an enigma's flittering."* Stevens would have been restless in any shape. His dissatisfaction drove him to find in words a more orderly shape. Yet his desire was not ultimately to be satisfied by even this "blind thing fumbling for its form" or its converse in *The Auroras of Autumn*, "form gulping after formlessness" (411). It was in the nature of his desire to be unsatisfied. He was of that company described in *The Auroras of Autumn*: "Unhappy people in a happy world" and "In these unhappy he meditates a whole" (420).

Chapter 6

"To picnic in the ruins that we leave": Stevens and Metonymy

By contrast to Dickinson's celebration of touch, Stevens might appear to celebrate sight. Quoting Mario Rossi in an epigraph to "Evening Without Angels," he identifies *"the great interests of man: air and light, the joy of having a body, the voluptuousness of looking."*[1] He appears in his poetry to retain a purely male interest in looking at women, or at least, he uses the gaze of a male speaker on a female object as the starting point for many of his early poems.[2] Nonetheless, the "masculinist overtones" that Gilbert and Gubar claim he adopts toward these women may reflect merely the shield of convention behind which he hides because, as we have seen, it is through the woman that he projects his own ambivalent desires and comes finally to express that part of himself drawn to them and from them.[3]

To use Luce Irigaray's opposition between the female sense of touch and the male gaze as a way of distinguishing between Dickinson and Stevens will not exactly lead us into the particular way in which this male poet works. Even more than Dickinson, Stevens writes from a sense of the discontinuous self that encourages him to seek out lines of contingency. He shares with her an interest in letters as tokens of contingency, links between reader and writer, and, like her, he writes about letters of the alphabet, letters of correspondence, and poems as letters to the world.

In this, he is no more feminized than she is if we mean by that term either Irigaray's celebration of the antimasculinist style or Lentricchia's denigrated version of the woman as consumer. Stevens is rather, with Dickinson, using the lyric form in a radical and experimental way to speculate on a place in the world, on a situation between parents and children, on the generation of reading and writing. In narrative, such rumination would be tied to the logic of cause and effect, to an explanatory organization, and to metaphors of growth. By contrast, the lyric genre allows for a metonymic chain of development in which one term substitutes for another, making connections without binding limitations.

Stevens came to the full and creative possibilities of the lyric genre gradually. At first, he used the lyric to indulge in a favorite theme of Romantic lyrics—dejection. For him, however, it took a strange turn since the melancholy of the young was exacerbated by arriving in midlife, and thus it was tinged with a fear of impotence. Sorrow is only pleasurable for the young when so much pleasure of all kinds remains. For the middle-aged, sorrow is often dull. And long before he grew too old to imagine anything but "long and sluggish lines," Stevens was haunted by the fear that he was not adequate to the poetic task.

Although it is true that often in his early works he could look upon a figure of a woman with the intention of improving the object of his gaze, as, for example, in "The Paltry Nude Starts on a Spring Voyage" (5–6), still he is much more concerned with his own imaginative failure than he is with objectifying the woman so that he might possess her. Her paltriness is his own, and in examining the links between them he finds that it is desire itself that must be affirmed, because only then will it be able to affirm the object of desire. In fact, the paltry nude in spring is all too much like the poet himself. A. Walton Litz has related this figure, an American version of Venus, to the ironic version of the beloved as Botticelli's "Birth of Venus" in "Le Monocle de Mon Oncle."[4] Unlike Botticelli's, however, the nude that Stevens calls into existence is "paltry," worthless, contempt-ible. Moreover, she is not rising out of the sea, but returning to it, starting "*for* the sea," "Eager for the brine and bellowing / Of the high interiors of the sea" because, with all her eagerness, she shares the mood of the speaker who observes her: "She too is discontent." He desires, he says, not this "Archaic" Venus, but some more powerful figure of his own imagining; likewise, the paltry nude "would have purple stuff upon her arms," a more stately existence than her present scudding. The speaker, trying to accom-modate her desire, claims his present vision is "meagre play " which is

> Not as when the goldener nude
> Of a later day
>
> Will go, like the centre of sea-green pomp,
> In an intenser calm,
> Scullion of fate,
> Across the spick torrent, ceaselessly,
> Upon her irretrievable way. (6)

Despite his own imaginative hopes, however, both "paltry" and "gold-ener" nudes are moving irretrievably away from the speaker, each a "Scullion" of fate but not of the male onlooker, and the speaker here, as dismissive of one nude as he is enthusiastic about the other, is yet oddly diffident about his own fated isolation from both women. The desire to possess, at the nerve ends of male erotic experience according to Irigaray, is less powerful here than the desire to imagine someone worthy of desire. Even that "goldener nude / Of a later day" will not be an object to possess; she too will go "*ceaselessly*, / Upon her *irretrievable* way" (italics added), also preferring the "high interiors of the sea" to "salty harbors." She will simply be more worthy of the desire she evokes.

Stevens's imaginative need is clearer, perhaps, in "Evening Without Angels" where it is "Sad men" who cannot relish Rossi's "*joy of having a body*" and "*voluptuousness of looking*" and instead make "angels of the sun." To them, the speaker says, "Let this be clear that we are men of sun / And men of day and never of pointed night". Men in their sadness are too quick to relinquish desire, assuming that they "repeat antiquest sounds of air / In an accord of repetitions." Not so, writes Stevens: "If we repeat, it is because the wind / Encircling us, speaks always with our speech." "Light, too, encrusts us making visible / The motions of the mind" and "desire for day / Accomplished in the immensely flashing East," and "Desire for rest, in that descending sea / Of dark". "Bare earth is best" the poem concludes, "Where the voice that is in us makes a true response, / Where the voice that is great within us rises up " (137–138).

The "paltry nude" is just an object of such "Sad men" and not of that moment when the imagination rises up and lifts the world above its "attendant ghosts." The "*voluptuousness of looking*" with the etymological roots of the noun in the "will" or "hope" has its end in affirmation rather than possession. In giving voice to such looking, the "true response" will be a celebration and a searching out of joy.

In his provocative study of Stevens as feminized by his poetic vocation, Frank Lentricchia does not agree. He sees possessions and possessiveness as central to Stevens's poetics, citing for support an early journal entry where the beginning poet writes, "It is a great pleasure to seize an impression and lock it up in words: you feel as if you had it safe forever" (S and P, 48) and a letter to his wife Elsie where he says "You know that I do with you as I like in my thoughts: I no sooner wish for your hand than I have it—no sooner wish for anything to be said or done than it *is* said or done; and none of the denials you make me are made there. You are *my* Elsie there" (L 96). These passages confirm Lentricchia's sense that:

> The aesthetic for Stevens is a lyric process of making interior, from the real space
> of the streets of New York to the private space of his room and then into the
> psychic space of consciousness (perilously sealed now to the outside) where
> pastoral experience can be made safe. (Lentricchia, 152)

Moving the exterior into the interior has been the way of lyric poets
from the Romantics on; it is not entirely Stevens's way.[5] Aware of the split
between the exterior and the interior as the Romantics also were, Stevens
is even more acutely concerned with the inadequacy and fragmentation of
his own interior. As a poet writing in midlife, he appears to feel the
diminishment of a youthful appetite and power to possess and makes an
attempt to compensate for it with an instinct educated by age for the truly
exquisite and inaccessible. Such *"voluptuousness"* will depend on an anti-
Romantic objectification and a preference for metonymy over metaphor.
In failing to tie Stevens's bourgeois taste to this preference, Lentricchia,
who certainly does not fail to notice the poet's enthusiasm for consumer
capitalism, places him nonetheless in the precapitalist aesthetics of the
pastoral. In this, he verifies Stevens's formalist critics whose work he sets
out to disprove.

The eagerness of the poet to lock a woman in his thoughts and then to
boast to her of his capture, which Lentricchia cites as evidence of his poetic
habits, are expressions of the man at twenty-seven, perhaps not entirely an
impetuous lover, but not the poet who waited for more than a decade to
publish his first volume of poems. The letters and journal entries on which
Lentricchia builds his case express artless sexual fantasies that have little in
common with either the permanence of art that the Romantic poets celebrated or the impermanence of potency that Stevens was to make the
subject of many poems. When Stevens told his fiancée that they were easier
with each other in letters than when they were together because "you are
more perfectly yourself to me when I am writing to you" (L 96), he may
have been still hoping for the immediate gratification of enjoying the
woman he had perfected in writing.

By the time he came to refine his fantasies in his poetry, however, he was
more able to chronicle an inaptitude for sexual possession than a fantasy of
gratification. In "Le Monocle de Mon Oncle" he admits that "This luscious
and impeccable fruit of life" remains "Untasted." Every appearance of the
woman in this poem resists possession. The "Mother of heaven" cannot be
possessed even by mocking without the danger of self-mockery. The already interiorized paramour is remembered only as "the radiant bubble

that she *was*" (italics added). The "fiery boys" make an odd match with "sweet-smelling virgins," the guffawing "centurions" with "dainty" "muleteers." Even the couple "hang like warty squashes" apart. The male dream of possession is resisted by the incontrovertible fact of contingency. Two by two, the couples stand together but apart.

"Le Monocle de Mon Oncle" is not a poem in the Romantic tradition about filling empty interior spaces, consuming the external world. It is rather a poem that moves along surfaces, as its speaker pursues "the origin and course / Of love". Attempting to discourage what he considered a "too close" analysis of the poem, Stevens said, "I had in mind simply a man fairly well along in life, looking back and talking in a more or less personal way about life" (L 251). For him, the "personal" is neither the deeply revelatory nor the purposefully symbolic, as Stevens suggests in claiming that the "much-crumpled thing" is not "sex appeal" nor is "Mother of Heaven" a symbolic reference (L 251). The personal here is rather an effort to link contingent moments in a life of love and even more in a life of thinking about love. Looking back, Stevens's middle-aged speaker is looking to connect past and future, fearing that there are no links, that he is at a stopping point in middle age where "No spring can follow past meridian."

The crux of his problem is genealogical. Inept at finding a suitable tone with which to link himself to his own creative source, he is equally uncertain about his heirs. In middle age he appears uneasy both as son and as father, moving uncomfortably between a muse-like figure he addresses as "Mother of heaven, regina of the clouds," and his role as "a man of fortune greeting heirs". With the "Mother of heaven," he assumes the tone and grammar of a child, boasting with sad admission, "'There is not nothing, no, no, never nothing, / Like the clashed edges of two words that kill.'" In the confessions of sexual inadequacy that are to come, this simile will reverberate as sex and text follow the same line of development. Moreover, the speaker himself is not certain about his intentions, asking, "so I mocked her" "Or was it that I mocked myself alone?" Unable to settle on a tone with the Mother-muse, he cannot find the right attitude toward his heirs, admitting that even in his greetings, "These choirs of welcome choir for me farewell." Considering himself a link between generations, this speaker is self-conscious about his failures.

His interest is not property, as Lentricchia might argue, but propriety. "Shall I uncrumple this much-crumpled thing?" he asks, as if he might be able to straighten out the circuitous course of both textual and sexual matters. Harold Bloom has suggested that he is referring here with bitter humor both to the abortive first lines of the poem that he has kept crumpling and recrumpling in an effort to start and at the same time to his own sexual organ (39). The two are linked in this poem of much crumpled things where "Utamaro's beauties sought / The end of love in their all-speaking braids" and "not one curl in nature has survived" where the "fruit of life" is "the book in which to read a round," and "amorists'" "scrivening / Is breathless to attend each quirky turn" of their "amours". But sex and text, crumpled or uncrumpled, are disjunctive, as he says:

> If sex were all, then every trembling hand
> Could make us squeak, like dolls, the wished-for words.
> But note the unconscionable treachery of fate,
> That makes us weep, laugh, grunt and groan, and shout
> Doleful heroics, pinching gestures forth
> From madness or delight, without regard
> To that first, foremost law. Anguishing hour! (17)

The "wished-for words" will never come from "that first, foremost law." In his impetuous youth the poet had gone oblivious to this unconscionable treachery: "Every day, I found / Man proved a gobbet in my mincing world" he remembers, But in later life he discovers that in the course of love, change is all, and he can console himself only with the pleasure of distinctive and minute changes, realizing that "until now I never knew / That fluttering things have so distinct a shade."

The distinctions that were to interest him may have found expression in his gourmandizing and his collecting of objets d'art, as Lentricchia argues, but these very habits depended on propriety, the noting and caring for external details. In his poetry, these collectors' habits were confirmed early by the Imagist insistence on precise diction, concrete imagery, and exactness of cadence and sound.[6] His insistence on distinct shades and shadings of colors, as in "Sea Surface Full of Clouds," may be simply an effort to revive an exhausted imagination, using language as if it were a stimulant, as A. Walton Litz suggests, but it coincides with the later reasoning of "Le Monocle de Mon Oncle" that prefers "fluttering things" to gobbets.[7] Objectifying the world by its colors is the tactic of several early poems: "Anecdote of the Prince of Peacocks," "Banal Sojourn," "Disillusionment of Ten O'Clock," "Six Significant Landscapes," and "The Public Square," for example, where Stevens apprehends a world that will not be minced.

Stevens's habit of conspicuous consumption, his day-to-day life as a collector, did have its expression in his poetry. He externalizes the internal in "Theory," for example: "I am what is around me." The metonymic chain of identity is the opposite of the Romantic ploy of moving the exterior into the interior, picking the daffodils off the hillside and putting them in the mind, which J. Hillis Miller has described.[8] Stevens's poetic energies flow in channels of contingency. He comes to the radical insight into his own way of thinking by equating it with that of women: "Women understand this " he writes, half in an effort to trivialize his own sense and half in a desire to draw back from his own bravado. He takes the denigration of women who guarantee *their* identity in the external prop and turns it, in what is to be the first stage of a slow but complete identification with the feminine in his poetry, by suggesting that women understand correctly the contingency of self. He develops his idea by metonymy where the portrait and its background are related:

One is not duchess
A hundred yards from a carriage.

These, then are portraits:
A black vestibule;
A high bed sheltered by curtains.

These are merely instances. (86–87)

The distinction between interior and exterior on which Lentricchia has insisted is obliterated in Stevens's sense of the contingency of self. "I am what is around me" may be the boast of the capitalist, but it is also the modest admission of the imaginative pragmatist who finds himself and his world simultaneously composed and recomposed in changing relations. The idea that external details constitute the self is behind the early play *Carlos Among the Candles* in which, Stevens says, he "intended to illustrate the theory that people are affected by what is around them" (L 201, fn 4). He goes on to explain, "This is an old idea, insofar as it relates to environment in a general sense. But the idea is just as valid if applied to the minutiae of one's surroundings."[9]

This theory of contingency works both ways, as Stevens suggests in "Adagia": "Nothing is itself taken alone. Things are because of interrelations or interactions" (OP 189). He talks of "the exquisite environment of fact" and he goes on to claim, "To be at the end of fact is not to be at the beginning of the imagination but it is to be at the end of both" (OP 190, 200). If "I am what is around me," "what is around me" is also dependent on what I am, Stevens could insist, revising radically the spiritual impact of Emerson's famous dictum, "What we are, that only can we see" (*Nature, Selected Prose*, 38). For Stevens, the duchess' carriage and not her soul is the clear indication of her identity.

For a poet, "the exquisite environment of fact" is always implicated in the existence his writing will have in the world. That potential audience is to the poet what the carriage is to the duchess, so that no poet can utter with confidence the boast of the anxious poet that "We knew for long the mansion's look / And what we said of it became / A part of what it is" (159). Such a claim must also rely for verification upon an audience; part of what a poet is is an audience who will read him in the future. And of this, no poet can be certain.

"A Postcard from the Volcano" becomes then a lament for a future audience that may never know the poet. Stevens expresses here what Rorty claims is the conscious need of the strong poet "to *demonstrate* that he is not a copy or replica," which is "merely a special, optional form of an unconscious need everyone has: the need to come to terms with the blind impress which chance has given him, to make a self for himself by redescribing that impress in terms which are, if only marginally, his own."[10]

Writing is the subject of writing "A Postcard from the Volcano," and the special genealogical consequence of writing is the postcard's focus. A postcard has writing on the back and a picture on the front: but, writing *from* the volcano, the poet situates himself in the scene of his own obliteration and assumes the melancholy of the already forgotten or obliterated poet. He addresses a fellow sufferer on the subject of their readers yet to come who "Will speak our speech and never know." What bothers him is genealogy. He will have no heirs, no one to realize, as Rorty says, "that his metaphoric redescriptions of small parts of the past will be among the future's stock of literal truths" (42).

In this poem, the poet who writes about the children yet to come writes also after the children have come and gone. This confusion of timing matches the confusion of place in writing on a postcard where the scene of writing takes place on the back of the scene, in this case, of the destruction of writing.

This confusion is what Jacques Derrida claims he likes: "What I prefer, about post cards, is that one does not know what is in front or what is in back, here or there, near or far. . . . Nor what is the most important, the picture or the text, and in the text, the message or the caption, or the address."[11] He goes on:

> Now, my post card, this morning when I am raving about it or delivering it [*quand je la délire où la délivre*] in the state of jealousy that has always terrified me, my post card naively overturns everything. In any event, it allegorizes the catastrophic unknown of the order. Finally one begins no longer to understand what to come [*venir*], to come before, to come after, to foresee [*prévenir*], to come back [*revenir*] all mean— along with the difference of the generations, and then to inherit, to write one's will, to dictate, to speak, to take dictation, etc. (21)

Although Bloom claims that "A Postcard from the Volcano" "achieves the most mature balance in *Ideas of Order*, between the pride of a poet's belief that in dying he leaves behind a legacy that alters 'the look of things' and the final transumptive or projective undoing of *Harmonium*'s great Whitmanian trope of the sun" (114), the balancing of moods seems less central to the dynamics of the poem than what Derrida calls the unknown in the order of contingency.[12] The poet is concerned to show how much we add to what is around us and how little we are credited by our heirs, but in both matters he is interested in the genealogy of house and children.

And genealogy, tracing the family tree, is a peculiar form of reading and writing that links past with present, moves along lines of contingency that threaten to fade in time when children "picking up our bones" cannot generate the metonymic chain that would allow them to decipher either the life or the legacy. By contrast to these unborn children "still weaving budded aureoles," the poet as genealogist can trace his family line that is yet to come and write up his still-to-be-conceived extinction from the record. Part of what we add to what is around us, then, may be our own future obliteration by the children who will not know that we have added *them*. But the speaker here has also been a child, and part of what he himself feels is that legacy of earlier poets who made the "windy sky" cry out "a literate despair." He started out in life in "A dirty house in a gutted world" that he inherited, and he has moved on to create the "shuttered mansion-house" that his heirs will inherit and disown.

"A Postcard from the Volcano" is Stevens's "letter to the World," a brief, more open exchange than Dickinson's, but no less insistent on itself as correspondence and on the hazards of linking poet and world, word and word. If Stevens narrows Dickinson's "World" into the genealogical link of children to come, they are children, like Dickinson's readers, who, he

fears, will not judge tenderly of him. Both Dickinson and Stevens allego-
rize, as Derrida says, the "catastrophic unknown of the order" of reader
and writer. The writer creating her or his own reader reverses the order of
writing and reading, of what comes, comes before, or comes after, or
comes back. Writing on the "blank walls," the poet simultaneously erases
himself, making in the process of making the present act of creation a
future of destruction where some distant children:

> Will say of the mansion that it seems
> As if he that lived there left behind
> A spirit storming in blank walls, (159)

The postcard forces us to ask what comes before: the message or the
picture, the writer or the reader. In "A Postcard from the Volcano,"
Stevens plays with Derrida's differences of generation (reading and writing) along with differences of generation (genealogical).

These same differences still concern him in the later *Esthétique du Mal*,
where Stevens again locates the scene of writing on the volcano. But this
volcano is truly a picture postcard version of the real thing, and the writer
is somewhat like the ephebe at his attic window in *Notes Toward a Supreme
Fiction*, removed from actual danger and equally removed from the hazards
of meditation. Stevens writes, "He could describe / The terror of the sound
because the sound / Was ancient " (314). Remote in time, the volcano is
also remote in place for this writer who writes because he is not at home.
Writing is the route that brings us home and forever estranges us from
where we are. Stevens opens the poem on aesthetics which, he told John
Crowe Ransom, he considered the equivalent of aperçus (L 469):

> He was at Naples writing letters home
> And, between his letters, reading paragraphs
> On the sublime. Vesuvius had groaned
> For a month. It was pleasant to be sitting there (313)

His comfort is short-lived because he realizes that:

> Except for us, Vesuvius might consume
> In solid fire the utmost earth and know
> No pain (ignoring the cocks that crow us up
> To die). This is a part of the sublime

From which we shrink. And yet, except for us,
The total past felt nothing when destroyed. (314)

The writer, who cannot avoid complicity in catastrophe because he alone
memorializes it, can be only falsely consoled by the books that have "Made
sure of the most correct catastrophe." Writing as a way of controlling fear
and organizing pain is always a falsification. It is as bad as the sympathy of
the "over-human god " "Who has gone before us in experience " (315).

Writing too comes before us always as a guide, "as if we were sure to find
our way" from it. All that saves us from the pity of the "too, too human
god" and our own desires to imitate his powers in writing the impossible
"Livre de Toutes Sortes de Fleurs d'après Nature" is the "genius of mis-
fortune," "that evil in the self, from which / In desperate hallow, rugged
gesture, fault / Falls out on everything" (316). "The imperfect is our paradise" Stevens writes in "The Poems of Our Climate" (194), anticipating
the affirmation here of both "being, wrong and wrong," and always trying
nonetheless to rescue the rose from nature in the style of the hot-hooded
Spaniard. In a too, too human world containing still those "attributes /
With which we vested, once, the golden forms" "we forego / Lament,
willingly forfeit the ai-ai" and celebrate contiguity and "dear relation," the
near, the closer still, the touch.

Turning from the exaltations of the "golden forms" Stevens turns inevitably to the "minutiae" and familial relations, as if he would enjoy one
extreme or the other. Divested of divinity, man has "this familiar, / This
brother even in the father's eye, / This brother half-spoken in the mother's
throat" (317). "Exquisite in poverty" the poet may be, but not content, and
the next four sections (vi–ix) move him from this impoverishment to the
"nostalgias" in sections x and xiii when he disentangles himself from "sleek
ensolacings." First, the relation of the mother is examined:

He had studied the nostalgias. In these
He sought the most grossly maternal, the creature
Who most fecundly assuaged him, the softest
Woman with a vague moustache and not the mauve *Maman*. (321)

He claims these relations with women, "The gross, the fecund, proved him
against the touch / Of impersonal pain." Thus he is acknowledging however diffidently that the consolations of the familial are as fictive as those
of the religious.

The other line of relationship, with the father, is restrictive not by its "sleek ensolacings" but by "the unalterable necessity / Of being this unalterable animal" (324). Caught between the woman's essentially maternal nostalgic wish to prove her beloved as her children against pain, and the father's relentless, if fated, submission of his son to the limits of existence, the son first announces himself among "Natives of poverty, children of malheur, / The gaiety of language is our seigneur "(322) and then corrects himself finally to conclude: "The greatest poverty is not to live / In a physical world, to feel that one's desire / Is too difficult to tell from despair " (325).

The poem had started as a letter home, and it has moved far from its opening writer seated at a cool cafe in Naples, listening to Vesuvius groan, reading a book on the sublime, and trying to remember phrases of pain and torture. Writing and catastrophe are linked throughout the poem where genre and form mark death, pain, and loss as, for example, the "elegy he found in space" (ii), the "stanzas" that "hang like hives in hell" (iii), "The prince of the proverbs of pure poverty" (ix), "the major / Tragedy" (xiii). Writing home and writing about loss are the same act in *Esthétique du Mal* where "Natives of poverty" are "children of malheur." The generation of reading through writing and of children through parents is still the central unity in Stevens's aesthetics.

What comes before and what after, children or parents, mood or word, is again the subject of another poem about generation which plays on the links or correspondences in correspondence. *The Comedian as the Letter C* also treats the correspondence between the person and what is around him, between reader and writer, between word and world, and the letter of the alphabet as the letter of correspondence.

Stevens's various explanations of the poem always insist that it plays upon the sound of the letter "C" which, he argued, has a comic aspect (L 294, 351–352, 778). The passages that he cites as evidence include "Exchequering from piebald fiscs unkeyed" where, he claims, "the sounds squeak all over the place" (L 352). This kind of oral impressionism, reminiscent of Poe's insistence on the melancholy tone of "Nevermore," may seem mere frivolity on Stevens's part, except that he made the same point so often when the subject of the poem's title came up that it forces an inquiry into its serious intention.

Stevens's poem poses the question: if sounds are, in themselves, comic, then does the sound of the letter "C" come before and thus create the comedy or does it reflect a comedy already in play? It is a topic that interested the Modernists in their early poetry where they were trying to bring poetry closer to the effects of music. Buttel, one of the few critics who takes Stevens's statement seriously, says:

> The various C sounds, along with all the other sounds in "The Comedian," would appear to well up from mysterious sources in nature (the "speech belched out of hoary darks / No way resembling" Crispin's), and these sounds the poet must bring into the musical order of the poem—"syllable / To blessed syllable affined, and sound / Bubbling felicity in cantilene." Thus the sounds which are a part of nature become a part of the nature of the poem; in this case the scoring encompasses both exuberant wit and more exalted harmonies. And the fact that the sounds of C are "both hard and soft" reflects an aspect of Crispin's problem: he must reconcile his fastidiousness with the rawness of his experience. (142)

The relation of the imaginative man to his environment is also where Daniel Fuchs locates the comedy in *The Comedian as the Letter C*. Fuchs says, "The central incongruity and source of comedy in the poem is precisely the juxtaposition of the everyday and our, alas, archaic, abortive impulse to rise high above it."[13] He relies here on Stevens's statement to Renato Poggioli, who was translating his poems, that it is an "anti-mythological poem": "The central figure is an every-day man who lives a life without the slightest adventure except that he lives it in a poetic atmosphere as we all do. This point makes it necessary for a translator to try to reproduce the every-day plainness of the central figure and the plush, so to speak, of his stage" (L 778). But Stevens comments from the ending of the poem when Crispin settles for the quotidian. Such comments do not recollect the course of the poem quite accurately here, however, since Crispin's life is full of activity, moving from "Bordeaux to Yucatan, Havana next, / And then to Carolina" (29). It may have been a "Simple jaunt" but it was full of more than everyday commonness as Crispin, "Stopping, on voyage, in a land of snakes, / Found his vicissitudes had much enlarged / His apprehension " (31).

Trying to avoid the "every-day plainness" of his life, Crispin himself thinks that he can escape by deliberately putting himself in the way of an elaborate adventure. Stevens says, "Life, for him, was not a straight course; it was picking his way in a haphazard manner through a mass of irrelevancies. Under such circumstances, life would mean nothing to him, however pleasant it might be" (L 293). Crispin's error is imagining that he can escape chance. "Imagination gives, but gives in relation," Stevens wrote to

Hi Simons about *The Man with the Blue Guitar*, and it is an insight that Crispin, who is too impatient to wait for the gift, fails to glean (L 364). As a result, he has to travel far and wide, cross seas to find what he might have learned at home:

> The natives of the rain are rainy men.
> Although they paint effulgent, azure lakes,
> And April hillsides wooded white and pink,
> Their azure has a cloudy edge, their white
> And pink, the water bright that dogwood bears. (37)

Crispin himself is not a "rainy man" but a planter, a colonist rather than an adventurer, neither "nincompated pedagogue" nor "Preceptor of the sea" but a homebody. Crispin's gift is for the quotidian. Thus, when "The fabulous and its intrinsic verse / Came like two spirits parleying," for Crispin to "catechize" (31), he relinquishes the opportunity, moving on to a "new reality" and "let that trifle pass." Finally, in discovering that "his soil is man's intelligence" (36), he is able to relent and determine that:

> Hence it was,
> Preferring text to gloss, he humbly served
> Grotesque apprenticeship to chance event,
> A clown, perhaps, but an aspiring clown. (39)

Chance event brought him home to a "prismy blonde" and there he was released into speech and action: "he poured out upon the lips of her / That lay beside him, the quotidian" thus producing from this quotidian four daughters, a future figured here as voices:

> four blithe instruments
> Of differing struts, four voices several
> In couch, four more personae, intimate
> As buffo, yet divers, four mirrors blue
> That should be silver, four accustomed seeds
> Hinting incredible hues, four selfsame lights
> That spread chromatics in hilarious dark,
> Four questioners and four sure answerers. (45)

Like the turnip "Sacked up and carried over seas," "And sown again" that "Came reproduced in purple, family font, / The same insoluble lump", so in his daughters Crispin has reproduced himself in four variations. They are "True daughters both of Crispin and his clay." They arrive to remind him of his arrival home. Crispin is their progenitor; he has come before them. Yet he has come to himself only after their appearance. So he has come after them, as well.

Coming after and before and back to his home and family, Crispin's story is one of the correspondence between the person and what is around him. But in the disjunction between the elaborate language of the poem and its simple plot, that correspondence becomes a question of style. "Portentous enunciation", "Prolific and tormenting tenderness / Of music" are forced into the service of this "skinny sailor's" story in such a way as to render problematic the correspondence between the style and the man, form and content. Helen Vendler notes that *The Comedian as the Letter C* "belongs, in the spectrum of poetic effort, at the end where we find anagrams, schemes, acrostics, figure poems, double sestinas, and so on— the poetry of ingenuity, the poetry with overt verbal designs on its readers" (*On Extended Wings*, 39). But to what end?

The sound of the letter "C" rather than the sense seems to direct the organization of such lines as "sound / Bubbling felicity in cantilene " or "All this with many multings of the man, / Effective colonizer sharply stopped / In the door-yard by his own capacious bloom " (43, 44). The sound exceeds its referential usefulness, but as one variation of the sound of "C" follows another it establishes its own momentum. The sounds of the letter "C" are varied, as Stevens notes in a letter: they are "both hard and soft, include other letters like K, X, etc." (L 778). Part of the play of the poem comes in the play between sounds of the letter "C"; part comes too from the extenuation of the correspondence between sound and sense. "Exchequering from piebald fiscs unkeyed" draws out that correspondence in the thinnest possible link.

Despite all that Stevens said about his intentions in the poem and despite the disjunction between the language of its narrative and that of its rhet-oric, critics continue to read the poem as if it were simply an overwrought epic or mock-epic. They read for the ending, and, even when they note that the ending allows, enigmatically, at least two different and equally plau-sible meanings, they can conclude that Stevens's aim in the poem is to convey the significance of Crispin's voyaging.[14]

The extent to which Stevens frustrates such a reading, however, encourages a reconsideration of the ending, where Stevens writes:

> Or if the music sticks, if the anecdote
> Is false, if Crispin is a profitless
> Philosopher,
>
>   . . . .
>
> And so distorting, proving what he proves
> Is nothing, what can all this matter since
> The relation comes, benignly, to its end? (45–46)

The "relation" of music to meaning, of sound to sense, of fancy to reality, is finite. The end of the poem is the end of all such relating. The letter "C" as a sound or as a sound corresponding to a comic meaning is the creation of the poet alone. Once the poem is over, the relation is over, and the poem ends on one last fanciful gorging of plain and common things: "So may the relation of each man be clipped."

This line that seems intent on concocting "doctrine" from the anecdotes of Crispin also turns the poem back into itself and to the relations Crispin has established in his daughters. He had planned "Loquacious columns by the ructive sea" and instead had created "four blithe instruments / Of differing struts," certainly as loquacious as any column. Chance, to which he had finally served his apprenticeship, allowed him more than he had originally sought for himself. His ending in marriage and fatherhood is an ending in relation, the comic ending.

"So may the relation of each man be clipped" concludes the poem by recalling, revising, and coming back to section vi, "And Daughters with Curls." Curls and clipping are an enigmatic combination for Stevens, who asked in "Le Monocle de Mon Oncle," "Alas! Have all the barbers lived in vain / That not one curl in nature has survived?" In this rhetorical question, Bloom reads "poets" for barbers, and for "curl" he reads whatever the imagination has contrived to add to nature, claiming futher that the question "could take a Paterian or Wildean answer that nature does imitate the barbers" (39–40). In *The Comedian as the Letter C*, the clipper may be the man himself, the barber-poet, who has created daughters with curls to be clipped and trimmed and fashioned into a poem. The poem may end then not in lament, but in the satisfaction of the procreator.

The "relation of each man" figured in letters, daughters, fathers, mothers, preoccupied Stevens in the 1940s when he engaged in a lengthy effort to trace his genealogy. Joining the Saint Nicholas Society of New York, whose residents trace their lineage to a native or resident of the city or state of New York prior to 1785, Stevens read a poem at the society's centenary Easter Monday Festival in 1945, which took as its subject the relations established by tradition.[15] He writes in "Recitation After Dinner":

Is it experience, say, the final form
To which all other forms, at last, return,
The frame of a repeated effect, is it that?
Are we characters in an arithmetic
Or letters of a curious alphabet;
And is tradition an unfamiliar sum,
A legend scrawled in script we cannot read? (OP 115)

The answer, as in "Dutch Graves in Bucks County," is that we are not so organized as letters of the alphabet nor can we read ourselves in such an orderly fashion. Rather, tradition is the process by which "The son restores / The father," "bears him out of love, / His life made double by his father's life." This is, however, tradition tricked out for the Saint Nicholas Society, "Aeneas seen, perhaps, / By Nicholas Poussin, yet nevertheless / A tall figure upright in a giant's air." It is not a process that Stevens in his less nostalgic moments can believe.

"Dutch Graves in Bucks County" disclaims such piety, as the speaker directly cuts himself off from his ancestors whom he addresses as "semblables" even when he claims that they do not resemble him: "you, my semblables, in the total / Of remembrance share nothing of ourselves"; "Know that the past is not part of the present"; "know that this time / Is not an early time that has grown late"; "know that your children / Are not your children, not your selves." Nor will those who come after share "our stale perfections": rather, "seeking out / Their own, waiting until we go / To picnic in the ruins that we leave." No relation was ever more clipped than this, and yet, the poem concludes, "Time was not wasted in your subtle temples. / No: nor divergence made too steep to follow down" (291–293).

"Down" here has some of the effect of "Time will write them down" in "It Must Change," canto x, in *Notes Toward a Supreme Fiction*. The relation of past to present, of present to future, never has the order of even a curious alphabet and much less the "unfamiliar sum" of addition. Nor is it a legend scrawled in script we cannot read. It is rather a "divergence" that, no matter how steep, is always down and always one we shall follow. We can read the script in the Dutch graves of Bucks County, if we are Dutch and intent on tracing genealogical lines. But it is the universal lesson that we shall read: "Time was not wasted in your subtle temples" because time is the essential medium of waste and preservation.

For Stevens, genealogy, "This structure of ideas, these ghostly sequences / Of the mind, result only in disaster," as he writes in "The Bed of Old John Zeller." That is what genealogy is, "the habit of wishing, as if one's grandfather lay / In one's heart and wished as he had always wished". But he does not, and "It is more difficult" "to accept the structure / Of things as the structure of ideas" (326). The structure of things is always to deconstruct itself, to fall into ruin, and the poet who wants to write it *down* is himself susceptible to the same structural law.

But it is less difficult, however hard, to acknowledge the crumbling structure of things in the generation just prior to one's own. The death of ancestors has only to tell us that we too will die, and it is this easing into death that Stevens learned from his study of genealogy. Tracing the origin and course of his own family line, he came at last to his mother and then to his father. If Dickinson imagined words as love tokens able to bind writer to reader, as physical certainties above the threat of metaphysical possibilities, Stevens imagined words as familial bonds linking one generation to the next: the letter as the begetter, the father, in *The Comedian as the Letter C*, the letter as part of an alphabetical order and as a son carrying a father out of love in "Recitation after Dinner," the letter as the end "Spelled from spent living and spent dying" "In a storm of torn-up testaments" in "Dutch Graves in Bucks County."

As Stevens worked through the links that words create from father to son, he moved toward the end of all such linkage. He had always had in mind that end in neglect where children will speak his speech and never know it is his, and he could begin to imagine an end of imaginative powers when, as he says in "Long and Sluggish Lines," "It makes so little difference, at so much more / Than seventy, where one looks, one has been there before" (522), but death as the end of life, something other than the mother of beauty, he came upon by turning back to that original trope and considering in old age the figure of the mother that had played so fully in his early poetry. The one he had addressed early in "To the One of Fictive Music" as "Sister and mother and diviner love, / And of the sisterhood of the living dead" (87) and had such difficulty addressing in "Le Monocle de Mon Oncle" returns in all her ambiguity.

At the end of life, Stevens looked for that assurance offered at the beginning of life from the mother, and, as we have seen, he reimagined his needs in his grandson in "Questions Are Remarks," where the grandson asks, "'Mother, what is that'" and not "'Mother, my mother who are you,' / The way the drowsy, infant, old men do " (463). The mother as guardian, as guarantor of beauty and knowledge, becomes in old age the mother as enigma, "regina of the clouds." She may even be age itself, as in "Madame La Fleurie" where "with the great weightings of the end" "he brings all that he saw into the earth, to the waiting parent. / His crisp knowledge is devoured by her, beneath a dew." "His grief is that his mother should feed on him, himself and what he saw, / In that distant chamber, a bearded queen, wicked in her dead light " (507).

Stevens was too committed to the mother as muse to give this devouring mother, once the source of beauty and now the wicked spirit of death, more than passing notice. More than the earthmother, the woman for Stevens was required to be not a symbol but a sign, a link with past and future, as in "The Owl in the Sarcophagus" where she is one of three forms (peace, sleep, and the mother) that "are not abortive figures, rocks, / Impenetrable symbols, motionless " (432). Stevens redescribes the earthly mother here:

And she that in the syllable between life

And death cries quickly, in a flash of voice,
Keep you, keep you, I am gone, oh keep you as
My memory, is the mother of us all,

The earthly mother and the mother of
The dead. (432)

Memory, the mother of the muses, becomes in this elegy for his friend Henry Church, all that assuages him. The maternal instinct to "keep," to keep and to keep on speaking, is the expression of the poet's creativity. The mother "cries quickly" in alarm and fully alive in "that syllable between life / / And death". If peace is "that figure stationed at our end, / Always in

brilliance, fatal, final, formed / Out of our lives to keep us in our death,"
(434), the mother seems posed to keep us in our life. She "stood tall in self
not symbol, quick / / And potent, an influence felt instead of seen. / She
spoke with backward gestures of her hand" (435).

These backward gestures are repeated in a summary address to the
mother:

> O exhalation, O fling without a sleeve
> And motion outward, reddened and resolved
> From sight, in the silence that follows her last word— (435)

Bloom calls this "brilliant in its precise nonimaging," but also "obscuran-
tist" since "this is death the mother, or the final ambiguity of remembrance,
as it fades, with life" (289). Stevens himself concludes that "These are
death's own supremest images, / The pure perfections of parental space "
(436). And in these lines. Stevens passes beyond the death of even memory
to suggest that death makes us children again, vulnerable, dependent,
afraid, at the same time that it makes us once again adult, aware of our
mortality as no child will ever be and aware too that we alone now move
toward the "perfections of parental space." Among the "forms" that are not
"Impenetrable symbols, motionless " the mind is also motionless, and, to
content itself, "It is a child that sings itself to sleep," in a gesture that Bloom
has suggested is characteristic of such later poems as "An Old Man Asleep"
or "A Child Asleep in Its Own Life" (291). But the child asleep rests in the
mother's care. His is the peace of place, of being at last at home.

The mother in "The Owl in the Sarcophagus" moves "With a sad splendor, beyond artifice" (435), and it is this elegiac motion that characterizes
the mother in *The Auroras of Autumn*. The mother is the first muse: "The
mother's face, / The purpose of the poem " (413). But the mother "they
possess" is the nurturer, not the creator: the one "Who gives transparence
to their present peace." Associated with warmth, gentleness, and softness,
the mother is associated also with death: "she too is dissolved, she is
destroyed. / She gives transparence. But she has grown old " (413). The
father here is linked with life or activity. For him, "The cancellings, / The
negations are never final " (414). "He says yes / To no; and in saying yes
he says farewell " (414). The offspring of this couple is the poet whose
inspiration comes directly from the winds of chance as they blow about
these figures and are ordered by them. For the mother:

A wind will spread its windy grandeurs round
And knock like a rifle-butt against the door.
The wind will command them with invincible sound. (414)

For the father, "Master O master seated by the fire"

Profound, and yet the king and yet the crown,
Look at this present throne. What company,
In masks, can choir it with the naked wind? (415)

The invincible wind is stripped naked, as it moves from mother to father, moves to inspire this son of both parents. The father will not give up his throne to the son; rather he himself "fetches" (goes or comes after, brings or takes back) his own choiring festival: "tellers of tales / and musicans who mute much, muse much, on the tales"; "negresses to dance"; "pageants out of air" (415).[16] But he also fetches "his unherded herds, / Of barbarous tongue" (415). Bloom calls this father a "failed translator, of desire into fiction" (268). More than that, this father is hoarding his resources; he is a "fetcher" and not a begetter.

Something is strangely amiss in these familial relations. "There is no play," Stevens writes (416). The mother who is possessed, the father who will not be dethroned, these parents defy the law of generation, and the son finds "there are no lines to speak."

The genealogical lines are broken here, and with them language degenerates into "This loud, disordered mooch" (415). The connection between genealogy and language has been developing in Stevens's poetry since *The Comedian as the Letter C* where the comedian eventually translated his letter into a procreative role, the letter as father. Here, the reversions of filiation lead to the surrealistic theatre of section vi: "filled with flying birds, / Wild wedges, as of a volcano's smoke, palm-eyed / And vanishing" (416). Identifying the father's theater with the volcano, Stevens returns to his obsession with writing at the place of obliteration, with writing always at the moment of erasure, that he first expressed in "A Postcard from the Volcano." Writing about the father's creation, the son, who had earlier tried to write "Farewell to an idea" of both the mother and the father, must now discover that he cannot rid himself of the disorder in the family which finds its natural counterpart in the galactic chaos of the aurora borealis. "He opens the door of his house / On flames." "And he feels afraid " (416–417).

This disorder is familial. Stevens's fear may be explained by Lacan, who has identified the law of the father as "identical to an order of Language." Lacan says:

> For without kinship nominations, no power is capable of instituting the order of preferences and taboos which bind and weave the yarn of lineage down through succeeding generations. And it is indeed the confusion of generations which, in the Bible as in all traditional laws, is accused as being the abomination of the *verbe* and the desolation of the sinner.[17]

Failing the language of the father, the son must think back through the mother to "a time of innocence" that

> we partake thereof,
> Lie down like children in this holiness,
> As if, awake, we lay in the quiet of sleep,
>
> As if the innocent mother sang in the dark
> Of the room and on an accordion, half-heard,
> Created the time and place in which we breathed . . . (418–419)

Like Crispin, the speaker of *The Auroras of Autumn* settles for the quotidian, becomes "as Danes in Denmark all day long," and settles for his life "In hall harridan, not hushful paradise" (421). He has found a place, and, he discovers, his search has been *for* place, for words that will "solemnize the secretive syllables" that fill the blank between life and death, that will create a space for himself.

From the early volcano of "A Postcard from the Volcano" to the father's late volcanic theater in *The Auroras of Autumn*, Stevens has associated writing with catastrophe, and catastrophe with a disturbance at the center of the family. Curiously reversing the generational order, Stevens treats in his early poems the disturbance created by the yet to be born heirs who will disinherit the poet by not ackowledging his letters, whereas in his later poems he sees the father as disturbing the catastrophic unknown of the order of reading and writing. In this confusion of generations, Stevens indicates the tottering of the orderly principle in the family that forces him to turn from the father to the mother for a place to breathe. Stevens's "letters of a curious alphabet" are attempts to articulate an order of language outside the father's which retains still a desire for a place in that order, even as they acknowledge that all such relations are clipped. Stevens's poetry moves, finally, outside the theater of the father to that other real comfort of the mother where he may be a child again. Writing letters and using alphabetic letters to trace correspondences indicate Stevens's futile search for relations of continuity in a violent world in which language has become this "disordered mooch."

Chapter 7

"A world impossible for poets": Stevens and His Audience

Different in details though their circumstances were, Dickinson and Stevens shared a longing for an audience they never were to have. She remained generally unpublished; he had a long middle period in his creative life in which he went, if not entirely unread, at least not read sympathetically. From these circumstances, she developed a fantasy of a reader-lover erotically charged and passionately attached to her, and he developed an equally fantasized dream of a reader-mother and a reader-brother. Again, hers is the intimate, his the social connection.

Wallace Stevens's creative life spanned two events that posed particular problems to a poet for whom writing was an activity of generation. Neither the Depression nor World War II was an easy subject for poetry or for a poet who may have wanted to generate a creative link with his audience but who also felt himself, first and last, inadequate to the task. Clearly, the terms of the Depression and the war were not the poet's, and Stevens turned to the first subject only after being provoked by a review of *Ideas of Order* in *The New Masses* by the Marxist critic Stanley Burnshaw. Nonetheless, once having taken up the subject, Stevens used it to launch a lengthy and troubled exploration of the relations of a poet to his audience in times of economic depression. And later, he continued his inquiry in thinking about the war. The course of his contemplation on the poet's social role was not simple nor did it produce his greatest poetry, but it may be followed as an important indication of Stevens's concern for the reader whom he, like Dickinson, never had.

Although the conventional view of Stevens is of a poet removed from social and political interests, in fact, he used the events of his own troubled times as a basis for contemplating just how much the imaginative poet shared with the common imagination. The Marxists were revolutionaries; so too the poet. And, for Stevens, the Marxists were not obtuse readers of poetry; they simply did not know how to read poetry with the greatest sensitivity to the revolutionary impulse in their own attitude; they needed to imagine a hero but, in Stevens's view, they needed the poet to instruct them in how not to let their limited imaginations obstruct the creation of the true hero they wanted. The poet as a guide and parental imagination for his readers had an early start in Stevens's work, but the role assumed a prominent place after the publication of *Ideas of Order*.

Writing in 1936 to his publisher, J. Ronald Lane Latimer, he said,

> You ask whether I should continue to write if no one but myself would ever see my work. There is no reason to believe that anyone will ever see any more of my work. . . . I think that I should continue to write poetry whether or not anybody ever saw it, and certainly I write lots of it that nobody ever sees. (L 305–306)

But just a few months earlier in an exchange of letters with Latimer about Stanley Burnshaw's review of *Ideas of Order*, Stevens had appeared directly concerned with the audience he knew he had, commenting,

> The review in MASSES was a most interesting review, because it placed me in a new setting. I hope I am headed left, but there are lefts and lefts, and certainly I am not headed for the ghastly left of MASSES (L 286).

A few weeks later, to Latimer who had asked him if he accepted "the common opinion" that his "verse is essentially decorative," he wrote,

> I was on the point of saying that I did not agree with the opinion that my verse is decorative, when I remembered that when HARMONIUM was in the making there was a time when I liked the idea of images and images alone, or images and the music of verse together. I then believed in *pure poetry*, as it was called. . . . I don't at all like the words *decorative* and *formal*. . . . I don't like any labels, because I am not doing one thing all the time. (L 288–289)

In the same letter, he mentioned "Mr. Burnshaw and the Statue" as a poem responding directly to Burnshaw's review which attempted to "apply the point of view of a poet to Communism" (L 289).

This exchange of letters with Latimer indicates the wide swings in Stevens's attitude toward his audience that may have developed in the thirties but never quite stabilized; by turns indifferent and receptive, he was never easy with his readers. He had had occasion to brood on the subject after the critical neglect of his first book and the long creative hiatus before his second book, which itself soon began to receive mixed reviews. He had never been impervious to his audience because, as he says in "The Noble Rider and the Sound of Words," the audience will "do for the poet what he cannot do for himself, that is to say, receive his poetry" (NA 30). To make that reception as generous as possible, the poet himself had to assume a certain initial receptivity, and, in a number of minor poems and the failed *Owl's Clover*, Stevens began to develop the position of the poet as himself receiving his readers, a "pater patriae," supported by a maternal muse.

Stevens's first ideas about his reader and reading began to germinate before he ever encountered Burnshaw and began to think of a potential Marxist audience. "The Reader," published in *Ideas of Order*, was the first of at least four poems about readers in which he uses the same combination of elements to describe the reading process as an effacement of the text and a direct confrontation with nature.[1] In "The Reader," Stevens wrote:

No lamp was burning as I read,
A voice was mumbling, "Everything
Falls back to coldness,

Even the musky muscadines,
The melons, the vermilion pears
Of the leafless garden."

The sombre pages bore no print
Except the trace of burning stars
In the frosty heaven. (147)

Reading blank pages that produce speech in the dark is an odd feat, and yet it is a common strategy in Stevens's poems about readers. In "Phosphor Reading by His Own Light," "The page is blank or a frame without a glass," and "The greenness of night lies on the page":

The green falls on you as you look,

Falls on and makes and gives, even a speech.
And you think that that is what you expect,

That elemental parent, the green night,
Teaching a fusky alphabet. (267)

In "The House Was Quiet and the World Was Calm," "The reader became the book; and summer night / / Was like the conscious being of the book" (358). "The words were spoken as if there was no book, / Except that the reader leaned above the page" (358). "The summer night is like a perfection

of thought" (358). Again, in "Large Red Man Reading," someone is reading aloud to "ghosts that returned to earth to hear his phrases," "to hear
him read from the poem of life " (423). He "spoke the feeling for them,
which was what they had lacked " (424).

Reading in these poems is always reading aloud, as a parent reading to
a child from a familiar book that each has memorized. It is an enterprise
of the night, not of darkness only but of "that elemental parent, the green
night," which, like the imagination it nourishes, is both generative and
obfuscating. It gives, but gives in relation, as Stevens said elsewhere,
teaching out of its own darkness "a fusky alphabet." Reading is leaning, as
Stevens says in "The House Was Quiet and the World Was Calm," where

> the reader leaned above the page,
> Wanted to lean, wanted much most to be
> The scholar to whom his book is true (358)

In this pose, the reader, even in the dark, bends to his task in the attitude,
if not of prayer, at least of the needy and the faithful.

Stevens himself read widely, but he appears here to be writing not so
much about his own habits of daily reading as about the special kind of
reading in which one looks for what one lacks or reads with the faith that
the book is "true." This kind of reading he had experienced as a child with
his mother, as he recalls in writing about her when she was dying:

> Fortunately for mother she has faith and she approaches her end here (unless her
> mind is too obscured) with the just expectation of re-union afterwards; and if
> there be a God, such as she believes in, the justness of her expectation will not
> be denied. I remember how she always read a chapter from the Bible every night
> to all of us when we were ready for bed. Often, one or two of us fell asleep. She
> always maintained an active interest in the Bible, and found there the solace she
> desired. (L 172–173)

Although Stevens goes on to admit that "she was, of course, disappointed,
as we all are," he pictures the reader in his poems as he does his mother here
as a reader to children, as the believer inculcating those who listen, as the
scholar who wants the book to be "true." At the heart of his feeling for his
dying mother is the nostalgia for a nurturing presence already lost to him.
Reading is a way of recovering that loss as memory restores a life and the
promise of life to the mother.

Such reading is not an easy task. "It is difficult to read" Stevens admits in "Phosphor Reading by His Own Light," but difficult because, even if the reader knows what he or she expects, as Phosphor does and presumably as Stevens' mother did, he or she is always remade in the reading (267). Especially when reading by his own light, Phosphor remains in the dark of "That elemental parent" in whom he will be reborn.

Reading for Stevens is then always a scene *mise en abîme*, a parent reading to a child from a parent reading to a child. Even reading by his own light and thinking he knows what he expects, Phosphor will still learn what it is he expects by reading what it is he can read. Who goes to dine in Stevens must feast on what is put before him, unlike Dickinson's more actively participatory diner. The parent text is the ample provider in Stevens, or, rather, the parent text provides what the parent text has been provided.

The parental relationship of the writer to the reader is stressed even when Stevens turns to address the poet in "Prelude to Objects":

Poet, patting more nonsense foamed
From the sea, conceive for the courts
Of these academies, the diviner health
Disclosed in common forms. Set up
The rugged black, the image. Design
The touch. Fix quiet. Take the place
Of parents, lewdest of ancestors.
We are conceived in your conceits. (195)

This second birth through the parental poet is itself a double conception in "common forms" and in the uncommon poetic "conceit." The "rugged black" and fixed "quiet" are far removed from the "conceit," "an intricate or far-fetched metaphor, which functions through arousing feelings of surprise, shock or amusement," as the *Princeton Encyclopedia of Poetry and Poetics* defines it.[2] Although the speaker can argue that "It comes to this: / That the guerilla I should be booked / And bound," he cannot settle on the nature of the binding, common or decorative. Nonetheless, conception through reading is what both poet and reader desire.

Naturally, the poet wants to see "his imagination become the light in the minds of others" and "to help people to live their lives," as Stevens argued in "The Noble Rider and the Sound of Words" (NA 29). And the poet conjures for himself ideal readers like the ghostly readers who return to hear the poetry of earth in "Large Red Man Reading." Stevens writes, "in those thin, those spended hearts," "the literal characters, the vatic lines " "Took on color, took on shape and the size of things as they are" (424). Here, Bloom's argument that "Stevens passes beyond irony to a pure celebration of his own poetry" (296) locates only half the meaning. Self-congratulatory though he is, he is even more intent on summoning up out of the heavens a reader who will also celebrate him. But again, this reader, like Phosphor, wants to learn what he thinks he knows.

Against this portrait of the ideal reader whom Stevens conceived and reconceived, Stanley Burnshaw stands out as an exception. He reveals himself to be someone who reads only in the clear light of Marxist sympathies in the review of Haniel Long's *Pittsburgh Memoranda* and Stevens's *Ideas of Order* entitled "Turmoil in the Middle Ground" that he wrote for the leftist journal *The New Masses*. Not for him the disappearance of the book and the revelation of nature and the vatic lines. He pays Stevens (and Long) the highest compliment by separating them from those contemporary poets who "have all tramped off to some escapist limbo where they are joyously gathering moonshine."[3] By contrast, Stevens and Long are, in Burnshaw's view, poets of the middle ground, "acutely conscious members of a class menaced by the clashes between capital and labor," "in the throes of a struggle for philosophical adjustment." He considers them "potential allies as well as potential enemies," hoping that Stevens will "sweep his contradictory notions into a valid Idea of Order" (366). Burnshaw, a poet himself, identifies Stevens as "a man who, having lost his footing, now scrambles to stand up and keep his balance" (365).

Judging from remarks he made later in the *Sewanee Review*, we may see that Burnshaw imagined that he was praising Stevens even when he could admit that he was proceeding in an atmosphere where "tentativeness and humility were unthinkable" (358). Stevens's response in a letter to Latimer was less than cordial:

> The rich man and the comfortable man of the imagination of people like Mr. Burnshaw are not nearly so rich nor nearly so comfortable as he believes them to be. And, what is more, his poor men are not nearly so poor. These professionals lament in a way that would have given Job a fever. (L 286)

He concluded, "MASSES is just one more wailing place and the whole left now-a-days is a mob of wailers" (L 287). Reading for Burnshaw was not self-making, not a leaning over the page in search of the truth, not a submission to that "elemental parent," but a categorizing of texts as true or false.

Yet something about the wailing wall of Burnshaw's reading and writing interested Stevens, and he set to work on an immediate reply in poetry, adding "Mr. Burnshaw and the Statue" as Part II of a series he had been working on. Part I, "The Old Woman and the Statue," had already been published in *Southern Review*. There the statue had served as a symbol for art. In "Mr. Burnshaw and the Statue" Stevens wrote, "the same statue is also a symbol, but not specifically a symbol for art; its use has been somewhat broadened and, so far as I have defined it at all, it is a symbol for things as they are" (L 290).

Some years later, Stevens wrote of a shorter version of the poem (Parts I, II, and III, Part V starting at the second line, and Part VI) that it "consists of a narrative interrupted by two apostrophes to one's celestial paramours, which are in reality short hymns of reconciliation" (L 367). The full poem has an additional apostrophe, but the direction of the poem remains the same. Its narrative is devoted to how things are; its apostrophe to how they should be. In both circumstances, the poem is commenting on a reading of reality.

If the statue represents "things as they are," the poem is quick to state in its opening line, "The thing is dead" (OP 78). And, in a Marxist state, "The stones / That will replace it shall be carved, '*The Mass / Appoints These Marbles Of Itself To Be / Itself*'" (OP 80).

Against the rigidity of this Marxist reading, the poet enjoins the "celestial paramours" to "Chant sibilant requiems for this effigy" and "Bring down from nowhere nothing's wax-like blooms, / Calling them what you will but loosely-named / In a mortal lullaby" (OP 79). The requiem for the dead, the lullaby for the newly born, are "loosely-named " songs of reconciliation to a world of change. Nothing will be changed by these songs (the apple "red, will not be redder " nor "the ploughman in his bed / Be free to sleep there sounder"), but change will be acknowledged, and "this gawky plaster will not be here" (OP 79). In the lullaby of these "celestial paramours," whom Stevens identifies as "all the things in our nature that are celestial" (L 367), he introduces once again the mother figure, the nurturing impulse of the parent. Stevens explains, "The music makes them" (L 367), noting the way in which the artist, like Phosphor reading in his own light, both makes and is remade in his art.

Unlike the "bare and blunt" statue of the Marxist, the paramours' music will disclose

a place
Of fear before the disorder of the strange,
A time in which the poets' politics
Will rule in a poets' world. Yet that will be
A world impossible for poets, who
Complain and prophesy, in their complaints,
And are never of the world in which they live. (OP 80)

And suddenly, the paramours will have created a time for poets who, like Burnshaw at the wailing wall, are like leftists who "Complain." The Marxists, like the Romantics, are never "of the world in which they live." So Stevens undoes the rigidity of the Marxists and converts them from the social realists they probably imagined themselves to be into true literary revolutionaries.

The "Mass" and the "Mesdames," once opposites and now oddly reconciled in their encouragement of exile from the world, both must listen to the "solemn voice, not Mr. Burnshaw's" deliver his panegyric to waste, both "the hopeless waste of the past" and "the hopeful waste to come" (OP 80–81). Change is hymned by a less solemn voice persuading them that "It is only enough / To live incessantly in change" (OP 82). Although the muses sang "A tragic lullaby," again as a mother soothing a baby, they have now to learn that "change composes, too, and chaos comes / To momentary calm" (OP 82).

These "damsels" are enjoined:

In the glassy sound of your voices, the porcelain cries,
The alto clank of the long recitation, in these
Speak, and in these repeat: *To Be Itself,*
Until the sharply-colored glass transforms
Itself into the speech of the spirit,

. . . .

until the waterish ditherings turn
To the tense, the maudlin, true meridian
That is yourselves when, at last, you are yourselves. (OP 83)

These lines would appear to be a rather severe indictment of Burnshaw's "turmoil in the middle ground." Yet, when Stevens finished this poem, he wrote to Latimer, "It is simply a general and rather vaguely poetic justification of leftism; to the extent that the Marxians are raising Cain with the peacocks and the doves, nature has been ruined by them" (L 294–295). So the solemn voice in his poem had warned the "Mesdames" that "it is not enough to be reconciled / Before the strange," "It is not enough / That the vista retain ploughmen, peacocks, doves," "It is not enough that you are indifferent" (OP 81–82). "It is only enough / To live incessantly in change." And presumably in the "maudlin, true meridian" of themselves, the mesdames rise to the occasion.

So, confronted by the obtuse reading habits of Burnshaw, Stevens turns to show him how to read in his own way but with greater sensitivity. He had told Latimer that he did "very much believe in leftism in every direction, even in wailing." Then, he goes on to write, "These people go about it in such a way that nobody listens to them except themselves, and that is a [sic] least one reason why they get nowhere. They have the most magnificent cause in the world" (L 287).

Presumably, in "Mr. Burnshaw and the Statue" Stevens had hoped to make a wider audience listen to a magnificent cause. That he imagined he had failed is suggested by his refusal to include "Mr. Burnshaw and the Statue" or *Owl's Clover* in his collected poems. That he had indeed failed to win over the particular reader he had named is evident in the statement that Burnshaw made some twenty-five years later in reflecting on the incident: "Like others interested in Wallace Stevens, I try to read what I can about his meanings, for despite the zeal of his commentators, I still find it hard to understand some of the most attractive poems, especially one directed to me that appeared a quarter-century ago" (*Sewanee Review*, 355).

In this same article, Burnshaw's attempt to set his own review and Stevens's work in the context of the time can perhaps explain some of Stevens's interest in what he imagined might be his audience among the leftists. Describing the excitement stirred by *The New Masses* among literary figures of all kinds, Burnshaw notes, "the world of books had suddenly come alive with excitement. . . . Literature was reaching sectors of the population that one never regarded as part of the reading public" (359). He goes on, "This startling experience, this sense of direct relationship with one's readers, was not only new in American letters; it could go far to sustain those writers within the Left who were wrestling with their private angels" (359).

Stevens was aware of this new excitement and change, admitting that his own thoughts about what a poet should be and do were constantly changing, and claiming that if he had once been interested in *"pure poetry"* and still liked it, he was also aware that "we live in a different time, and life means a good deal more to us now-a-days than literature does" (L 288). Stevens's awareness of the changing times may not have been identical to Burnshaw's, but, like his critic, the poet was responding to the excitement occasioned by the left in literary matters. The connection was made directly when, asked by Latimer if he felt there was an essential conflict between Marxism and the sentiment of the marvelous, Stevens replied in a manner that suggested his willingness to remain open to both:

> I think we all feel that there is conflict between the rise of a lower class, with all its realities, and the indulgences of an upper class. This, however, is one of the very things which I at least have in mind in MR. BURNSHAW. My conclusion is that, while there is a conflict, it is not an essential conflict. The conflict is temporary. The only possible order of life is one in which all order is incessantly changing. Marxism may or may not destroy the existing sentiment of the marvellous; if it does, it will create another. (L 291–292)

In this light, not just "Mr. Burnshaw and the Statue" but Part I of *Owl's Clover*, "The Old Woman and the Statue," as well as Part IV, "A Duck for Dinner," may be seen as efforts on Stevens's part to incorporate the Marxist reader and reading of reality into his poetry. Helen Vendler's extensive commentary on *Owl's Clover* scants its social commentary, which she claims elicits two kinds of poetry from Stevens, the poetry of satire and the poetry of pity, but chiefly proves that Stevens "never deceived himself about the apparent irrelevance of poetry to practical social problems" (*On Extended Wings*, 100). Yet, Stevens's letters of the period and his commentary much later about *Owl's Clover* to Hi Simons show him directly concerned about the relation of poetry to social problems and the role of the poet in society. If *Owl's Clover* is not an entirely successful poem, it might be because, for the time of its composition, Stevens did deceive himself into thinking that he could address not just social problems but a segment of society from which he had hitherto held himself aloof.

Of all the readers that he might have wanted to court and incorporate in his poem, the Marxist reader or the destitute old woman, depressed and a product of the depression, may seem the most intractable. And yet, in including them in his poem, Stevens was following the familiar strategy of much of his earlier poetry of setting up what Alan Perlis identifies as "'straw dog' protagonists." In "Sunday Morning," *The Comedian as the Letter C*, "A High-Toned Old Christian Woman," and "Mrs. Alfred Uruguay," among others, he develops a reader of reality whom the poem's speaker attacks.[4]

But the old woman in "The Old Woman and the Statue" is not entirely debunked. Her "harridan self and ever maladive-fate" has its place in relation to the statue of marble horses; she does what the sculptor cannot do for himself, and that is receive his art (OP 77). Although she is "the bitter mind / In a flapping cloak," "that tortured one, / So destitute that nothing but herself / Remained and nothing of herself except / A fear too naked for her shadow's shape," she exists outside the sculptor's imagination and thus exceeds his imaginative reach (OP 76). She proves that the poet in the Depression must work harder to reach her. He had "foreseen" "autumn," the seasons of change; he had "devised" "white forelegs taut," the stillness of art in this changing world. "But her he had not foreseen," and she is his audience (OP 76). In his lack of foresight, his creation fails:

> The mass of stone collapsed to marble hulk,
> Stood stiffly, as if the black of what she thought
> Conflicting with the moving colors there
> Changed them, at last, to its triumphant hue. (OP 76)

"Without her, evening like a budding yew / Would soon be brilliant, as it was, before" her (OP 77). The old woman will disappear, eventually, and then "the horses would rise again" (OP 78). But, for the moment, the old woman's reaction changes the statue.[5] Stevens wrote that the poem:

> deals specifically with the status of art in a period of depression, it is, when generalized, one more confrontation of reality (the depression) and the imagination (art). A larger expression than confrontation is: a phase of the universal intercourse. There is a flow to and fro between reality and the imagination. (L 368)

The irony here is that the audience of the Depression attacked Stevens for being merely decorative, for not caring about social issues, whereas Stevens imagined that he could reach them by being more decorative, by resisting the old woman's desire to turn everything to black.

Although the old woman is not like the reader leaning over the page in "The House Was Quiet and the World Was Calm," she shares with those other figures of Stevens's poems about readers the darkness in which they read. Her "chalky brow scratched over black / And black by thought that could not understand / Or, if it understood, repressed itself / Without any pity in a somnolent dream" (OP 76). Still, in "thinking of heaven and earth and of herself / And looking at the place in which she walked " (OP 77), she is that common viewer and reader that seeks always after the uncommon vision which neither sculptor nor poet can neglect. Art must always confront the "black" of her not understanding. "Cross-reflections, modifications, counter-balances, complements, giving and taking are illimitable" between depression and art, as Stevens says (L 368). The poet's role in these interchanges is to respond, to nurture them and be nurtured by them, moving always in ceaseless change.

A different kind of reader, although no less a product of depression and the Depression, is the Bulgar of "A Duck for Dinner" whom Stevens identifies as a "socialist," not the socialist as he used to be depicted, "dirty, hairy, and in rags," but the socialist who has done very well by himself and, as Stevens suggests, is "entitled to a new image" (L 371). In "A Duck for Dinner," the Bulgar as socialist is not too unlike, in his eating habits at least, the "diplomats of the cafes" in Part III of *Owl's Clover*, "The Greenest Continent," presumably those members of the indulgent upper class whom he opposes, who "expound" over "Fromage and coffee and cognac" (OP 88). The Bulgar says, "'After pineapple with fresh mint / We went to walk in the park'" where the workers walk and rise above their work to think about art: "'what these hands from Sweden mean, / These English noses and edged, Italian eyes, / Massed for a head they mean to make for themselves, / From which their grizzled voice will speak and be heard'" (OP 91). But the Bulgar, who, we may judge, may have misinterpreted the workers' interests entirely, seems to retreat in disgust from what he calls their:

> "Geranium budgets, pay-roll water-falls,
> The clank of the carrousel and, under the trees,
> The sheep-like falling-in of distances,
> Converging on the statue, white and high". (OP 93)

Although Stevens's later comments about these workers fail to recall their "sheep-like" nature (L 371), it is, in fact, this negative image that he elaborates in section IV of the poem where the band's playing of "Concerto for Airplane and Pianoforte, / The newest Soviet reclame" is called

"Profound / Abortion" (OP 93). He propounds "Perennial doctrine and most florid truth" "As the man the state, not as the state the man"; yet he asks,

> In an age of concentric mobs would any sphere
> Escape all deformation, much less this,
> This source and patriarch of other spheres,
> This base of every future, vibrant spring,
> The volcano Apostrophe, the sea Behold? (OP 94)

Stevens comments, "Given the mobs of contemporary life, however, it is impossible to project a world that will not appear to some one to be a deformation. . . . At a time of severely practical requirements, the world of the imagination looks like something distorted. A man who spouts apostrophes is a volcano and in particular the volcano Apostrophe. A man full of behold this and behold that is the sea Behold" (L 372).

Vendler dismisses this enigmatic statement too quickly when she sees it as the discouragement behind the satiric portions of *Owl's Clover* and the explanation of why Stevens never wrote again against the backdrop of the masses (*On Extended Wings*, 101). Its oddity of attribution erupts from the strained language in *Owl's Clover* and arrests attention on the subject that has been central in Stevens's writing of this period: the relationship of poet to reader, especially the reader as typically characterized in his poetry both as a listener and as one of the mob.

Identifying poetry with the apostrophe and apostrophe's agent "Behold" is not an uncommon strategy for a lyric poet, but imagining apostrophe as a volcano toys with that attribution in ways that undermine and intensify its force. If, as Jonathan Culler claims, "to apostrophize is to will a state of affairs, to attempt to call it into being by asking inanimate objects to bend themselves to your desire," then to identify the apostrophe with the volcano unites creation and destruction, equates animation with violence.[6]

The volcano is one of Stevens's favorite locations for poetry and writing, as we recall from "A Postcard from the Volcano." Yet its violence seems at odds with the animation intended by the poet in apostrophe. In this oxymoronic figure, Stevens expresses more than his discouragement with the poetry readers among the socialists; he attempts to find a place for the poet among the revolutionaries. If, as he says, "At a time of severely practical requirements, the world of the imagination looks like something distorted," (L 371) in fact the distortion or "deformation" of art will coincide with a radically disruptive social and political atmosphere. The "volcano Apostrophe" may be dormant, as the future in the poem that "never comes," but when it erupts it is more truly explosive than anything the hot-air social orator can imagine, "he that / Confounds all opposites and spins a sphere" "With a tendency to bulge as it floats away" (OP 93–94). The "volcano Apostrophe" of the poet neither bulges nor floats away; rather it erupts and animates the new world, and, in this, it resembles the revolutionaries, the truly explosive and distorting element in the "concentric mobs."

"A Duck for Dinner" goes on to elaborate the role of the poet among the masses:

> Ethereal compounder, pater patriae,
> Great mud-ancestor, oozer and Abraham,
> Progenitor wearing the diamond crown of crowns,
> He from whose beard the future springs, elect.
> More of ourselves in a world that is more our own. (OP 95)

Unlike the confounding orator, the compounding poet assumes a paternal role, taking up the task of nurturing from the maternal "celestial paramours" of "Mr. Burnshaw and the Statue" and looking forward to the "subman" of Part V, "Sombre Figuration," of Owl's Clover, whom Stevens describes as another parental figure:

> He was born within us as a second self,
> A self of parents who have never died,
> Whose lives return, simply, upon our lips,
> Their words and ours. (OP 97)

The subman represents the imagination as the subconscious, as Stevens notes (L 373), but it is the subconscious associated with memory, the mother of the muses, and with the generative and parental nature of memory. Stevens says, "We fear because we remember" (L 373), and it is this subconscious fear that must be assuaged by the parental muse that fosters it. So the poet is a conservator of the past as well as an explosive force for the future. Litz calls him "the hero in an age 'grown weary of the man that thinks'" (226).

The muse as interior paramour has dominated critical discussions of Stevens, but the parental and family muses, mother and father, "sister and solace, brother and delight," form a recurrent motif in his poetry of this period at a time when Stevens was seeking an accommodation with the masses he imagined as an audience. The need he projected on them for nourishment and sustenance overwhelmed the Romantic poet's conventional need to be aroused and impassioned. Clearly, this parental muse also fulfilled Stevens's own deepest imaginative longing. He himself lived every day in a world of "severely practical requirements," and thus he could recognize the repression of the imagination in that world.

The search for parental nurturing persists in "Sombre Figuration" as the subman, that self constantly nourished by undying parents, shades into the portent, another "anthropomorphic mythical creation," as Vendler calls these figures (*On Extended Wings*, 87), which is both a place and a time, a menace and a solace. Stevens writes, it "may itself be memory" "And memory's lord is the lord of prophecy" (OP 99). The portent is then also a nurturer, a caretaker of the past and itself a protector of the future. "A wandering orb upon a path grown clear," the portent seems to also "teach a fusky alphabet" (OP 99).

Owl's Clover does not rest in the company of this double lord of memory and prophecy. Like all children of doting parents, the reader and the poet himself, as part of that community of readers, can stand only so much solace. "Sombre Figuration" ends, and ends *Owl's Clover*, on this note of rebellion in

> a passion merely to be
> For the gaudium of being, Jocundus instead
> Of the black-blooded scholar, the man of the cloud, to be
> The medium man among other medium men. (OP 101)

So, in a gesture familiar from the ending of *The Comedian as the Letter C*, the poem ends with a "fling of the cloak " but "the cloak to be clipped." The medium man reasserts himself as Stevens reaches out of the poem toward Stanley Burnshaw for whom he has redefined the turmoil in the middle ground as a turmoil of the present against the burden of the past and the promise of the future. It is a turmoil between a mob that does not want to be nurtured by the past and future and a poet who conceives of his role as animating that mob, of calling into being by the "volcano Apostrophe" a better world.

In his direct address to a particular reader as well as in his stated concern to apply poetry to social issues, Stevens reveals a conception of an audience that his academic critics have tended to overlook. Bloom minimizes Stevens's efforts to address a leftist audience, claiming that "Mr. Burnshaw and the Statue" "collapses into a hysteria of bad wit" and finds the poem impressive only where "Stevens is able to repress his social and poetic anxieties into his own variety of the American Sublime" (118). Vendler admits that it was probably not possible "in the thirties to pass over the relation of the poet to the convulsions of the social order," but she asserts that the theme did not suit Stevens (*On Extended Wings* 118). Marjorie Perloff is even more adamant about Stevens's *"aesthetic detachment"* from society.[7]

Stevens himself confirmed these critics' views of the kind of audience he imagined in "The Noble Rider and the Sound of Words," a talk he gave at Princeton University in 1941 at the behest, indirectly, of his wealthy friend Henry Church. He claimed that every poet had an instinct to address himself to someone, and, to that audience and in that atmosphere, he tailored his instinct accordingly, writing, "It is of the essence of that instinct, and it seems to amount to an instinct, that it should be to an elite, not to a drab but to a woman with the hair of a pythoness, not to a chamber of commerce but to a gallery of one's own" (NA 29). It is probably correct to assume that Stevens would not have considered Mr. Burnshaw one of his own.

Moreover, Stevens acknowledged there his agreement with Charles Mauron that "the artist transforms us into epicures," that he gives "life whatever savor it possesses," and that the "poetic process is psychologically an escapist process" (NA 30). Earlier, in writing about the same subject to Henry Church, Stevens admitted that "poetry is, after all, the field of exceptional people," and then goes on to state:

> Again, if it is objected that this is carrying humanism to a point beyond which it ought to be carried in time of so much socialistic agitation, the answer must be that humanism is one thing and socialism is another, and that the mere act of distinguishing between the two should be helpful to preserve humanism and possibly to benefit socialism. (L 278)

But the serenity of these convictions about the distinction between humanism and socialism, odd categories that approximate poetry and politics, is not evident in the poetry Stevens was writing during this period and published in *Parts of a World* in 1942.

In this volume of poetry, as even his earliest reviewers noticed, he extended and deepened his concern with society.[8] Recently, David Bromwich has pointed to the debate in *Parts of a World* between two versions of pragmatism in which Stevens gradually shifts from an allegiance to Nietzsche's superman to James's tough-minded world-maker, and he claims, "One effect, then, of Stevens's engagement with the pragmatic idea of world-making, was to show how a personal reading of life might include a concern with his fellow readers."[9]

Bromwich argues that in his portrait of the common soldier in "Examination of the Hero in a Time of War," Stevens closed the distance between misery and the sort of mastery he had once supposed to exist by contrast with it, and he claims that such a contraction could occur only when the whole life of the community was in question. Bromwich concludes, "This is another way of saying that the most pronounced anti-Nietzschean moment of his poetry involves a certain sacrifice of his own inventions" (20). But, as we shall see, in the conclusion of the poem Stevens reclaims some of those inventions. He seems in the end simply unwilling to sacrifice certain imaginative extravagances.

Stevens's interest in the community and in his fellow readers had not begun in *Parts of a World*. The shifts in that volume owe their inception to the considerable interest Stevens evidenced in the 1930s in Communism and in a potential audience for poetry on the left. Common to both decades is a parental muse, fostering a poet who would nourish and sustain his audience.

"Examination of the Hero in a Time of War" is the poet's inquiry into his own imaginative resources "in the presence of the violent reality of war" when "consciousness takes the place of the imagination," as Stevens said in his prose statement on the poetry of war. In such a time, the hero is not so much an imaginative as a public creation. The public knows the old aggrandizement of the hero, "Creature of / Ten times ten times dynamite " (273), and "They are sick of each old romance " (274). Yet in their desire for a new version of the hero, the flat statement that "The common man is the common hero" does not quite satisfy them either. Even the poet remains unsatisfied and asks, "Unless we believe in the hero, what is there / To believe?" (275).

Stevens enjoins the poet to create his own hero: "Devise. Make him of mud, / For every day." The hero will be "of summer's / Imagination, the golden rescue: / The bread and wine of the mind, permitted / In an ascetic room " (275). Even if, as Stevens goes on to write, the hero will be "the extremest power / Living and being about us and being / Ours, like a familiar companion " this hero will give, as the poet must, whatever savor life has. His "bread and wine" will nourish us even in a time of war with its ascetic imaginative tendencies.

The problem with the hero is that he nourishes an imagination that falsifies the consciousness of war. He is soon "Painted by mad-men, seen as magic, / Leafed out in adjectives as private / And peculiar and appropriate glory " (277). And, in return, the hero gets drunk on his own bread and wine:

> Hip, hip, hurrah. Eternal morning . . .
> Flesh on the bones. The skeleton throwing
> His crust away eats of this meat, drinks
> Of this tabernacle, this communion,
> Sleeps in the sun no thing recalling. (278)

Feeding on the hero-worship that his mere existence inspires in a time of war, this hero is one effort on the poet's part to suggest how consciousness becomes inflated by a public imagination in wartime. Even in peacetime, the imagination had its dangerous moments, as Stevens suggests in *Notes Toward a Supreme Fiction* when he admits: "so poisonous / / Are the ravishments of truth, so fatal to / The truth itself " (381). And the poet no sooner reduces the hero than the hero enlarges himself or is enlarged by the public willingness to "nourish ourselves on crumbs of whimsy" (278), to worship "the human / Accelerations that seem inhuman " (279). The poem's speaker attempts to hold the hero to the literal, not the allegorical, by fiat, but he works against not only his own but the imagination of the masses:

> These letters of him for the little,
> The imaginative, ghosts that dally
> With life's salt upon their lips and savor
> The taste of it, secrete within them
> Too many references. (279)

Although Stevens tries to "Destroy all references" by acknowledging that the "hero is his nation" (279), nonetheless the public, this nation in its "thousand crystals' chiming voices" will not stop its hymns for the hero. He writes, "After the hero, the familiar / Man makes the hero artificial." But he concludes "Examination of the Hero in a Time of War" by returning to the desire for the hero:

> How did we come to think that autumn
> Was the veritable season, that familiar
> Man was the veritable man? So
> Summer, jangling the savagest diamonds and
> Dressed in its azure-doubled crimsons,
> May truly bear its heroic fortunes
> For the large, the solitary figure. (281)

For Bromwich, the light of the hero here is "an elegiac after-glow" (23). But summer "jangling" its diamonds recalls the "Ethereal compounder, pater patriae," "Progenitor wearing the diamond crown of crowns" in "A Duck for Dinner" (OP 95), whom Stevens identifies as the "artist, that is to say, the man of imagination, . . . the patriarch wearing the diamond crown of crowns, that is: the crown of life, as compared with the starless crown with which THE GREENEST CONTINENT concluded" (L 372).

Bromwich has his seasons mixed up. The summer-artist comes before, not after, the fall-familiar man; nurturing, not elegizing, an imaginative apprehension of the hero. Although Bromwich admits that Stevens never gave up his interest in the Nietzschean hero, he overlooks the extent to which Stevens associated his own summertime interest in "heroic fortunes" with those of his fellow readers. It was *their* hero-worship, not his own, that he attempted unsuccessfully to deflate in "Examination of the Hero in a Time of War." The hero, like the poet, is a nurturer of fantasies and ideals, and, in examining the hero, Stevens could also explain how hard it is for the "man-sun" as poet as well as hero to restrain himself to the "man-man."

The war hero was more useful to Stevens than the Marxist or the old woman of the Depression had been as an allegorical figure because, although he represented as they did the common man, he was always capable in the public imagination of "brave quickenings" (279). The hero "Acts in reality, adds nothing / To what he does " (279). But his very existence makes others add their chiming voices and hymns of praise. He is both the perfect subject for the poet and an exemplar of the poet himself who adds nothing to reality and yet changes it. The common hero, like the poet, can never escape his audience, "a profane parade" by whom he is made a hero whether he wills it or not, as the poet is made in his readers.

This connection between poet and hero is made fast in the note to the soldier that forms the epilogue of *Notes Toward a Supreme Fiction*. There Stevens says, "there is a war between the mind / And sky," "a war that never ends. / / Yet it depends on yours " (407). Although the soldier's war ends, and "after it you return," the poet says to the soldier, he goes on to announce, "The soldier is poor without the poet's lines" (407). The epilogue concludes:

> How simply the fictive hero becomes the real;
> How gladly with proper words the soldier dies,
> If he must, or lives on the bread of faithful speech. (408)

Here, the bread and wine on which the hero nourishes the crowd is transformed into the poet's words nourishing the hero. Poet-hero-community are bonded by words that must sustain them.

The relationship of common hero to common crowd and to the poet, longing to share their quite different attributes and also kinship in their family union, absorbed Stevens's imagination in these years and encouraged him to recast the poet's familial role from parent to brother. In "Chocorua to Its Neighbor," Stevens takes up again the image of the "highest man" that he had imagined in "Examination of the Hero in a Time of War." "He rose because men wanted him to be," Stevens has the mountain Chocorua, the poem's speaker, state, although the mountain goes on to qualify itself as Stevens had done in the earlier poem:

> They wanted him by day to be, image,
> But not the person, of their power, thought,
> But not the thinker, large in their largeness, beyond
> Their form, beyond their life, yet of themselves,
> Excluding by his largeness their defaults. (299)

Although Chocorua asserts that there are others like him and identifies them as leaders ("captain squalid", the "great / Cardinal", the "scholar") and as parental figures (the "mother"), he finally identifies this "eminence" as:

Not father, but bare brother, megalfrere,
Or by whatever boorish name a man
Might call the common self, interior fons.
And fond, the total man of glubbal glub,
Political tramp with an heraldic air, (300–301)

This "eminence" is "an enkindling, where / He is, the air changes and grows fresh to breathe." He grows out of the hero: "Integration for integration, the great arms / Of the armies, the solid men, make big the fable " (301). But he is the "brother," the "common self," even when he is also, by Chocorua's testimony, "the companion of presences / Greater than mine " (302).

Trying to settle on the relationship of this "eminence" to the common, Stevens has Chocorua look toward another poem, admitting that "He was the figure in / A poem for Liadoff, the self of selves" (297). In "Two Tales of Liadoff," Stevens first presents Liadoff practicing "epi-tones" on a black piano while the townspeople crowd into a rocket and blow themselves up. Far from fiddling as Rome burned, Liadoff appears to be responding directly, if synaesthetically, to the common fate: "what they said, as they fell, / Was repeated by Liadoff in a narration / Of incredible colors ex, ex and ex and out?" (347). In the second tale of Liadoff, the town's violent activity is reduced; "the rocket was only an inferior cloud," the speaker realizes. But then he must also admit that Liadoff's playing was equally inferior, his "epi-tones" "Voluble but archaic and hard to hear" (347). "There was no difference between the town / And him," the speaker says, indicating perhaps the inevitable intercourse between the poet and his town, between the common and the poetic imagination.

But Stevens was not finished with this theme. In "Credences of Summer," in an effort to celebrate "midsummer" when "the mind lays by its trouble" he locates what "must comfort the heart's core against / Its false disasters—" first in the familial: "these fathers standing round, / These mothers touching, speaking, being near " (372). Beyond that, he places it in the communal "Axis of everything, green's apogee / / And happiest folk-land, mostly marriage-hymns " (373). But the speaker does not long remain content with such content. He questions the relation of the one to the many, of the leader to the nation, of the son to his town:

And is the queen humble as she seems to be,

The charitable majesty of her whole kin?
The bristling soldier, weather-foxed, who looms
In the sunshine is a filial form and one
Of the land's children, easily born, its flesh
Not fustian. The more than casual blue

Contains the year and other years and hymns
And people, without souvenir. The day
Enriches the year, not as embellishment.
Stripped of remembrance, it displays its strength—
The youth, the vital son, the heroic power. (374–375)

Both Vendler and Bloom find Stevens's confidence here in the day, the youth, in the one as enrichment for the many, a blustering and false solution (*On Extended Wings*, 238 and 248). As an answer to the questioning of the one, it does not long serve, and Stevens eventually retreats to that point where "what is possible / Replaces what is not " (376). Even there, however, he "supposes" a relationship between the one and the many as:

> The trumpet supposes that
> A mind exists, aware of division, aware
> Of its cry as clarion, its diction's way
> As that of a personage in a multitude:
> Man's mind grown venerable in the unreal. (377)

This "personage in a multitude" is strangely aloof, not one of the folk in the "happiest folk-land" but a solitary in the unreal. So too, the "cock bright" of Canto IX that Bloom sees as a parody of the trumpet, casting doubt on the qualified raptures of earlier cantos (251). The question remains, however, and, like the trumpet, the bird elicits from the poet the same concern for a potential audience. First addressed as "Soft, civil bird," the bird is seen as part of its town, a "civil" and civic bird. But the bird even on its bean pole has a vantage point removed from the civil center, and may, the poet suggests,

>   detect
> Another complex of other emotions, not

So soft, so civil, and you make a sound,
Which is not part of the listener's own sense. (377)

So the civil bird and his civil listener are separated.

The concluding canto removes the scene from the real world of bird and bean pole to the theater, where the whole question of performer and listener is reformulated by making the listeners the performers or, rather, presenting "the personae of summer" as "characters / Of an inhuman author" (377). They are "mottled," decked out as fools in "the manner of the time / Part of the mottled mood of summer's whole, / / In which the characters speak because they want / To speak " (378) and not because they represent their author or address a particular audience. This fantasy of unauthored characters "speaking / Their parts as in a youthful happiness" reinstates the opening celebratory mood, but as a play and not as "the very thing and nothing else," not as a real life with those parental figures that "comfort the heart's core against / Its false disasters" (372). The poem ends then in the false freedom of the present, the "gaudium of being," that concluded "Sombre Figuration" with the same devil-may-care spirit.

Developing this mood and its theatrical metaphor, the later poem, "In a Bad Time," recasts the parental comforts of the heart's core into a questioning of the self, imagined as the "beggar" but nonetheless a performer who must "strut bare boards": "What has he that becomes his heart's strong core?" (426) The answer comes:

He has his poverty and nothing more.
His poverty becomes his heart's strong core—
A forgetfulness of summer at the pole. (426)

To this "muse of misery " the speaker urges, "Speak loftier lines. / Cry out, 'I am the purple muse.' Make sure / The audience beholds you, not your gown" (427). Bereft of parental comforts himself and living in a world where he "gazes on calamity" and "thereafter he belongs to it," this beggar creates for himself and for his audience a new and royal lineage. Neither he nor the audience can be disinherited for long, and yet the heritage here is a false genealogy, "leafed out in adjectives," a separation of the dissembling poet from his community. Stevens had descended a long way from Hoon's purple descent and confidence that "I was the world in which I walked, and what I saw / Or heard or felt came not but from myself" (65). This later "purple muse" must make his boast against his poverty and in the presence of an audience that will not fail to notice the disparity between his boasts and his gown.

The poet and his audience continued to concern Stevens, and in "Reply to Papini" he excuses the poet from that ancient, lofty, and public role, urged in a letter of Celestin VI, Pope to the poets, quoted by Giovanni Papini and used here as the poem's epigraph: *"In all the solemn moments of human history . . . poets rose to sing the hymn of victory or the psalm of supplication. . . . Cease, then, from being the astute calligraphers of congealed daydreams, the hunters of cerebral phosphorescences"* (446). Stevens opens, "Poor procurator, why do you ask someone else / To say what Celestin should say for himself?" For Stevens, the poet, unlike the pope, does not "stand there making orotund consolations. / He shares the confusions of intelligence" (446). He is again one with his community, and he does not write hymns of victory because "a politics / Of property is not an area / / For triumphals" (447). But the poet is, as part of the brotherhood of this community, also the son of experience, albeit a special son:

> This is the centre. The poet is
> The angry day-son clanging at its make:
>
> The satisfaction underneath the sense,
> The conception sparkling in still obstinate thought. (448)

In the counterpoint between the Holy Father and the poet, Stevens defends the son against the father's outmoded expectations, presenting him as one who "Increases the aspects of experience" by anticipating the future. His anger is not the pope's anger at his flippancy but an impatience with the "make," the "conception sparkling" that he cannot quite forge out of "obstinate thought."

Stevens's interest in his audience outlasted his response to Stanley Burnshaw and the critics of the thirties who argued that he was too removed from social issues to appeal to them, and it outlasted his meditations on how in wartime consciousness took the place of imagination. If, as Stevens said to the mobs of the Depression, imagination would seem a distortion and if to those same mobs during wartime the work of the imagination appeared to be a struggle with heroic fact, still the poet worked on, responding to these changes and making those changed conditions respond to him.

In Stevens's later years, he was finally accorded the public attention that he had made the subject of some of his most strained verse. It is in these later and occasional speeches, accepting the awards that were given to him, that Stevens had his final say on the ever-changing role of the poet in the world. He maintained his earliest sense that the poet is nourished by his time. Accepting the National Book Award in 1951, he said:

> There is about every poet a vast world of other people from which he derives himself and through himself his poetry. What he derives from his generation he returns to his generation, as best he can. His poetry is theirs and theirs is his, because of the interaction between the poet and his time, which publishers, booksellers and printers do more than any others in the world to broaden and deepen. (OP 254)

In 1955, accepting the National Book Award, he again considered the poet in his relation to his audience, claiming that when the poet comes out of his cavern to confront a great crowd, he must first "put on the strength of his particular calling as a poet, to address himself to what Rilke called the mighty burden of poetry" (OP 289). The poet's "belief in the greatness of poetry is a vital part of its greatness, an implicit part of the belief of others in its greatness" (OP 289). From his own writing, he claimed to have learned of "the greatness that lay beyond, the power over the mind that lies in the mind itself, the incalculable expanse of the imagination as it reflects itself in us and about us" (OP 289). Although he admitted that awards and honors had nothing to do with the work of the imagination, still he accepted them "as tokens of the community that exists between poetry on the one hand and men and women on the other" (OP 289).

Yet, he found even in these years of public attention that he remained still riveted to "the conception sparkling in still obstinate thought," the "angry day-son clanging at its make," and in accepting the Gold Medal from the Poetry Society of America, he pointed to that space:

> There is no doubt that poetry does in fact exist for the thoughtful young man in Basel or the votary in Naples. The Marxians, and for that matter a good many other people, think of it in terms of its social impact. In one direction it moves toward the ultimate things of pure poetry; in the other it speaks to great numbers of people of themselves, making extraordinary texts and memorable music out of what they feel and know. In both cases it makes itself manifest in a kind of speech that comes from secrecy. Its position is always an inner position, never certain, never fixed. It is to be found beneath the poet's word and deep within the reader's eye in those chambers in which the genius of poetry sits alone with her candle in a moving solitude. (OP 253)

In this valedictory to his long and fruitful career, Stevens turned to that paradox that had also served Dickinson as the link between poet and reader: "'Secrets' is a daily word / Yet does not exist" (P 1385), she wrote. The kind of speech that comes from secrecy never really comes fully out of the dark. The words of the poet cannot quite bring the "conception sparkling" out of "obstinate thought," nor can the reader fully focus what lies deep within his vision. And yet, in the effort to overreach themselves, poet and reader engage in that same creative and self-engendering act by which they are reborn in words. The genius of poetry that "sits alone with her candle in a moving solitude" is the maternal muse that elicits their rebirth, nurtures their adventures in "the incalculable expanse of the imagination as it reflects itself in us and about us."

Stevens's devotion to that muse had never faltered in the course of his career. Although he had famously called her his "interior paramour," this muse is more frequently figured in parental and familial metaphors. In this use, Stevens drew on a rich literary history, but, beyond that, he relied on a fundamental conceptual structure that underlies linguistics, philosophy, and anthropology, as Mark Turner points out in an interdisciplinary study of kinship metaphors, *Death is the Mother of Beauty*. Turner claims that "One way to understand the abstract notion *metaphor* is in terms of what we know about *kinship*."[10] Although, as literary critics, we may think of the kinship metaphors as distinctive, individual creations, Turner suggests that, in fact, kinship metaphors reveal a mental model used to produce and understand certain kinds of language about mind and that kinship metaphors provide basic metaphors we use to understand mental creation.[11]

Thus, both Stevens's inventiveness and his awareness that he had never been inventive enough to capture "the huge, high harmony that sounds / A little and a little, suddenly, / By means of a separate sense " (440) rely on the basic conceptual pattern of kinship, the confidence that "The essential poem begets the others " (441). The "giant on the horizon" is not "Too exactly labelled," and yet he is exactly labelled as "a close, parental magnitude, / At the centre on the horizon, concentrum, grave / And prodigious person, patron of origins " (443).

The "parental magnitude" nourished Stevens's imagination from the beginning when he could summon into being that "Sister and mother and diviner love." There, he hoped both to inherit her strengths and to overcome her, to get back from her "The imagination that we spurned and crave" (88). As he continued to write, he grew more conscious of his own parental role and could exclaim in "The Lack of Repose," "What a thing it is to believe that / One understands, in the intense disclosures / Of a parent in the French sense." (303).

As he grew old, he did not return to childhood, but he came to frame his imaginative need in questions about the parental: "Who is my father in this world, in this house / At the spirit's base?" he could ask in "The Irish Cliffs of Moher" (501). And he urged, "Go back to a parent before thought, before speech, / At the head of the past " (501). This, he imagined "is not landscape, full of the somnambulations / Of poetry"; "This is my father or, maybe, / It is as he was, / / A likeness, one of the race of fathers: earth / And sea and air " (502). The parent as time and place and time and place as a parent to the somnambulant poet is a basic kinship pattern by which literary and common language understands its growth and being.

One of the strangest uses of the kinship metaphor is "Madame La Fleurie" where Stevens jumbles many of the elements he had used to describe the poet and his reader and the poet as a reader: the glass, darkness, the parent text. He writes:

> He looked in a glass of the earth and thought he lived in it.
> Now, he brings all that he saw into the earth, to the waiting parent.
> His crisp knowledge is devoured by her, beneath a dew. (507)

The poem concludes in this terrible address to the mother:

> The black fugatos are strumming the blackness of black . . .
> The thick strings stutter the finial gutturals.
> He does not lie there remembering the blue-jay, say the jay.
> His grief is that his mother should feed on him, himself and what he saw,
> In that distant chamber, a bearded queen, wicked in her dead light. (507)

Among the attributes of kinship patterns is the inheritance of characteristics and belief, and Stevens had presented the poet as nurtured by the parent in "Anatomy of Monotony":

> If from the earth we came, it was an earth
> That bore us as a part of all the things

It breeds and that was lewder than it is.
Our nature is her nature. (107)

"Madame La Fleurie" has simply reversed that process, transfering the
attributes of the child to the parent. And yet we see how uneasy we are in
any deliberate reversal of kinship relations. We may inherit from parents
their nurturing instincts, but when we pretend to endow parents with the
need for those same instincts, even when we collude with the parents, we
are stunned by the inappropriateness of the interchange. The poet's grief
is understated horror at finding that the mother too has desires.

   This "wicked" queen and progenitor made lewd by an imagining of her
lewdness is a bold articulation of Stevens's imaginative need for comfort at
the end and the deep emotional poverty and undernourishment of a lifetime's desire. His late poems were not all so bitter, and in "The Sail of
Ulysses" he locates

   In the generations of thought, man's sons
   And heirs are powers of the mind,
   His only testament and estate. (OP 129)

Finally, in "The Sail of Ulysses," Stevens identifies himself with that more
potent parental figure, the woman as sibyl, the woman as progenerative,
"the sibyl of the self" "whose jewel found / At the exactest central of the
earth / Is need" (OP 130). And "For this, the sibyl's shape / Is a blind thing
fumbling for its form" (OP 130). Thus Stevens returns mystery to the
female, the progenerative need to create which can never be mastered, can
only be inherited.

Chapter 8

"So summer comes in the end to these few stains": Conclusion

"That is solemn we have ended / Be it but a Play" Dickinson advises, opening a poem with an uncharacteristic reverence that she subverts almost immediately in the poem's conclusion which reads on, "or later, / Parting with a World / We have understood for better / Still to be explained" (P 934). Endings are not conclusions in Dickinson, and their solemnity is easily undercut by the promise of something made better because still to be explained.[1] This opening of the ending may be, as Cristanne Miller suggests, a nineteenth-century anticipation of possibilities for an *écriture féminine*, but, as it is repeated in the mitigations of Stevens's endings, we might consider it here by way of conclusion as an attribute of that lyric impulse to add rather than add up and a possible source of the tension between the lyric genre and a teleological American culture.[2]

Because Dickinson's penchant for writing beyond the ending, for imagining that "This World is not Conclusion," is most evident in her obsession with the subject of death, it is generally discussed in the context of her religious beliefs and doubts. But, as Robert Weisbuch has astutely noted, death is not "so much a theme with assignable topics of rational discourse" "as a raw material for speculations, even for speculations about the limits of speculation" (79). Weisbuch goes on to develop his idea by organizing this raw material in a typological interpretation of death that indicates Dickinson's reliance on and departure from the Christian tradition of typology.[3]

His insight might serve as well to open an inquiry into how, as Dickinson began to develop the American lyric poem through an experimentation with form, it became the first expression of a pragmatism that would replace Romanticism. In its resistance to the ending, Dickinson's lyric acknowledges the contingency of starting points and the impossibility of the end. The Romantic project of secularizing Christianity, of discovering new vocabularies to bring hidden secrets to light, is here surrendered to the pragmatic possibility of describing the world as it appears, neither hidden nor secret, but simply the world as it appears to one unique individual.

In this context, the example of Wallace Stevens is useful because his poems also evince a reluctance to end. However, what is considered a question of religious or philosophical speculation in criticism of Dickinson's poetry is treated as a matter of style in Stevens criticism. Helen Vendler, for example, has suggested the variety of stylistic forms by which his poems evade or mitigate conclusion.[4] It may be, however, that neither religion nor style is sufficient to explain the problematic of ending in these two poets. The ending may be, rather, the point at which these two poets wrest imaginative literature from the teleological ambition of American cultural history. Dickinson's doubts and what Vendler calls Stevens's moods are evidence of a creative energy that insists on itself and will not be drained into the moral purpose of American literature. Their endings can never be final because, as Rorty says, "The world is out there, but descriptions of the world are not" ("The Contingency of Language," 5), and the poet's efforts at description can never get completed.

Going on, moving from contingency to contingency, will be a way of proceeding in the lyric, as Stevens suggests in "The Ultimate Poem Is Abstract": "If the day writhes, it is not with revelations. / One goes on asking questions." (429). The continuity of the questions is made necessary by a lack of revelations that allows the poet to create in the lyric poem his own momentum of arbitrary revelations, and he can conclude simply from his ongoing questioning: "That, then, is one / Of the categories. So said, this placid space / / Is changed. It is not so blue as we thought" (429). Stevens plays here with a poetic version of Kant's categorical imperative, writing as though the maxim from which he writes were to become through his will a universal law of nature.

To achieve this end, Stevens uses the nonspecific "that" and "it"; these open-ended terms summarize what has never been detailed and leave the poet free to create categories, to change the space he occupies, to revise his own thinking, and not to represent a preexisting world, to match his thoughts to an origin outside themselves. Stevens's use of the nonspecific "it" is reminiscent of Dickinson in such poems as "It was not Death" (P 510) where "it" remains mysterious and significant and capable of endlessly proliferating rather than of precisely distinguishing. This endless process is further detailed as Stevens goes on in "The Ultimate Poem Is Abstract" to elaborate through abstractions on the poem's avoidance of both a conclusion and an ultimate end:

> It is an intellect
> Of windings round and dodges to and fro,

Writhings in wrong obliques and distances,
Not an intellect in which we are fleet: present
Everywhere in space at once, cloud-pole

Of communication. It would be enough
If we were ever, just once, at the middle, fixed
In This Beautiful World Of Ours and not as now,

Helplessly at the edge, enough to be
Complete, because at the middle, if only in sense,
And in that enormous sense, merely enjoy. (429–430)

But what is "it"? Would "it" ever be enough to satisfy the poet's will to multiply references: "It is not so blue", "It is an intellect", and "It would be enough"? The "lecturer / On This Beautiful World of Ours" may compose himself from a fixed position, but such composure and completion can never satisfy the poet. The poet can never "merely enjoy" except in his "windings round."

And what would it mean to "merely enjoy"? Enjoy what? The ending here trails off even as it tracks back to the "middle, fixed" where it would be "enough to be / Complete". The language doubles on itself, canceling its references. To be at the middle and at the end simultaneously, to be enough and complete at the same time, is impossible. Even the repetitions here work to dissolve meanings, as the enigmatic and nondirectional "only in sense" is changed into the abstraction, "in that enormous sense". To be either "complete" or "at the middle" "if only in sense" may be to live a purely sensual life, reduced to the senses, and there to "merely enjoy" mere sensual pleasures, or it may be to make a sense out of the world that allows one to enjoy it. Either way, the ending opens out rather than closes the subject.

Like Dickinson's, Stevens's lyric impulse is not an intellect in which he is fleet nor does it eventuate in a form in which, however brief, he can be fleet. But it is a form perfectly suited, in its writhings and dodgings to and fro, to challenge fixities of identity, of language, and of audience. Dickinson uses it to protect, while still inquiring into, the privacy of the self that had been so violated by the ideology of self-reliance in nineteenth-century America. For Stevens, "lol-lolling the endlessness of poetry" (458) is a way of being in the world, of using whatever is at hand (here, a quotation from Lorca sent in a letter by one friend added to an anecdote in a letter from another friend), in order to hold off the final knowledge which would be death and death to poetry: "as if to know became / The fatality of seeing things too well " (459).[5]

The lyric is a process of incompletion for Stevens. It does not marmore-alize objects or states of mind; rather it provides him the power to "make the visible a little hard / / To see," as he claims in "The Creations of Sound" (311). It is a way of adding to experience. The poet as "secondary expositor" is neither original nor originating, but additional. It may be that the poet's images are merely an addition and an artifice, as in "Add This to Rhetoric" when again the unspecified "it" "is posed and it is posed. / But in nature it merely grows." Or the lyric may indicate that despite all poetic contri-butions, nature is what is added as "To-morrow when the sun, / For all your images, / Comes up as the sun " (198). The poet may want "the figure and not / An evading metaphor " (199). But his advice remains: "Add this. It is to add " (199).

Adding, dodging to and fro, Stevens in the lyric has the freedom of the "angel in his cloud" circling around without actually acceding to a center in *Notes Toward a Supreme Fiction*, who, he writes:

Leaps downward through evening's revelations, and
On his spredden wings, needs nothing but deep space,
Forgets the gold centre, the golden destiny. (404)

That destiny, so much desired and so far removed from twentieth-century poets, could be forgotten in a lyric form of endlessly elaborating anecdotes and, in being so forgotten, could be seen as part of the "rodomontadean emptiness" of the past. Stevens uses the movement in space, the contin-gencies of the lyric, to direct attention to that present of which he imagines himself a part, but only a part, never—even there—the "gold centre."

The poet's part is to add to experience, as Stevens points out in discuss-ing the difference between poetry and philosophy in "A Collect of Phi-losophy." There, he claims the poet and philosopher are united in "their habit of probing for an integration," but separated in the kind of integra-tions for which they search. He distinguishes the two:

The philosopher searches for an integration for its own sake, . . . the poet searches for an integration that shall be not so much sufficient in itself as sufficient for some quality that it possesses, such as its insight, its evocative power or its appearance in the eye of the imagination. The philosopher intends his integration to be fateful; the poet intends his to be effective. (OP 276)

The distinction is made more clear in Stevens's claim that the "philosopher's native sphere is *only* a metaphysical one. The poet's native sphere is the sphere of which du Bellay wrote, 'my village . . . my own small house'" (OP 277) (italics added). Forgetting the "gold centre " Stevens's poet, like his angel, can also evade "*only* a metaphysical" sphere and reside instead in his own world where his aim is that of the pragmatist: "to be effective."

To be effective is to go on; it is decidedly not to be fateful, final, finished. For Stevens, the endlessness of poetry is a way of being in the world, an assurance like Penelope's in "The World as Meditation" that "The barbarous strength within her would never fail" (521), and a belief like Georges Enesco's in the epigraph to that poem: "*J'ai passé trop de temps à travailler mon violon, à voyager. Mais l'exercice essentiel du compositeur—la méditation—rien ne l'a jamais suspendu en moi . . . Je vis un rêve permanent, qui ne s'arrête ni nuit ni jour* " (520). Such an activity could go on even beyond the end for Stevens who imagines in "The Plain Sense of Things" that "It is as if / We had come to an end of the imagination " and still can write, "Yet the absence of the imagination had / Itself to be imagined." (502–503).

Lyric poetry is, for Stevens, a conversation that continues. Even his envoi will be "genial," as Milton Bates points out in reviewing the mythology of self he finds in "Conversation with Three Women of New England."[6] In that poem, Stevens addresses what Bates considers each of his animae or modes of self: the idealist in quest of "Sole, single source and minimum patriarch" "in that ever-dark central"; the realist for whom "the capital things of the mind / Should be as natural as natural objects"; and the pragmatist who concludes, "The author of man's canons is man, / Not some outer patron and imaginer " (OP 134). Stevens concludes the poem with another "is it enough," a way of having a choice not between but of all such possibilities:

Or is it enough to have seen
And felt and known the differences we have seen
And felt and known in the colors in which we live,
In the excellences of the air we breathe,

The bouquet of being—enough to realize
That the sense of being changes as we talk,
That talk shifts the cycle of the scenes of kings? (OP 134–135)

This ever-changing "sense of being" is not frivolous nor does its resistance to finality and definitiveness derive from what Lentricchia identifies
rather broadly as the "culture's debunking feminization of poetry and its
concomitant masculinizing of economic activity" (222). It is rather the
means by which lyric poetry not only elicits but expresses the resistance of
American culture because such poetry will not verify the need of the culture
to have a purpose.[7] The teleological view of America, so dominant in the
culture from its Puritan origins onward, has no place in a lyric poem, and
the lyric poem has no place in that history.

The lyric poet is, as Stevens describes him, dilatory and perhaps without
purpose, but not feminized. He is an impoverished fearful figure, and not
the powerful activist hero of the marketplace. But, the "ephebe" of *Notes
Toward a Supreme Fiction*, for example, in his "attic window," his "mansard
with a rented piano" is, like the world around him, the day that writhes
without revelations, as Stevens addresses him, "You writhe and press / A
bitter utterance from your writhing, dumb" (384). Neither feminized, if we
mean by that term what Lentricchia seems to identify as frivolous and
nonessential, nor masculinized by economic endeavor, he is rather imaged
as the nonsexual tramp, a Charlie Chaplin figure in "that old coat, those
sagging pantaloons." Still, he has the poet's charge, as Stevens writes:

It is of him, ephebe, to make, to confect
The final elegance, not to console
Nor sanctify, but plainly to propound. (389)

In spite of his duty to confect elegance, he is seen in most guises as a figure
in need, a figure of desire. Even when he is addressed as Santayana "On the
threshold of heaven," "The human end in the spirit's greatest reach, / The
extreme of the known in the presence of the extreme / Of the unknown "
(508), he is seen as:

Impatient for the grandeur that you need

In so much misery; and yet finding it

Only in misery, the afflatus of ruin,
Profound poetry of the poor and of the dead. (509)

And, in "Final Soliloquy of the Interior Paramour," where he rests with his muse "and, for small reason, think / The world imagined is the ultimate good" the paramour says that they collect themselves:

Within a single thing, a single shawl
Wrapped tightly round us, since we are poor, a warmth,
A light, a power, the miraculous influence. (524)

The poverty of Stevens's poet seems ill-matched to his task "to confect / The final elegance " (389). Yet, elegance is the only cure for such poverty; it is the only way of avoiding the ending in misery. From "The Latest Freed Man" "Tired of the old descriptions of the world" (204) to "The Weeping Burgher" who would "come as belle design / Of foppish line" (61), the speakers in Stevens's poems have followed the advice of *The Man with the Blue Guitar* who says:

Throw away the lights, the definitions,
And say of what you see in the dark

That it is this or that it is that,
But do not use the rotted names. (183)

The "rotted names," the poverty of a miserable end, inspire him para-doxically to elegance. By contemplating other names, he allows himself to go on, to find a place for himself, to add to what he sees, as he does in "Botanist on Alp (No. 1)," which opens with the statements, "Panoramas are not what they used to be", "And apostrophes are forbidden on the funicular" (134). He may be abjected by this banishment of the Romantic painter and poet since he can also lament, "in Claude how near one was" "To the central composition, / The essential theme" (135). And, he does not appear to be certain that the decreation of the Romantic creation has led to anything, since he suspects, "the panorama of despair / Cannot be the specialty / Of this ecstatic air" (135). Yet it is in the addition of this language that the speaker moves out of dejection. The movement from "despair" through "specialty" to "ecstatic air" is a trick of sounds that lifts the poem from one range of experience to another. In the next poem, "Botanist on Alp (No. 2)," Stevens settles on the middle ground of delight between Romantic hope and Modernist despair. He writes:

Chant, O ye faithful, in your paths
The poem of long celestial death;

For who could tolerate the earth
Without that poem, or without

An earthier one, tum, tum-ti-tum,
As of those crosses, glittering,

And merely of their glittering,
A mirror of a mere delight? (136)

Not a mirror up to nature, but a poem that is "A mirror of a mere delight" composes in its repetitive sounds the addition that is art, the double of desire in its desiring. So "tum, tum-ti-tum " with its added beat, which seems at first just a way of marking time, proves to be a reproduction in sound of the same repetitive action that, in sight, might be mere glittering and that, in poetry, is the lyric poem. "Mere delight" in the crosses glittering in the sun on the convent roofs, even when the angels and believers are both gone, is a way of enduring by going on, by questioning, by finding a way of tolerating the earth.

Stevens's delight in contingency sets him apart from his contemporary Eliot, who, he felt, was always striving after perfection. In "The Creations of Sound," Stevens is moved to tell Eliot "that speech is not dirty silence / Clarified. It is silence made still dirtier" (311). Flawed words, stubborn sounds, dirtier silence, these are the sources of Stevens's creative urge, all that keep him tolerant in and of this earth.

And yet, in this Stevens seems to have abandoned the "final elegance" that he would have the poet "confect" in *Notes Toward a Supreme Fiction*. He may seem to, but his notion of elegance is quite other than that of "Mrs. Alfred Uruguay" who said, as she was riding up the mountain, "'I fear that elegance / Must struggle like the rest '"; "'I have said no / To everything, in order to get at myself'" (248–249). Like Dickinson's "Soft Cherubic Creatures," Mrs. Alfred Uruguay's denials are inadequate: "Her no and no made yes impossible" (249). In contrast to her is the "figure of capable imagination" going down the hill as she goes up. He is "A youth, a lover with phosphorescent hair, / Dressed poorly, arrogant of his streaming forces " (249). He is "Impatient":

> And, capable, created in his mind,
> Eventual victor, out of the martyrs' bones,
> The ultimate elegance: the imagined land. (250)

Elegance, then, for Stevens is not that false refinement of taste, not Mrs. Alfred Uruguay in her velvet dress. It is rather a matter of selection, of inclusion, of capacity, of capability. It is the arrogance of the poorly dressed who will pass by without notice the poverty of the overdressed who can "never be more / Than to be " (249). Such elegance is not "dirty speech / Clarified" (311), to return to Stevens's image of Eliot.

Eliot was, for Stevens, "a man / Too exactly himself " (310). "His poems are not of the second part of life" he could argue. Stevens preferred the poet as "an artificial man," "a secondary expositor," as I have noted earlier. In contrast to the philosopher whose probing is "deliberate," the probing of such a poet is "fortuitous" (OP 277). "The poet's native sphere, to speak more accurately, is what he can make of the world," Stevens claims (OP 278). It may be only by chance that he finds the "flawed words and stubborn sounds" and yet, Stevens argues, he works to create confidence in the world or, as he quotes from Jean Paulham: *la confiance que le poète fait naturellement— et nous invite à faire—au monde*" (OP 278). The poet does not work in such a way because he has confidence or because he is confident in himself or in his ability; rather he works because confidence in the world is a good working hypothesis. As an example of such a usable method, Stevens points to the posthumously published writings of Planck, the most convinced determinist, who came in the end to see that determinism could not be liberated from the human aptitude to foresee events, and thus, because the absolute could not be made independent of men, it had to be judged neither true nor false, but rather a good working hypothesis (OP 280).

In Stevens's poetry, the working hypothesis is an adding that does not require an adding up, two distinct activities for which he had two different figures. The one who wants to add up never gets the sum quite right: he is the "dark rabbi" of "Le Monocle de Mon Oncle" who "Observed, when young, the nature of mankind, / In lordly study "; he is Crispin as "a profitless / Philosopher, beginning in green brag" in *The Comedian as the Letter C*. He is one of those who "will get it straight one day at the Sorbonne" in *Notes Toward a Supreme Fiction*. These figures are always somehow off the mark. It is the one who adds without regard to the final sum who comes closest to the fullness that is himself. He is the self as "a rose rabbi" of "Le Monocle de Mon Oncle" who "pursued / And still pursue[s], the origin and course / Of love" and who until now "never knew / That fluttering things have so distinct a shade." He is Crispin "proving what he proves / Is nothing."

The poet who adds relies on the dependence of words on place, of finding the words for place, as Stevens suggests in commenting on the poet: "Up to the point at which he has found his subject, the state of vague receptivity in which he goes about resembles one part of something that is dependent on another part, which he is not quite able to specify" (OP 277). In the late poem "The Planet on the Table" the speaker says, "Ariel was glad he had written his poems. / They were of a remembered time / Or of something seen that he liked " (532). And he concludes:

> It was not important that they survive.
> What mattered was that they should bear
> Some lineament or character,
>
> Some affluence, if only half-perceived,
> In the poverty of their words,
> Of the planet of which they were part. (533)

The "affluence" of the planet and the "poverty" of words seem ill-suited to each other, imbalanced and nonresponsive. Stevens returns to that problem again in replying to the comment of Pope Celestin VI that poets used to "*sing the hymn of victory or the psalm of supplication*" and now are only "*the astute calligraphers of congealed daydreams*" (446). He writes, "Is Celestin dislodged? The way through the world / Is more difficult to find than the way beyond it." (446). Still, he adds, "The poet / / Increases the aspect of experience, / As in an enchantment, analyzed and fixed / / And final" (447–448). The "way through the world" is the twentieth-century poet's way, and no matter how impoverished he may be, he shares and adds to the affluence of the world.

Stevens writes in "The Bouquet":

The rose, the delphinium, the red, the blue,
Are questions of the looks they get. The bouquet,
Regarded by the meta-men, is quirked
And queered by lavishings of their will to see. (451)

"The bouquet is part of a dithering" to such men, but there is that other view of "A soldier, an officer," who "bumps the table. The bouquet falls on its side. / He walks through the house, looks around him and then leaves " (453). In a world of such a soldier, the poet must add that "The bouquet has slopped over the edge and lies on the floor " (453). It is he who will notice the excess even of disarray.

"Add this. It is to add," the lyric poet reminds us. Stevens liked summer in an age of autumnal poets. It is not that, in "The Beginning," he did not hear "the first tutoyers of tragedy / Speak softly, to begin with," or that he could not announce "So summer comes in the end to these few stains" (428, 427). It is rather that, for him, the poet in all seasons was there to "increase the aspect of experience." Even "After the leaves have fallen," and "A fantastic effort has failed," even then, Stevens could go on in "The Plain Sense of Things" to say, "all this / Had to be imagined as an inevitable knowledge, / Required, as a necessity requires " (503).

The "ultimate elegance" then returns finally in its other guise as simplicity. The poet, for all his apparent lol-lolling and endless elaborating, has been engaged in that most arduous effort of taking from complexity the simplest, most precise, and thus elegant, proof. His knowledge is "inevitable," "Required," and not frivolous or merely decorative.

Stevens fits into a literary tradition of pragmatism which Richard Rorty has defined, as I have noted before, as "the conscious need of the strong poet" "to come to terms with the blind impress which chance has given him and to make a self for himself by redescribing that impress in terms which are, if only marginally, his own."[8]

Dickinson's case is somewhat different. She wrote in an age in which she would never be regarded as a copy or replica and in which her own need to come to terms with the blind impress of chance was always in danger of being overwhelmed by the eccentricity of the chance that drew her first to poetry. Yet, unique as she imagined her own experience and special as she appeared to be, she had no way of proceeding except by offering an alternative description of the world to go along with the powerful description of what Emerson called the "centered mind."

As a woman, Dickinson had to be a pragmatist because she could never subscribe to any but her own description of the world. She anticipated the revolution in thinking that came toward the end of the nineteenth century for the male figures that Rorty discusses, in which it "became possible to see a new vocabulary not as something which was supposed to replace all other vocabularies, something which claimed to represent reality, but simply as one more vocabulary, one more human project, one person's chosen metaphoric." Among the men, it became possible, according to Rorty, "only when one's aim becomes an expanding repertoire of alternative descriptions rather than The One Right Description" (39–40). Slightly before those figures that Rorty discusses—Freud, James, Nietzsche—experienced that change in which the world and the self were de-divinized, Dickinson had to believe in order to write that neither the self nor the world is, as Rorty explains, "quasi persons, neither wants to be expressed or represented in a certain way" (40).

Redescribing the self in terms appropriate to her own sense of things could generate a certain hyperbolic playfulness as she boasts, "I'm Nobody! Who are you? / Are you—Nobody—Too?" and offers the invitation, "Then there's a pair of us / Don't tell! they'd advertise—you know!" (P 288). But it could also turn from play to a serious contemplation of her public presence:

> How dreary—to be—Somebody!
> How public—like a Frog—
> To tell one's name—the livelong June—
> To an admiring Bog!

The lyric poem allows Dickinson to convert a nonexistent public audience, which she had imagined as an encoring "House" in "I cannot dance upon my Toes," into what is, for her, a more manageable "admiring Bog." It allows her, too, to see that not being "Somebody" to that audience gives her the freedom to question the very conception of self that "Somebody" implies. Her speakers could imagine their identity as a process of change. Arguing on the analogy of the running years, Dickinson writes:

> I find my feet have further Goals—
> I smile upon the Aims
> That felt so ample—Yesterday—
> Today's—have vaster claims—

I do not doubt the self I was
Was competent to me—
But something awkward in the fit—
Proves that—outgrown—I see—[9](P 563)

She can acknowledge a past self and point to a future self without drawing
them together in a logical progression of cause and effect. Always starting
again, the lyric speaker can acknowledge the inadequacies of all that she has
started before without confirming the conviction that this time she will tell
or see everything. "We see—Comparatively," the speaker in P 534 admits,
suggesting, "Perhaps 'tis kindly—done us—" and goes on:

To spare these Striding Spirits
Some Morning of Chagrin
The waking in a Gnat's—embrace—
Our Giants—further on—

An identity that is always a process of becoming, a disappointment of
actualization, is conceived in terms that will challenge the identity of the
Transcendental ideal that dominated Dickinson's generation. Her pragmatic hero realizes her potential and must realize it again. She finds herself
in change, always outgrowing what appeared to be a fully competent self
yesterday, and not in that Transcendental state, slightly out of sight. She
is all activity, unlike the Transcendental hero who is beyond activity.[10] As
opposed to this static state, Dickinson imagines constant change—the
"Giants" always further on. If her "Striding Spirits" have something of the
moral earnestness of the Transcendental hero, their purpose is mocked and
reduced by the "Gnat's embrace" in which they find themselves. We "see"
and live "Comparatively," that is, by an addition that is not an evolution
toward some state of perfection but a constant moving on in a life where,
Rorty says, "there is nothing to complete, there is only a web of relations
to be rewoven, a web which time lengthens every day" ("The Contingency
of Selfhood," 42–43).

Dickinson upsets the conventional hierarchy of superior ideal and inferior real, and makes the ideal's opposition not the real but the vital, as she
writes:

Ideals are the Fairy Oil
With which we help the Wheel

> But when the Vital Axle turns
> The Eye rejects the Oil. (P 983)

Ideals are only secondary helps, not primary movers. Whatever turns the "Vital Axle" makes such help unnecessary. The enigma here is the "Eye" that rejects the oil of ideals as it starts to move, just as oil spits out of the axle as it turns. The "Eye" sees on its own, sees what it sees, and not what it would see. Yet Dickinson was never content to limit herself to her present abilities. She writes, "If What we could—were what we would— / Criterion—be small—" (P 407). Her speakers are not content there; they prefer the impossible: "It is the Ultimate of Talk— / The Impotence to Tell—" (P 407). Thus, like the self that is always moving away from the competence of yesterday, the poet's interest in language is in the language that she does not yet have the power to use.

Often her speakers do not have language because they have not been in the place that provided it, both literally, as in this poem:

> Bred as we, among the mountains,
> Can the sailor understand
> The divine intoxication
> Of the first league out from land? (P 76)

and figuratively, as in this poem:

> I found the words to every thought
> I ever had—but One—
> And that—defies me—
> As a Hand did try to chalk the Sun
>
> To Races—nurtured in the Dark—
> How would your own—begin?
> Can Blaze be shown in Cochineal—
> Or Noon—in Mazarin? (P 581)

Usually the inability to put a word to a thought comes from the inadequacy of the thought. But the speaker here has had a thought that has literally dislocated her, and she describes the experience by suggesting that she can know what she has learned only from the places where she has been.[11]

Thus, Dickinson's sense of individuality is quite parochial compared with the universality of Emerson's representative man. In regarding the individual as always changing and always rooted in a place that is changing, however, Dickinson moves beyond the Transcendental hero toward a more pragmatic conception of self, articulating a sense of the open-endedness of identity that twentieth-century philosophers were to posit in their reaction against idealism.

Because she fit uneasily into her time, she took the opportunity to go beyond it. Skilled as she was in presenting the tentativeness of identity, she has often been misread as speaking from a vulnerable, victimized, power-less position when, in fact, she would not have believed in the opposites of these states as constituting true identity. Only the "Soft—Cherubic Creatures" with the "Dimity Convictions," refined "Horror," and shame at "freckled Human Nature" had any faith—and that the most false—in their invulnerability.

She has been judged by the values of a male-dominated culture from which she was and chose to be excluded. But that exclusion freed her from the limitations of that culture, from the identity it might have allowed, and from the poetic language it would have encouraged. She could then admit that she had thoughts for which there were no words, that she "had been hungry, all the Years" (P 579), that she "felt a Cleaving in my Mind—" (P 937). Her vulnerability is all her strength against the rock of the Transcen-dental ideal. In the lyric, she could find a voice for those moments of inadequacy that the Transcendental hero could express only by denial or in a state of depression. She could give words to those times when the mind does not know itself and yet cannot be still. And she could find a way to evoke the irreducible, the enigmatic, that surplus in her experience of herself.

Stevens lacked Dickinson's vulnerability to circumstance. He was not a woman, restrained from publishing, removed from society, living in the age of the Transcendental ideal. Yet, he wrote lyric poems that, like hers, evoke the tentative, the marginal, the eccentric ranges of experience. He used the lyric genre to dodge to and fro, to turn this way and then that, to try out a variety of voices and identities, and always to recommence in change. Perhaps in American literature the lyric is the only genre open to either gender that will express the vulnerable yet extravagant individual whose whimsy is fateful.[12]

Dickinson and Stevens made poetry out of their "fated eccentricity" which had to be read as a requirement even by that audience, composed of "Soft Cherubic Gentlewomen" or "Mrs. Alfred Uruguay" or the soldier. Their achievement is to remind American readers that elegance does not have to struggle like the rest. It is required, as a necessity requires.

Notes

CHAPTER ONE

1. Eleanor Cook points out that the Greek *symballein* (our symbol) means "throw together" so that "Ver" "mont," green mountain, self-symbolizes. *Poetry, Word-Play, and Word-War in Wallace Stevens* (Princeton, N.J.: Princeton University Press, 1988), 298. I want to distinguish Stevens's improvisational style from what George Bornstein has called his "provisionality" in "Provisional Romanticism in 'Notes Toward a Supreme Fiction,'" *The Wallace Stevens Journal* 1 (Spring 1977): 17–24. Bornstein looks at his habit of false starts and misleading clues, whereas what I mean to emphasize is his genuine openness to whatever comes from random and arbitrary interactions.

2. Wallace Stevens, "Introduction," *Kora in Hell: Improvisations* in William Carlos Williams, *Imaginations* (New York: New Directions, 1970), 5.

3. His letters are full of comments about the little time he has free from business for poetry. A note to Marianne Moore in 1927 might serve for many such examples: "The extreme irregularity of my life makes poetry out of the question, for the present, except for momentary violences" (L 249). His secretary claims that he walked to work when he was in good health, a distance of three or four miles, and in these long walks he jotted down lines for his poetry, polishing it later. See Marguerite Flynn's reminiscences in Peter Brazeau's *Parts of a World: Wallace Stevens Remembered* (New York: Random House, 1977), 34.

4. Milton Bates discusses Stevens's pragmatism as part of his religious development in *Wallace Stevens: A Mythology of Self* (Berkeley: University of California Press, 1985), 203–212.

5. In an interesting discussion of Stevens's shift of allegiance from Nietzsche to James, David Bromwich reads this comment as the poet's rebuke to a Jamesian geniality. I take it to be an early premonition that the work of the hands is in pitching rather than in piecing together, in assaying rather than in completing the world. See "Stevens and the Idea of the Hero," *Raritan* 7 (Summer 1987): 1–27.

6. Gorham B. Munson, "The Dandyism of Wallace Stevens," in *Wallace Stevens: The Critical Heritage*, ed. Charles Doyle (London: Routledge and Kegan Paul, 1985), 79. This volume provides a summary history of the critical reception of Stevens.

7. Hugh Kenner, *The Pound Era* (Berkeley: University of California Press, 1971), 517. Harold Bloom, *Wallace Stevens: The Poems of Our Climate* (Ithaca, N.Y.: Cornell University Press, 1976). The debate concerning Stevens's reputation continues. See, for example, Marjorie Perloff's relegating of Stevens to the great tradition of Romantic visionary humanism in "Pound/Stevens: Whose Era?" *New Literary History* 13 (1982): 485–514 and Frank Lentricchia's description of the poet as a victim of bourgeois capitalism in *Ariel and the Police: Michel Foucault, William*

James, Wallace Stevens (Madison: University of Wisconsin Press, 1988), 135–244. A special issue of *The Wallace Stevens Journal* takes up the question of Stevens and politics in an effort to indicate his poetic interaction with the political events of his day. See *The Wallace Stevens Journal* 13 (Fall 1989). For a careful guide to the history of Stevens's criticism, see Melita Schaum, *Wallace Stevens and the Critical Schools* (Tuscaloosa: University of Alabama Press, 1988).

8. Frank Lentricchia. *Ariel and the Police*, 135–244.

9. See Lentricchia, *Ariel and the Police*; Sandra Gilbert and Susan Gubar, *The Madwoman in the Attic: The Woman Writer and the Nineteenth-Century Literary Imagination* (New Haven, Conn.: Yale University Press, 1979), 581–650; and the discussions of their debate: Donald E. Pease, "Patriarchy, Lentricchia, and Male Feminization," Sandra Gilbert and Susan Gubar, "The Man on the Dump versus the United Dames of America; or, What does Frank Lentricchia Want? " and Frank Lentricchia, "Andiamo!" in *Critical Inquiry* 14 (Winter 1988): 379–414.

10. William Carlos Williams, *In the American Grain* (New York: New Directions, 1933), 178–179.

11. Williams expresses the anti-Puritan sentiment of his day here. In discussing Anne Bradstreet, Adrienne Rich makes the point that versifying was not an exceptional pursuit in that society, and, in fact, even much later than Bradstreet, Cotton Mather cautioned against a "Boundless and Sickly Appetite for Reading of Poems." "Foreword" to *The Works of Anne Bradstreet*, ed. Jeannine Hensley (Cambridge, Mass.: Harvard University Press, 1967), xiii.

12. In their immensely influential book, *The Madwoman in the Attic*, Gilbert and Gubar discuss the importance of Dickinson's choice of what they call "the most Satanically assertive, daring, and therefore precarious of literary modes for women: lyric poetry" (582). Their assessment here derives more from English than from American literature, where the lyric has been considered a woman's genre. Nineteenth-century critics, calling for an American literature, argued for the epic as the only suitable genre for the American experience, relegating the lyric to minor writers and women. Even in the twentieth century, the poets themselves aspired to the epic or the long poem as their major work. See my *On the Modernist Long Poem* (Iowa City: University of Iowa Press, 1986).

13. Richard Mather's preface to *The Bay Psalm Book* is one expression of the New England Puritans' fear of the sensuality of rhyme and rhythm. See *The Bay Psalm Book: A facsimile reprint of the first edition with a list of later editions*, ed. Wilberforce Eames (New York: Artemis, 1973). Michael Wigglesworth's undergraduate oration, "The Praise of Eloquence," explains how thoroughly tied to conversion eloquence must be. Anne Bradstreet's meditations include the admonition, "Sweet words are like honey: a little may refresh, but too much gluts the stomach," *The Works of Anne Bradstreet*, 273. I cannot do justice here to the New England Puritans' defense of the plain style and their concomitant aversion to an art that might simply please. A brief survey of these views may be found in *The American Puritans: Their Prose and Poetry*, ed. Perry Miller (New York: Doubleday, 1956).

14. See Marjorie Perloff's "Pound/Stevens": Whose Era?" Although Perloff associates Stevens with content and Pound with style, in fact her objection to the

"desperately triumphant poetic humanism" of Stevens is an objection to his Romantic style rather than to his thought. For a complete survey of the poet's critical reception, see Schaum's *Wallace Stevens and the Critical Schools.*

15. F. O. Matthiessen's commanding *American Renaissance: Art and Expression in the Age of Emerson and Whitman* (New York: Oxford University Press, 1941) established the terms in which American literature could be defined. Even more recently, Sacvan Bercovitch has used those terms to indicate their origins in the Puritan period in *The Puritan Origins of the American Self* (New Haven, Conn.: Yale University Press, 1975).

16. *Southern Literary Messenger* 6 (September 1840): 709.

17. *The Knickerbocker: or, New-York Monthly Magazine* 12 (November 1838): 383.

18. *North American Review* 46 (January, 1830): 279.

19. *North American Review* 82 (January 1856): 274.

20. *Literary Essays of Ezra Pound*, edited with an introduction by T. S. Eliot (New York: New Directions, 1968), 299–300.

21. William Carlos Williams, *Paterson* (New York: New Directions, 1963), vii.

22. See Bercovitch, *Puritan Origins*, 165–185. For more on the representative self, see Mark R. Patterson, *Authority, Autonomy, and Representation in American Literature, 1776–1865* (Princeton, N.J.: Princeton University Press, 1988).

23. See James Clifford's discussion of this evolutionary process in "On Ethnographic Self-Fashioning: Conrad and Malinowsky," in *Reconstructing Individualism: Autonomy, Individuality, and the Self in Western Thought*, ed. Thomas C. Heller et al. (Stanford, Calif.: Stanford University Press, 1986), 140–162.

24. See Myra Jehlen's *American Incarnation: The Individual, the Nation, and the Continent* (Cambridge, Mass.: Harvard University Press), 84.

25. Richard Rorty, *Contingency, Irony, and Solidarity* (Cambridge: Cambridge University Press, 1989), 40.

26. See Alicia Suskin Ostriker's discussion of Dickinson in *Stealing the Language: The Emergence of Women's Poetry in America* (Boston: Beacon Press, 1986), 37–43.

27. In an interesting discussion of what he calls "democratic social space," Philip Fisher comments on individuality that is relevant to Dickinson's case. He says, "features of individuality become of value as features of an outsider who has been given his position by means of the unintelligibility of the world. A world strongly marked by output—late nineteenth-century capitalism, for example—does not raise the question of observation, nor the question of individual differences that would lead to the strong concern with nuances of individualism. Because it is within the sphere of differing interpretations that uniqueness becomes clear, the transparent social life of work and output is free of uniqueness. It is bland in the Emersonian sense or universal and blank as we find personality in Whitman or Theodore Dreiser. Individuality is itself the product of social damage" (89). See "Democratic Social Space: Whitman, Melville, and the Promise of American Transparency," *Representations* 24 (Fall 1988): 60–101.

28. Dickinson's conception of self and of individuality formed part of a nineteenth-century controversy in which women writers and subjects played an

increasingly important role. For a discussion of this controversy in England, see Mary Poovey's *Uneven Developments: The Ideological Work of Gender in Mid-Victorian England* (Chicago: University of Chicago Press, 1988). Mark R. Patterson finds that Emerson too took part in the inquiry into the self and concludes, "Redefining the independence of 'self-trust' from the possession of a material self, defined by imitation of custom, to the decentered, liberated self, bound to the universal interest, Emerson attempted to fit democracy to his ideals" (Patterson, *Authority, Autonomy, and Representation*, 155).

29. For a fruitful discussion of Dickinson as a Modernist and briefly for her relation to Stevens, see David Porter, *Dickinson: The Modern Idiom* (Cambridge, Mass.: Harvard University Press, 1981), 252–269.

30. Robert Weisbuch, *Emily Dickinson's Poetry* (Chicago: University of Chicago Press, 1972), 161. Although Weisbuch himself seeks to order Dickinson's poetry by identifying two patterns which he calls "regulation fiction" and "poems of epistemological quest," his readings of Dickinson's poems are sensitive to the many ways in which her poems defy such categories.

31. Perhaps the most interesting commentary on this relationship is Richard Wilbur's "Sumptuous Destitution," in *Emily Dickinson: A Collection of Critical Essays*, ed. Richard B. Sewall (Englewood, N.J.: Prentice-Hall, 1963), 127–136. He argues, using Dickinson's phrase, that once an object is magnified by desire it can never be wholly possessed.

32. For a discussion of this distinction, see Christopher E. G. Benfey, *Emily Dickinson and the Problem of Others* (Amherst: University of Massachusetts Press, 1984), 56. For a discussion of Stevens's interiorization of the external world of commodities, see Lentricchia, *Ariel and the Police*, 136–158.

33. For a full discussion of this pragmatic sense of self, see Richard Rorty, "The Contingency of Selfhood," in *Contingency, Irony, and Solidarity*, 23–43.

34. See the introduction to *Secretaries of the Moon: The Letters of Wallace Stevens & José Rodríguez Feo*, ed. Beverly Coyle and Alan Filreis (Durham, N.C.: Duke University Press, 1986), for a study of the pattern of Stevens's correspondence— first, "elation at the news of a new letter writer, followed by sympathy, then identity, then increasingly organized criticism of the literary life" (29).

35. *Sur Plusieurs Beaux Sujects: Wallace Stevens' Commonplace Book*, ed. Milton J. Bates (Stanford, Calif.: Stanford University Press, 1989), 25. Page numbers in the next few paragraphs are from this edition.

36. For an interesting discussion of Stevens's use of quotation, see Milton Bates's "Introduction," to *Sur Plusieurs Beaux Sujects*, 1–18.

37. See *Secretaries of the Moon*, where Stevens quotes this passage to José Rodríguez Feo with the warning, "Reality is the great *fond*, and it is because it is that the purely literary amounts to so little" (62).

CHAPTER TWO

1. See Stanley Cavell, *In Quest of the Ordinary* (Chicago: University of Chicago Press, 1988), 106–120.

2. Emerson was not without his own doubts about himself, but, as John Michael

notes, "the value of the inner self is proved in its relation to the outer world's judgment of it" (5). See Michael's entire study for a full reading of how much Emerson depended on community approval for his verification of the self. *Emerson and Skepticism: The Cipher of the World* (Baltimore: Johns Hopkins University Press, 1988). See also Julie Ellison's *Emerson's Romantic Style* (Princeton, N.J.: Princeton University Press, 1984). Ellison demonstrates how Emerson's thinking repeats rather than develops.

3. For a study of the gaps, abysses, and mysteries in Emerson's sentences and paragraphs, see Eric Cheyfitz, *The Trans-Parent: Sexual Politics in the Language of Emerson* (Baltimore: Johns Hopkins University Press, 1981), 10. In his immensely suggestive reading, Cheyfitz examines Emerson's identification of language with mother and father and claims that eloquence is a manifestation of the power of the father, a masculine power (41).

4. I take exception here to Cynthia Griffin Wolff's literal reading of Dickinson's statement that "When I state myself, as the Representative of the Verse—it does not mean—me—but a supposed person" (II, 268). Wolff claims that Dickinson "did not want the Voice of the verse to be incongruous or susceptible of dismissal; above all, she wanted to speak as a 'Representative Voice.'" *Emily Dickinson* (New York: Alfred A. Knopf, 1986), 177.

5. It is not only the feminists who have read for the plot. Early and late, narrativizing critics have worked on Dickinson. See, for example, Clark Griffith's *The Long Shadow: Emily Dickinson's Tragic Poetry* (Princeton, N.J.: Princeton University Press, 1968), which traces her traumatic relationship with her father as the source of her tragic poetry, or John Cody's *After Great Pain: The Inner Life of Emily Dickinson* (Cambridge, Mass.: Harvard University Press, 1971), which uses the poetry as a psychoanalytic case study of the poet. Among representative feminist readings of Dickinson are Margaret Homans, *Women Writers and Poetic Identity* (Princeton, N.J.: Princeton University Press, 1980), Joanne Feit Diehl, *Dickinson and the Romantic Imagination* (Princeton, N.J.: Princeton University Press, 1981), Barbara Antonina Clarke Mossberg, *Emily Dickinson: When a Writer is a Daughter* (Bloomington: Indiana University Press, 1982), Sandra M. Gilbert and Susan Gubar, *The Madwoman in the Attic: The Woman Writer and the Nineteenth-Century Literary Imagination* (New Haven, Conn.: Yale University Press, 1979), and Alicia Suskin Ostriker, *Stealing the Language: The Emergence of Women's Poetry in America* (Boston: Beacon Press, 1986). Based on a model of binary opposition, these readings of Dickinson stress the extent to which she was different because she was made to be by a society that restricted or represeed women's expression. Sacvan Bercovitch in *The Puritan Origins of the American Self* (New Haven, Conn.: Yale University Press, 1975) explores the strain on the individual imposed by the demands of American individualism in terms that explain the difficulties of reading Dickinson's poetry.

6. Wolff, *Emily Dickinson*, 177.

7. In talking about the brevity of Dickinson's poems, I mean only to suggest a general characteristic of all lyric poems and not to stress the particular ways in which Dickinson exploited brevity or limitation as a theme. For such treatment, see

Jane Donahue Eberwein's *Dickinson: Strategies of Limitation* (Amherst: University of Massachusetts Press, 1985).

8. See Sacvan Bercovitch's discussion of Emerson for a complete treatment of his sense of the public self. The whole question of privacy is a central concern for Dickinson. For example, in P 1385, she deals directly with the impossibility of publishing the private, making public the secret. Dickinson's privacy is an issue of some debate among her critics. She is charged with being too private by Elinor Wilnor, "The Poetics of Emily Dickinson," *ELH* 38 (1971): 126–154, and David Porter, *Dickinson: The Modern Idiom* (Cambridge, Mass.: Harvard University Press, 1981). Robert Weisbuch has defended her habit of privacy in *Emily Dickinson's Poetry* (Chicago: University of Chicago Press, 1972). More recently, Christopher E. G. Benfey has discussed the issue of privacy and secrecy as a longing for invisibility in *Emily Dickinson and the Problem of Others* (Amherst: University of Massachusetts Press, 1984).

9. Hawthorne's complaint about "the damned mob of scribbling women" was directed against women novelists. Cheyfitz points out Hawthorne's fears that the manly "garment" of American literature was fast becoming a feminine one (*The Trans-Parent*, 99). See Cheyfitz's entire discussion of Emerson and the femininization of language which he concludes with the statement that Emerson's call for "the kingdom of man over nature" "may be the siren song of a savage, hermaphroditic figure that, aligning itself with a growing feminine power, is luring us into drowning in a dream of the FATHER" (167).

10. Hamacher, "'Disintegration of the Will': Nietzsche on the Individual and Individuality," in *Reconstructing Individualism: Autonomy, Individuality, and the Self in Western Thought*, ed. Thomas C. Heller et al. (Stanford, Calif.: Stanford University Press, 1986), 110. Studying the transformation of the opposition between the individual and the social during the Progressive Era, Walter Benn Michaels claims that the loss of individualism is the dominant theme in American cultural studies rivaled only by the triumph of individualism, which is to say that social change in American life presents itself characteristically as an event in the history of the individual. See "An American Tragedy, or the Promise of American Life," *Representations* 25 (Winter 1989): 71–98. For an interesting discussion of the importance of individual character in an economy of debt, reciprocity, and obligation in Ralph Waldo Emerson, see Richard A. Grusin, "'Put God in Your Debt': Emerson's Economy of Expenditure," *PMLA* 103 (January 1988): 35–44.

11. For more on Nietzsche, the self, and contingency, see Richard Rorty, "The Contingency of Selfhood, in" *Contingency, Irony, and Solidarity* (Cambridge: Cambridge University Press, 1989).

12. I am indebted here to the arguments of Leo Bersani in *The Freudian Body: Psychoanalysis and Art* (New York: Columbia University Press, 1986), 82–83.

13. "'A Loaded Gun': Dickinson and the Dialectic of Rage," *PMLA* 93 (1978): 431.

14. *Dickinson: the Anxiety of Gender* (Ithaca, N.Y.: Cornell University Press, 1984), 18–19.

15. "'Vesuvius at Home': The Power of Emily Dickinson," in *On Lies, Secrets, and*

Silence: Selected Prose 1966–1978 (New York: Norton, 1979), 169. Rich gives this much repeated reading its most palatable form because she does understand that for Dickinson there is no split between masculine creativity and feminine receptivity. Other feminists have taken up the split that Rich identifies and have made more of it. See Diehl, *Dickinson and the Romantic Imagination*, 19–20.

16. I am indebted here to Giles Deleuze's discussion of repetition in *Différence et répétition* (Paris: Presses Universitaires de France, 1968), 96–168.

CHAPTER THREE

1. See Roland Hagenbuchle's discussion of the difference between Dickinson and Emerson in their concept of language. He argues that "Emerson's poet links words to things, man to nature; being both lover and 'Brother of the world' (JMN, V, 309), he is primarily an Orphic poet; in 'articulating' nature as 'Namer' (E, III, 21), he masters it (E, XII, 164). Dickinson's poet is preeminently a *philologos*, a lover of the word; to her the spirit is essentially *logos*; she links man to the eternal through language rather than via natural objects, though, she, too, is immensely moved by nature " (141). Hagenbuchle's argument is compelling, although I cannot agree with its premise that the reservoir for words is the same as Emerson's the universal mind. I want also to take quite literally his idea that Dickinson is a lover of words. See "Sign and Process: The Concept of Language in Emerson and Dickinson," *Emerson Society Quarterly* 25 (1979): 137–155.

2. For a discussion of poetry and privacy in Dickinson, see Benfey, *Emily Dickinson and the Problem of Others* (Amherst: University of Massachusetts Press, 1985), 56.

3. Walt Whitman is much more frequently linked with touch than Dickinson. He was quick to identify book and man. But he was altogether Emersonian in his interest in the opposition between the public and the private rather than in the social and the intimate. There is something very public about his invitations to intimacy. See Paul Zweig, *Walt Whitman: The Making of the Poet* (New York: Basic Books, 1984), for a complete discussion of Whitman's publicized private self. Also, for a comparison of Dickinson and Whitman, see Sandra Gilbert, "The American Sexual Poetics of Walt Whitman and Emily Dickinson," in *Reconstructing American Literary History*, ed. Sacvan Bercovitch (Cambridge, Mass.: Harvard University Press, 1986), 123–154.

4. Luce Irigaray, "Ce sexe qui n'en est pas un," in *New French Feminisms*, ed. Elaine Marks and Isabelle de Courtivron (New York: Schocken Books, 1981), 101.

5. For example, Hagenbuchle links Dickinson to Emerson, as I noted above, and differentiates between them only in their methods of tapping the source of language.

6. E. Miller Budick, *Emily Dickinson and the Life of Language: A Study in Symbolic Poetics* (Baton Rouge: Louisiana State University Press, 1985), 174.

7. One critic has concentrated on the ways in which the difficulties of Dickinson's poetry stem not from metaphorical but from metonymical reference. See Roland Hagenbuchle, "Precision and Indeterminacy in the Poetry of Emily Dickinson," *Emerson Society Quarterly* 20 (First Quarter 1974): 33–56. Hagenbuchle views me-

tonymy as tending toward indeterminacy, whereas I see Dickinson's use of metonymy as an effort to retain a hold on this world.

8. Dickinson's interest in sight and symbol has been thoroughly discussed. See,
for example, Weisbuch's discussion of the two worlds, one of vision and one of
veto, in *Emily Dickinson's Poetry* (Chicago: University of Chicago Press, 1972) and
Budick's *Emily Dickinson and the Life of Language*.

9. See Cristanne Miller's insightful discussion of the importance of letters to
Dickinson. She comments, "Dickinson's use of her poems in letters suggests one
way in which she may have intended them to be read: they are private messages
universalized by a double release from private circumstance" (15). *Emily Dickinson:
A Poet's Grammar* (Cambridge, Mass.: Harvard University Press, 1987), 1–19.

10. Edgar Allan Poe, "The Murders in the Rue Morgue," in *Selected Writings of
Edgar Allan Poe*, ed. Edward Davidson (Boston: Houghton Mifflin, 1956), 153.

11. In a related point, Benfey emphasizes Dickinson's interest in the body. Although he claims she is the poet of anorexia, he says that what makes Dickinson's
case against the skeptic is her awareness of the role of the body in ordinary human
experience. He claims that "it is only an acceptance of the body and not in a
skeptical denial of it that limits our sadistic rage for certainty." *Emily Dickinson and
the Problem of Others*, 108.

12. See Rich, "'Vesuvius at Home,'"; Sandra M.Gilbert and Susan Gubar, *The
Madwoman in the Attic: The Woman Writer and the Nineteenth-Century Literary
Imagination* (New Haven, Conn.: Yale University Press, 1979); and Joanne Feit
Diehl, *Dickinson and the Romantic Imagination* (Princeton, N.J.: Princeton Uni-
versity Press, 1981), who all emphasize the split between woman and poet.

13. See Mutlu Konuk Blasing's discussion of this poem for a parallel treatment
of the difference between name and thing and the pun of taking the "name of Gold"
rather than the "name of God." Blasing claims that "Dickinson's location of meaning in the literal difference of words informs her esthetic." *American Poetry: The
Rhetoric of Its Forms* (New Haven, Conn.: Yale University Press, 1987), 176–177.

14. Wolff, *Emily Dickinson*, 142–143.

15. Richard Rorty, "The Contingency of Language," in *Contingency, Irony, Solidarity* (Cambridge: Cambridge University Press, 1989), 7.

16. See Cameron's entire discussion of this poem for the number of insights her
hypothetical reading offers in *Lyric Time: Dickinson and the Limits of Genre* (Baltimore: Johns Hopkins University Press, 1979), 85–90.

17. Georges Bataille, *Erotism: Death & Sensuality* (San Francisco: City Lights
Books, 1986), 15.

18. Elaine Scarry, *The Body in Pain* (New York: Oxford University Press, 1985),
164.

19. Vivian Pollak has pointed out to me the strange coincidence of her use of the
same term "love tokens" to describe Edward Dickinson's letters to Emily Norcross
Dickinson. See her valuable *A Poet's Parents: The Courtship Letters of Emily Norcross
and Edward Dickinson* (Chapel Hill: University of North Carolina Press, 1988), xix.

CHAPTER FOUR

1. Geoffrey Hartman, *Saving the Text: Literature/ Derrida/ Philosophy* (Baltimore: Johns Hopkins University Press, 1981), 135–136.

2. Michel de Montaigne, "Of Experience," in *Selected Essays*, trans. Donald M. Frame (Toronto: D. Van Nostrand, 1943), 324.

3. Ralph Waldo Emerson, "The American Scholar," in *Selected Prose and Poetry*, ed. Reginald Cook (San Francisco: Rinehart Press, 1969), 44.

4. Thomas Wentworth Higginson, quoted by Thomas H. Johnson in his introduction to *The Complete Poems*, vi.

5. Thomas Wentworth Higginson, "An Open Portfolio," reprinted in *The Recognition of Emily Dickinson: Selected Criticism Since 1890*, ed. Caesar R. Blake and Carlton F. Wells (Ann Arbor: University of Michigan Press, 1968), 3.

6. For an interesting discussion of the nineteenth-century meaning of "spasmodic" as applied to literary works, see Jonathan Morse's "Emily Dickinson and the Spasmodic School: A Note on Thomas Wentworth Higginson's Esthetics," *New England Quarterly* 50 (September 1977): 505–509. Morse traces the term to the May 1854 issue of *Blackwood's Edinburgh Magazine*, where it is borrowed from Poe to describe "highly colored Byronisms expressed in great halting flows of metaphor" and art for art's sake. Higginson admired the "spasmodic school" and, in calling Dickinson's verse "spasmodic," may have been making it appear stronger, less Emersonian and more Byronic, in Morse's view.

7. For example, she wrote "One Sister have I in our house" to Sue Gilbert Dickinson (L, II, 342–343), "Sleep is supposed to be," a poem addressed to her father but sent to Sue Gilbert Dickinson (L, II, 344), "As by the dead we love to sit" to Mrs. J. G. Holland (L, II, 350), "Two swimmers wrestled on the spar" to Samuel Bowles (L, II, 363), "'Faith' is a fine invention" to Samuel Bowles (L, II, 364), and "Is it true, dear Sue?" (L, II, 373).

8. Although she does not discuss Dickinson, Patricia Yaeger has an interesting discussion of women's hunger for language and their productive use of it in *Honey-Mad Women: Emancipatory Strategies in Women's Writing* (New York: Columbia University Press, 1988).

9. For an interesting discussion of the feminist interest in images of darkness, see Wendy Barker, *Lunacy of Light: Emily Dickinson and the Experience of the Metaphor* (Carbondale: Southern Illinois University Press, 1987).

10. Edward Dickinson's simultaneous encouragement and discouragement of his children's wide reading is treated in Jack L. Capps, *Emily Dickinson's Reading: 1836–1866* (Cambridge, Mass.: Harvard University Press, 1966), 11–16. See also Pollak's discussion of Dickinson's relation with her father in *Dickinson: The Anxiety of Gender* (Ithaca, N.Y.: Cornell University Press, 1984) and her discussion of Edward Dickinson's effort to encourage the reading of his future wife, Emily Norcross in *A Poet's Parents: The Courtship Letters of Emily Norcross and Edward Dickinson* (Chapel Hill: University of North Carolina Press, 1988) as a model of his instructive habits. Clearly, Dickinson had some ideas about her own reading requirements. See Margaret Homans's discussion of her acquaintance with women writers as it relates to her own efforts to find a poetic identity in *Women Writers and Poetic Identity*

(Princeton, N.J.: Princeton University Press, 1980), 162–214. Gilbert and Gubar also discuss Dickinson's father as he appeared to his daughter in two separate figures: the intense man who "'read lonely and rigorous books'" and a pompous public figure. *The Madwoman in the Attic: The Woman Writer and the Nineteenth-Century Literary Imagination* (New Haven, Conn.: Yale University Press, 1979), 597.

11. Although she is talking about poetic influence and not Dickinson's reading, Joanne Feit Diehl emphasizes just the opposite point. She notes that "Resentment and anxiety are the mirror emotions which reflect Dickinson's vision of reality. The fear she experiences when contemplating the advent of any possible happiness arises from an already present knowledge, a foreboding which could only appear to one who had experienced, if subliminally, the anguished sum of life's promise" (575). See her important article, "'Come Slowly—Eden': An Exploration of Women Poets and Their Muse" in *Signs* 3 (Spring 1979): 572–587. My emphasis on Dickinson's delight runs counter also to Richard Wilbur's point that "Sumptuous Destitution" is the major motif in her art. See Richard Wilbur, "Sumptuous Destitution" in *Emily Dickinson: A Collection of Critical Essays*, ed. Richard B. Sewall (Englewood Cliffs, N.J.: Prentice-Hall, 1963), 127–136. I think that the sumptuousness has been scanted in discussions of Dickinson, and, in attempting to right the balance between "sumptuous" and "destitution," I shall emphasize her delight. In coming to this conclusion, I have been helped by Yaeger's book *Honey-Mad Women* with its emphasis on woman's delight in words.

12. Gilbert and Gubar point to the "magnitude of the poetic self-creation Emily Dickinson achieved through working in a genre that has been traditionally the most Satanically assertive, daring, and therefore precarious of literary modes for women: lyric poetry" (*The Madwoman in the Attic*, 582). Although, as I have noted earlier, I think that their point about the lyric might be influenced by their interest in British literature, their emphasis on self-creation is important.

13. Feminist readings of Dickinson's deprivation tend to emphasize her vulnerability and defiance rather than the strength she derived from relying solely on her own resources. See Barbara Antonina Clarke Mossberg, "Emily Dickinson's Nursery Rhymes," in *Feminist Critics Read Emily Dickinson*, ed. Suzanne Juhasz (Bloomington: Indiana University Press, 1983), 45–66, and Vivian Pollak, "Thirst and Starvation in Emily Dickinson's Poetry," *American Literature* 51 (March 1979): 33–49. Mossberg reads Dickinson's use of hunger as a metaphor for powerlessness. Pollak sees it as an attempt to ward off the full woman's body.

14. For a related point, see Gilbert and Gubar's comments on hunger in nineteenth-century women's fiction where the food (and fiction) that sustains men contributes to the sickening of women in *The Madwoman in the Attic*, 374.

15. Vivian Pollak reminds me that the generosity and hospitality that I find in Dickinson's poems were not so apparent in certain real-life situations. She is right to be skeptical. My own sumptuous language is designed to suggest the overpowering energy of her creative power as it confronted a world that seemed, by contrast, often disappointing.

16. Ralph Waldo Emerson, *Nature* in *Selected Prose*, 38.

17. Ralph Waldo Emerson, *Selected Prose*, 526.

18. Henry David Thoreau, *Walden*, in *Walden & Civil Disobedience*, ed. Gwen Thomas (New York: W. W. Norton, 1966), 70.

19. Margaret Homans, "'Oh, Vision of Language!': Dickinson's Poems of Love and Death," in Juhasz, *Feminist Critics Read Emily Dickinson*, 125.

20. See Diehl's discussion of Dickinson's exclusion from public discourse for a provocative argument that differs substantially from my own. She claims that Dickinson's insistence on her own version of experience caused her to develop rhetorical strategies that undermined coherent, recognizable meanings. In Diehl's view, Dickinson approaches modernist theories of art because she "shapes a revisionary language that pursues the possibilities of internally generated meanings as it resists the confines of figuration, the potential clarities of signification," "'Ransom in a Voice': Language as Defense in Dickinson's Poetry," in Juhasz, *Feminist Critics Read Emily Dickinson*, 174.

21. In an interesting discussion of Dickinson's use of iambic pentameter, A. R. C. Finch argues convincingly that it codifies for her a patriarchal poetic tradition that she associates with the power of religion and public opinion, with formality, and with stasis. See "Dickinson and Patriarchal Meter: A Theory of Metrical Codes," *PMLA* 102 (March 1987): 166–176.

INTERCHAPTER

1. See, for example, Cynthia Griffin Wolff, *Emily Dickinson* (New York: Alfred A. Knopf, 1986), Sharon Cameron, *Lyric Time: Dickinson and the Limits of Genre* (Baltimore: Johns Hopkins University Press, 1979), and Barton Levi St. Armand, *Emily Dickinson and Her Culture* (Cambridge, Mass.: Cambridge University Press, 1984).

2. See Rorty's description of pragmatism in "Pragmatism, Relativism, Irrationalism," *Consequences of Pragmatism (Essays: 1972–1980)* (Minneapolis: University of Minnesota Press, 1982), 160–166.

3. For a full discussion of women writers and the Romantic movement, see Margaret Homans, *Women Writers and Poetic Identity* (Princeton, N.J.: Princeton University Press, 1980).

4. William James, "The Will to Believe," *The Will to Believe and Other Essays in Popular Philosophy* (Cambridge, Mass.: Harvard University Press, 1979), 33.

5. See Cameron, *Lyric Time*, 32–34.

6. See George Lessing's account of the incident of Stevens as an undergraduate reading a poem to Santayana and receiving one in reply, along with his full account of Stevens's formative years in *Wallace Stevens: A Poet's Growth* (Baton Rouge: Louisiana State University Press, 1986), 25–31.

7. For a valuable discussion of the idealist tradition, see Margaret Peterson's entire discussion of Stevens's connection with these philosophers in *Wallace Stevens and the Idealist Tradition* (Ann Arbor, Mich.: UMI Research Press, 1983), 66–88.

8. See Lessing's chapter on correspondence in which he describes the variety of Stevens's correspondents, *Wallace Stevens*, 226–241.

9. David Bromwich, "Stevens and the Idea of the Hero," *Raritan* 7 (Summer 1987): 20.

10. *Sur Plusieurs Beaux Sujects: Wallace Stevens' Commonplace Book*, ed. Milton Bates (Stanford, Calif.: Stanford University Press, 1989), 102.

CHAPTER FIVE

1. Frank Lentricchia's contention that Stevens is a feminized male, anxious about his identity in an age when poetry was not considered a fit occupation for a young man, has been developed through an argument with what he takes to be the "essentialist feminism" of Gilbert and Gubar. The entire discussion takes place on the level of economics and sociology so that it has very little to say about Stevens's actual poetic treatment of women. But it is of interest in its focus as it points to the whole question of gender relations in Stevens. See Lentricchia's *Ariel and the Police: Michel Foucault, William James, Wallace Stevens* (Madison: University of Wisconsin Press, 1988) and Sandra Gilbert and Susan Gubar's *No Man's Land: The Place of the Woman Writer in the Twentieth Century*, Vol. 1, *The War of the Words* (New Haven, Conn.: Yale University Press, 1988). The argument continues in *Critical Inquiry* 14 (Winter 1988): 386–406, 407–413, 379–385.

2. A very interesting discussion of the "cybernetic self" of the dramatic monologue may be found in Loy D. Martin, *Browning's Dramatic Monologue and the Post-Romantic Subject* (Baltimore: Johns Hopkins University Press, 1985).

3. Steven Shaviro does pause to consider the subject as "master of repetition," identifying him as "not a substratum to which varying predicates are superadded but a repeated projection of nonidentity" (226–227). He says that "repetition without identity is the movement that stops at the point of its preludes, a movement whose interminable latency is also its finality and its openness to continued alteration" (226). In his insistence on what he calls *disjunctive affirmation* in Stevens's poetry, Shaviro attempts to read the poetry beyond the "totalizing limitations of Western culture that," he claims, "it was Stevens's fortune and fate to transgress and to exceed" (231). See "'That Which is Always Beginning': Stevens's Poetry of Affirmation," *PMLA* 100 (March 1985): 220–233.

Although in her recent book on Stevens, Helen Vendler does not dwell on repetition, she is anxious nonetheless to connect Stevens's poetry to the general emotional experiences common to us all. She says, "Stevens is the poet of this overmastering and mercilessly renewed desire. Each moment at reflection, for him, is a rebirth of impulse toward fulfillment, as desire reaches for its object—sexual, religious, epistemological, or (encompassing them all) aesthetic." See *Wallace Stevens: Words Chosen Out of Desire* (Knoxville: University of Tennessee Press, 1984), 30.

4. Helen Vendler, *On Extended Wings* (Cambridge, Mass.: Harvard University Press, 1969), 202.

5. Harold Bloom, *Wallace Stevens: The Poems of Our Climate* (Ithaca, N.Y.: Cornell University Press, 1976), 216.

6. Drawing on J. Hillis Miller's two theories of repetition from *Fiction and Repetition* (repetition as copy and as an uncanny return), Mary Arensburg provides

an interesting reading of the central "Theatre of Trope" in *Notes*. She traces a filiative pattern in the generational descent of the ephebe and an affiliative repetition of various marriages, which are part of a more general scheme of canonical repetition in which going round is "a final good." See "'Spinning Its Eccentric Measure': Stevens's 'Notes Toward a Supreme Fiction,'" *The Wallace Stevens Journal* 11 (Fall 1987): 111–121.

7. Frank Doggett, *Stevens's Poetry of Thought* (Baltimore: Johns Hopkins University Press, 1966), 119.

8. I discount here Stevens's identification of the fat girl with earth in his letter to Henry Church (L 426).

9. Several articles in the special issue of the *The Wallace Stevens Journal* devoted to "Stevens and Women" focus on Stevens's obsession with his mother. C. Roland Wagner claims that "Ambivalent attachment to the nurturing, pre-Oedipal mother is central to our understanding of Stevens" in "Wallace Stevens: The Concealed Self," *The Wallace Stevens Journal* 12 (Fall 1988), 88. Maria Irene Remalho de Sousa Santos also argues that the woman in his poems is frequently the mother. See "The Woman in the Poem: Wallace Stevens, Ramon Fernandez, and Adrienne Rich." Mary Arensburg's study of the poetic process in Stevens as "a fantasy of desire" also depends for its full development on *Auroras of Autumn*, and toward that end her commentary on *Notes* is directed to the figure of Cinderella in canto viii. She draws on Paul Ricoeur's notion of the choice of the third woman in literature and folklore who is death to trace the process by which "Stevens invents a twentieth-century version of the American sublime that posits the fiction of the family romance as the indefinite and infinite whiteness that haunts the vestiges of our memories" ("White Mythology and the American Sublime: Stevens' Auroral Fantasy," in *The American Sublime*, ed. Mary Arensberg [Albany: State University of New York Press, 1986], 153, 156–158, 162). Her interest in the haunting of the sublime in Stevens's work encourages her to emphasize the ghostly woman over the desirous woman I discuss.

10. See "The Agency of the Letter in the Unconscious or Reason Since Freud" in *Écrits: A Selection*, trans. Alan Sheridan (New York: W. W. Norton, 1977), 166–167. I am also endebted here to Anthony Wilden's "Lacan and the Discourse of the Other" for a discussion of Lacan's views. See *Speech and Language in Psychoanalysis*, trans. and ed. Anthony Wilden (Baltimore: Johns Hopkins University Press, 1984), 238–249. Peter Brooks relies on Lacan to track the motivating force of plot to a desire that is unsatisfied and unsatisfiable since it is linked to memory traces and seeks its realization in the hallucinatory reproduction of indestructible signs of infantile satisfaction. He concludes, "Narratives portray the motors of desire that drive and consume their plots, and they also lay bare the nature of narration as a form of human desire: the need to tell as a primary human drive that seeks to seduce and to subjugate the listener, to implicate him in the thrust of a desire that never can quite speak its name—never can quite come to the point—but that insists on speaking over and over again its movement toward that

name" (61). See *Reading for the Plot: Design and Intention in Narrative* (New York: Vintage, 1985). I think that the same dynamics operates on a more intense level in poetry where the speaker is often addressing himself, seeking to seduce some part of himself.

11. Richard Rorty, "The Contingency of Language," in *Contingency, Irony, and Solidarity* (Cambridge: Cambridge University Press, 1989), 21.

CHAPTER SIX

1. See Stevens's comments on this quotation in *Sur Plusieurs Beaux Sujects*, 33–37, where he quotes his correspondence with Rossi on the quotation. Rossi redirects the association of poetry and pleasure and places it within ourselves.

2. See Frank Lentricchia's argument in *Ariel and the Police: Michel Foucault, William James, Wallace Stevens* (Madison: University of Wisconsin Press, 1988), 136–244, where he identifies Stevens the poet as a feminized male.

3. See Sandra Gilbert and Susan Gubar, *No Man's Land: The Place of the Woman Writer in the Twentieth Century*, Vol. 1: *The War of the Words* (New Haven, Conn.: Yale University Press, 1988), 155.

4. A. Walton Litz, *Introspective Voyager: The Poetic Development of Wallace Stevens* (New York: Oxford University Press, 1972), 92. Litz's study of Stevens's development points to an early interest in man's relation to the nonsymbolic universe directly in such poems as "Earthy Anecdote" and "Anecdote of Men by the Thousands." "We are where we live, and what we wear," Litz comments (78), but he finds that Stevens soon tired of these "theoretical" poems and moved on to a new boisterousness in poems such as "Depression Before Spring" (79). I would claim that Stevens retained an interest in the nonsymbolic universe throughout his career.

5. In *An Ordinary Evening in New Haven*, Stevens writes:

Professor Eucalyptus said, "The search
For reality is as momentous as
The search for god." It is the philosopher's search

For an interior made exterior
And the poet's search for the same exterior made
Interior: breathless things broodingly abreath

With the inhalations of original cold
And of original earliness. (481)

This passage would seem to contradict my point, and yet I think that Stevens's philosopher and his poet are one and the same, and that their activities rely entirely on a constantly changing reversal of interior and exterior and not a static hoarding in interior space.

6. See Robert Buttel's discussion of Imagism in Stevens's poetry in *Wallace Stevens: The Making of Harmonium* (Princeton, N.J.: Princeton University Press, 1967), 125–147.

7. Litz, *Introspective Voyager*, 147.

8. J. Hillis Miller, *Poets of Reality: Six Twentieth-Century Writers* (New York: Atheneum, 1969), 4.

9. Milton Bates argues persuasively for the separation of the various elements in Stevens's personality that I want to combine here. In his chapter "Burgher, Fop, and Clown," Bates is at pains to distinguish the stages of Stevens's development and the separation in his roles as insurance executive, aesthete in his early poetry, and, finally, self-mocking clown. I think that, for all the discontinuities in his life, he retained in every identity an interest in his surroundings. See Bates, *Wallace Stevens: A Mythology of Self* (Berkeley: University of California Press, 1985), 83–126.

10. Rorty, "The Contingency of Selfhood," in *Contingency, Irony, and Solidarity* (Cambridge: Cambridge University Press, 1989), 43.

11. Jacques Derrida, *The Post Card: From Socrates to Freud and Beyond*, trans. Alan Bass (Chicago: University of Chicago Press, 1987), 13.

12. See Lentricchia's whole discussion of this poem and its argument against Gilbert and Gubar's feminist position, as it comes to bear on the economics of their patriarchal myth in *Ariel and the Police*, 193–195.

13. Daniel Fuchs, *The Comic Spirit of Wallace Stevens* (Durham, N.C.: Duke University Press, 1963), 33.

14. See, for example, Rajeev S. Patke, *The Long Poems of Wallace Stevens* (Cambridge: Cambridge University Press, 1985), 8–38, and Leonora Woodman, *Stanza My Stone: Wallace Stevens and the Hermetic Tradition* (West Lafayette, Ind.: Purdue University Press, 1983), 147–163.

15. See Bates, *Wallace Stevens*, 281.

16. See what Lentricchia makes of that word in his discussion of "The World as Meditation," in *Ariel and the Police*, 243–244.

17. Jacques Lacan, "The Function of Language in Psychoanalysis," in *Speech and Language in Psychoanalysis*, trans. and ed. Anthony Wilden (Baltimore: Johns Hopkins University Press, 1984), 40.

CHAPTER SEVEN

1. The other poems are "Phosphor Reading by His Own Light" (1942), "The House Was Quiet and the World Was Calm" (1945), and "Large Red Man Reading" (1948). For an interesting examination of the ways these poems slide metaphor into metonymy, see Alan D. Perlis, "Wallace Stevens's Reader Poems and the Effacement of Metaphor," *The Wallace Stevens Journal* 10 (Fall 1986): 67–75.

2. *Princeton Encyclopedia of Poetry and Poetics*, ed. Alex Preminger (Princeton, N.J.: Princeton University Press, 1965), 148.

3. Stanley Burnshaw, "Turmoil in the Middle Ground," *The New Masses* 17 (October 1, 1935): 41–42, and quoted in "Wallace Stevens and the Statue," *Sewanee Review* 69 (Summer 1961): 363.

4. Perlis, "Wallace Stevens's Reader Poems," 70.

5. Litz calls "The Old Woman and the Statue" "effective rhetoric, with both poverty and eloquence, reality and imagination, evoked in moving language." He goes on, "It offers no resolution other than that of its own forms and harmonies,

but as a splendid drama of the confrontation between poverty and art it tells more than a dozen proletarian novels." *Introspective Voyager: The Poetic Development of Wallace Stevens* (New York: Oxford University Press, 1972), 211.

6. Jonathan Culler, *The Pursuit of Signs: Semiotics, Literature and Deconstruction* (Ithaca, N.Y.: Cornell University Press, 1981), 139.

7. Marjorie Perloff, "Revolving in Crystal: The Supreme Fiction and the Impasse of Modernist Lyric," in *Wallace Stevens: The Poetics of Modernism*, ed. Albert Gelpi (Cambridge: Cambridge University Press, 1985), 41–64.

8. See, for example, Weldon Kees, "Parts: But a World," *New Republic* 107 (September 1942): 387–388, in *Wallace Stevens: The Critical Heritage*, ed. Charles Doyle (London: Routledge & Kegan Paul, 1985).

9. See David Bromwich, "Stevens and the Idea of the Hero," *Raritan* 7 (Summer 1987): 20.

10. Mark Turner, *Death is the Mother of Beauty: Mind, Metaphor, Criticism* (Chicago: University of Chicago Press, 1987), 11.

11. Turner, both a literary critic and a cognitive scientist, has cataloged ten basic metaphor kinship inference patterns that inform our conceptual systems, cognitive processes, and common language, and that, we may see, inform Stevens's poetry: property transfer, similarity, group, inheritance, components and contents, order and succession, causation as progeneration, biological resource as parent, place and time as parent, and lineage in the world, the mind, and behavior. See *Death is the Mother of Beauty*, 195.

CHAPTER EIGHT

1. Critics writing from a variety of perspectives have discussed the problematic endings of Dickinson's poems. For example, Robert Weisbuch, claiming that because "possibilities are endless, Dickinson's poetry posits no final truths" (1), studies the two prevailing and apparently conflicting attitudes toward experience that run through her poetry: those of "visionary celebrant" and "skeptical sufferer." See *Emily Dickinson's Poetry* (Chicago: University of Chicago Press, 1972). A feminist reading of Dickinson concludes that her "poetry stylistically emphasizes the multiplying, rupturing aspect of creation over the positing, controlling one, or the feminine over the masculine form, and yet it ultimately achieves that 'bisexuality' Kristeva claims as the foundation for exploring meaning." See Cristanne Miller, *Emily Dickinson: A Poet's Grammar* (Cambridge, Mass.: Harvard University Press, 1987), 181.

2. See Helen Vendler's discussion of Steven's syntax in *On Extended Wings* (Cambridge, Mass.: Harvard University Press, 1969) for commentary on the variety of ways he chose to mitigate the endings of his poems (13–37). Also see the comments about Stevens's endings in *Harmonium* in Eleanor Cook's *Poetry, Word-Play, and Word-War in Wallace Stevens* (Princeton, N.J.: Princeton University Press, 1988), 99–114. Cook looks closely at "Sunday Morning" and the poems that end *Harmonium* for their exposure of Stevens as a poet against closure. Hers is an introduction to the essay she claims remains to be written on Stevens and the subject of endings, including matters of formal closure, doctrines of last things, evening, elegy, Virgilian closure. She finds "Sunday Morning" with its three pro-

posed endings a rich text for this subject and concludes that "Stevens' closure seems to me a paradoxical variation on Virgilian alternatives—a movement that is downward to shadow but also outward" (110).

3. David Porter also ties Dickinson to the Puritan tradition of typology, although he credits her with a movement toward a more skeptical attitude. See *The Art of Emily Dickinson's Early Poetry* (Cambridge, Mass.: Harvard University Press, 1966), 81.

4. For a discussion of Stevens's "paradoxical logic" in which "the atmosphere of false precision" is "deceptive," see Vendler, *On Extended Wings*, 13–37.

5. See Stevens's letter to José Rodríguez Feo in which he identifies the source of "The Novel" as a letter from this young friend (617) and the quotation from Lorca which had been sent to him by another friend, Thomas McGreevy (690).

6. Milton J. Bates, *Wallace Stevens: A Mythology of Self* (Berkeley: University of California Press, 1985), 297–299.

7. I do not mean to suggest that the speakers in *The Waste Land*, *The Cantos*, *Paterson*, and *The Bridge* represent American culture, but rather that they express their creators' efforts to speak for points of cultural crises, to tell the tale of the tribe, create the myth of America, articulate the dream of the whole poem. In their privacy, they can still imagine themselves to be representative Americans speaking for a culture in need of its poets. See my *On the Modernist Long Poem* (Iowa City: University of Iowa Press, 1987).

8. Rorty, *Contingency, Irony, and Solidarity* (Cambridge: Cambridge University Press, 1989), 43.

9. See Weisbuch's comment on this poem in the context of her constant desire to push beyond the barrier of the accessible. He says, "She can see the immortal self as a 'limitless Hyperbole,' limitless and more dynamic and desirous than ever before. Eternity need not epitomize completion, but endlessness," *Emily Dickinson's Poetry*, 175–176.

10. See Myra Jehlen's discussion of Ralph Waldo Emerson's need for the dialectic that would allow man to continue and expand in a world that was, ideally, beyond activity. *American Incarnation: The Individual, the Nation, and the Continent* (Cambridge, Mass.: Harvard University Press, 1986), 84.

11. Christopher Benfey sees in Dickinson a thematic of neighbors, nearness, and nextness, which often takes the form of a response to problems of knowledge. See his discussion, *Emily Dickinson and the Problem of Others* (Amherst: University of Massachusetts Press, 1984), 75.

12. I mean to suggest here that the lyric is the genre in American literature that has allowed for the widest range of self-expression because it has not been co-opted by the cultural imperatives of a national literature. It is the genre that has allowed American writers to experiment with form.

I do not agree with Lentricchia's suggestion that "high-modernist lyricism is the creation of radical privacy in the belief that feeling cannot be entrusted to social context," because "radical privacy" cannot be created in a poem that is to be published. See *Ariel and the Police: Michel Foucault, William James, Wallace Stevens* (Madison: University of Wisconsin Press, 1988), 222. Nor is social context easy to create in a short lyric poem, although the high-modernists Pound and Eliot could intersperse brief lyric interludes into their longer poems, thus, presumably, suggesting that feeling can be expressed in a social context.

Index of Works Cited

General Index

This book has been set in Linotron Galliard. Galliard was designed for Merganthaler in 1978 by Matthew Carter. Galliard retains many of the features of a sixteenth century typeface cut by Robert Granjon but has some modifications which give it a more contemporary look.

Printed on acid-free paper.